THE CONSTABLE HAS BLUNDERED

Library of Congress Cataloging-in-Publication Data

Signorelli, Walter P.
The constable has blundered : the exclusionary rule, crime, and corruption /
Walter P. Signorelli. -- 2nd ed.
   p. cm.
Includes index.
ISBN 978-1-61163-102-9 (alk. paper)
1. Exclusionary rule (Evidence)--United States. I. Title.

KF9662.S56 2011
347.73'62--dc23

                              2011036566

Carolina Academic Press
700 Kent Street
Durham, North Carolina 27701
Telephone (919) 489-7486
Fax (919) 493-5668
www.cap-press.com

Printed in the United States of America

THE CONSTABLE HAS BLUNDERED

The Exclusionary Rule, Crime, and Corruption

SECOND EDITION

Walter P. Signorelli

CAROLINA ACADEMIC PRESS
Durham, North Carolina

Contents

Introduction

For more than four decades in my roles as a police officer and as a criminal defense attorney, I have encountered problems created by the exclusionary rule, and I believe that the insidious effects of the rule have significantly undermined trust in the law enforcement community and the criminal justice system. In 1967, when I joined the New York City Police Department as a rookie police officer, the nation was experiencing a tumultuous period with anti-Vietnam war protests, the civil rights movement, and the burgeoning of an anti-establishment counterculture. It was an interesting time to be a police officer, and I was proud to be part of the law enforcement community. This was before the surfacing of the worst police corruption scandals in New York City history, before the 1971–1972 Knapp Commission investigation into police corruption that was later depicted in such popular films as *Serpico*, with Al Pacino acting as Officer Frank Serpico, and *The Prince of the City*, with Treat Williams acting as Detective Robert Leuci.

Most of the public was surprised and outraged at the extent of police corruption that existed at that time; however, little was done to determine or cure the underlying causes that led to such corruption. The police department restructured its organizational chart to increase supervision, accountability, and discipline, but these measures dealt more with the symptoms of corruption rather than with the causes. At a time when academics, politicians, and administrators had been focusing on the need to address the root causes of crime, delinquency, drug abuse, poverty, and racism, it was odd that the root causes of police corruption seemed not to be of concern. It was as though everyone believed the police were inherently corrupt and would always be corrupt. The only thing to do was to put in controls and to keep the corruption to a minimum.

Greed, egoism, and the opportunity for illegitimate gains are obvious causes of corruption, but they are not reserved to police officers and police work. What is unique to police work is the constant exposure to unsatisfactory and unjust outcomes in the criminal justice system. Police officers see hypocrisy everywhere in the system, and believe they are the scapegoats for the system's failures. They find themselves under constant criticism, and they respond with the colloquial maxim, "Damned if you do; damned if you don't."

The exclusionary rule is the most direct and consequential means of second-guessing and criticizing the work of police officers. The rule requires that evidence obtained in violation of constitutional rights cannot be used in a criminal trial. Officers, who believe that they acted properly while making an arrest or searching for evidence, find themselves criticized for their efforts and see criminals set free because of what the officers believe are impractical and, sometimes, incomprehensible rules. The suppression of otherwise reliable evidence negatively affects police morale and causes the resentment, cynicism, and rebelliousness that often are the precursors to corruption.

My first exposure to the exclusionary rule occurred with my first arrest. It was a routine case, but it introduced me to the ambiguities and injustices of the exclusionary rule that I would face for the next thirty years as an officer and for another ten years as a criminal defense attorney.

The case began when my partner and I were assigned to a patrol car in the Bedford-Stuyvesant section of Brooklyn. It was a summer day at a time when crime was on the rise because of an epidemic of heroin addiction in New York and other cities. The police radio dispatcher directed us to investigate a 911 call about suspicious men loitering in the hallway of an apartment building. Since we were not far from the location, we arrived within two minutes. The building was a rundown, four-story tenement, and we immediately noticed that the glass pane of the unlocked front door was broken. Upon entering the lobby, we observed two young men hurrying down the staircase toward us. To the right of the stairs was a window to a courtyard; to the left, a bank of mailboxes. My partner stopped and questioned the first man who came down the stairs, taking him toward the mailboxes. I attempted to stop the second man, who was about twenty-five years old, six-feet tall, of medium build, and wearing a red bandana on his head. He kept moving from side to side trying to get around me, but I blocked his path. He turned his back to me and, while trying to block my view, put or dropped a red and white Marlboro cigarette box on the windowsill as he moved toward the stairs. I picked up the Marlboro box, opened the lid, and saw a batch of glassine envelopes containing a white powder that looked like heroin. I said, "You're under arrest," but as I reached for my handcuffs, he bolted and ran up the stairs.

My partner stayed with the first man, while I chased the man wearing the bandana up five flights of stairs to the roof, across several rooftops, then down the stairs of another building to the street. I chased him through the streets, and after two blocks of zigzagging in and out of traffic and almost being hit by several cars, I caught and handcuffed him. As we caught our breath and walked back to the patrol car, he said, "I'm sorry for running."

In court, I charged the defendant with unlawful possession of narcotics and resisting arrest. During the booking process, he told me that he was actually glad to be arrested. He was strung out on heroin and needed help. He hoped that in prison he might get into a program.

At the arraignment, he was held in $500 bail, but he did not have the money and no one from his family would put up the bail for him. Within two weeks, the police laboratory confirmed that the white powder was indeed heroin, and the defendant's legal aid attorney made a motion to suppress the heroin on the grounds that it was seized in violation of the defendant's constitutional rights.

A hearing was held, and on direct examination by the district attorney, I testified to exactly what had happened, or what I thought had happened, and I hoped the defendant would be convicted: first, because he could have caused me to be killed, running across the rooftops and dodging traffic, and, second, because he needed to be incarcerated in order to get help for his drug addiction.

On cross-examination, the defense attorney asked me a series of questions. I testified that I saw the defendant put the Marlboro box on the windowsill. He asked me how he put it there. I said, "I don't know, he just put it there." He asked me how far he was from the windowsill. I said one or two feet. He asked whether he could reach the windowsill by extending his arm. I said yes. He asked whether he threw it to the windowsill. I said, "Not really, he let it go, then ran up the stairs." He asked how many inches were there between his hand when he let the Marlboro box go and the windowsill. I said, "I'm not sure."

The defense attorney did not ask me anything about the chase across the roofs or through the streets to apprehend the defendant, and on redirect testimony the district attorney was precluded from asking anything about the chase.

At the conclusion of the hearing, the judge ruled that the envelopes containing heroin must be suppressed and could not be used as evidence against the defendant. The judge explained that when the defendant put the cigarette box on the windowsill, it did not mean that he had abandoned the box. Legally, it was still in his possession, and I had violated his Fourth Amendment rights against unreasonable search and seizure by picking up the box and looking into it. According to the exclusionary rule, evidence obtained in violation of the Fourth Amendment could not be used in court against a defendant.

At first, I did not understand the ruling. However, when the assistant district attorney explained it, I realized my testimony was responsible for the judge's ruling. Had I testified that the defendant discarded the Marlboro box by throwing it or flipping it three or four inches to the windowsill, his intent to abandon the box would have been clear. In that case, seizing the box would have been constitutional, and the ruling would have been different.

The charges of possession of narcotics and resisting arrest were dismissed and the defendant was released, but I saw his reaction and he did not look overjoyed. Apparently, he had resigned himself to going into the correctional system and hoped someone there would help him.

Over the next few days, I grew angry with myself because, while reconstructing the events in my mind as impartially and as accurately as I could, I realized that clearer testimony would have shown that the defendant had in fact tossed the box several inches. He had not placed it on the windowsill, but had let it fall to the windowsill. He had not placed it on the windowsill in the sense of someone being careful with his possession, but he had let it fall about four or five inches while he turned his head away and moved toward the stairs. Unfortunately, I had not realized the importance of those inches and the physical and spatial movements. I had not realized what the defense attorney had been trying to prove, and I had provided him with the exact answers he needed.

What made me angrier still, and what I was confused about, was the dismissal of the resisting arrest charge. The judge had ruled that since there was no basis or probable cause to seize the heroin, the arrest of the defendant was invalid, and, consequently, the arrest was unauthorized and the defendant could not be convicted of resisting an unauthorized arrest. On the basis of that logic, it would seem that had I fallen off the roof or been hit by a car during the chase, my death or injury would not have been a basis for any charges against the defendant. The ruling seemed wrong to me then, and forty years later, it still seems wrong.

Later, during my police career, as a higher ranking officer in the New York City Police Department Patrol Bureau, Detective Bureau, Organized Crime Control Bureau, and Narcotics Division, I encountered the exclusionary rule in all its forms. I saw its demoralizing effect on young idealistic officers when clearly dangerous and guilty criminals got off because of the rule.

After I retired from the police and began practicing as a criminal defense attorney, I had to invoke the exclusionary rule even when I doubted that it was applicable to the circumstances of the case, otherwise I would have been subject to allegations of malpractice for not zealously representing my client. I saw criminal defendants, refusing to accept blame themselves, shift blame for their crimes to the police for not "getting them right," then switch the blame to their defense attorneys for failing to convince the court to suppress the evidence. In one case, a woman, who was arrested immediately after she bought heroin on a street corner, related that as the police approached her, she dropped the envelope of heroin on the ground and stepped on it to cover it. She complained that when the police made her move from the spot on which she was standing, they saw the envelope of heroin. She believed that they violated her constitutional rights by making her move and she wanted the heroin to be suppressed. Not once did she mention her own guilt, her own debilitating addiction, or the three young children she had left alone at home while she went out to get high.

Our greatest legal minds have debated and disagreed about the exclusionary rule for decades. They have debated fine legal points of whether it is a mandated right inherent in the Fourth Amendment or whether it is an optional remedy that can be modified on a case-by-case basis. They have debated whether Congress can overrule or modify judicial interpretations or whether only the judiciary can do so because of the Constitution's supremacy over legislation. They have debated whether the general deterrence the rule may provide outweighs the costs of the specific injustices it causes.

Simpler, ordinary people, victimized by crime, are not as conflicted. Those involved in cases in which dangerous criminals are freed because of technicalities complain that the system is broken, the cops and the district attorneys do not know what they are doing, and either a fix is in or a bias in the system works against true justice.

Questions need to be answered: After decades of expansion, does the exclusionary rule serve the cause of justice? Does it really deter police from committing constitutional violations? Does it cause corruption? Is it a detriment even to the criminals it releases? How does it affect the war on terrorism? Is it the best means of protecting privacy?

The purpose of this book is to examine the exclusionary rule and its consequences, including the historical development of the rule, its relation to crime rates, police performance, and the loss of confidence in the justice system. Specific cases are examined to illustrate the practical effects of the rule. Assumptions about the rule's deterrent value are scrutinized, and alternative methods of protecting individual rights are proposed.

THE CONSTABLE HAS
BLUNDERED

Chapter One

Unequal Justice

Written above the entrance to the United States Supreme Court are the words, "Equal Justice Under Law." The exclusionary rule subverts that ideal: two criminals who commit the same crime by the same means can receive different and unequal treatment by the criminal justice system, not on the basis of their own conduct, but rather on the basis of police conduct. Furthermore, two crime victims subjected to similar crimes can be treated differently and unequally: one might receive justice while the other might not, solely on the basis of police conduct of which they had no knowledge or responsibility.

The exclusionary rule is the primary means by which courts enforce constitutional restraints on law enforcement. It prohibits the use in a criminal trial of evidence that is obtained by the government in violation of the Bill of Rights, particularly the Fourth, Fifth, and Sixth Amendments of the Constitution. When the police conduct an unlawful arrest, search, or interrogation, the courts will suppress any physical evidence, confession, or information obtained directly from the unlawful conduct. The theory and stated purpose of the suppression remedy is to deter police and other law enforcement agents from committing the same kinds of violations in the future.

Whether the rule has accomplished its stated purpose is the subject of intense debate and many scholarly articles, and while the rule may have produced some positive effects on police conduct, its detrimental effects have far outweighed any benefits. It is not a cost-free remedy. The suppression of evidence can undermine otherwise viable prosecutions and can result in guilty defendants being released and victims of a crime losing their opportunity for justice. Furthermore, in addition to dispensing unequal justice for both defendants and victims, the rule has generated widespread police corruption, greatly increased perjury in our courts, incited animosity toward the police, spread a substantial disrespect for the law, and led to an overall increase in criminality.

In 1961, the United States Supreme Court extended the exclusionary rule for Fourth Amendment violations from federal courts to the courts of all fifty states.[1] Since then, with few exceptions, the rule has grown in application, complexity, and inconsistency. In addition to suppressing evidence to enforce the Fourth Amendment, courts suppress evidence to enforce other clauses in the Bill of Rights. Courts suppress physical objects, confessions, statements, documents, evidence analysis reports, identifications, and even testimony about observations of what an officer saw or heard.

A significant problem with all of this evidence suppression is that sometimes the evidence is suppressed, sometimes it is not, and the determinants are difficult to discern or justify. The criteria for applying suppression are different from court to court: federal courts use different criteria than state courts, and state courts vary from one to another.

Moreover, outcomes are inconsistent and unrelated to fairness or justice; they are often determined by nuances and chance factors. For example, in street encounters, evidence recovered by the police may be suppressed on the basis of how the police approached the suspects; consequently, two criminals who are arrested for committing the same crime of unlawful possession of a loaded gun might face different and unequal consequences. Were the first criminal to be approached by a police officer who had drawn his firearm, which would be tantamount to a seizure, the criminal might be able to successfully challenge the constitutionality of the seizure and, therefore, demand the suppression of the illegal gun he carried. On the other hand, were the second criminal to be approached by an officer who had not drawn his firearm, the second criminal might be unable to successfully challenge the admissibility of the gun he carried. As a result, the first criminal would either avoid trial entirely or would be acquitted, while the second criminal might have to stand trial and might be convicted.[2] These divergent results occur not on the basis of the defendant's guilt or innocence but on whether the police officers felt it was necessary to take out their guns.

In addition, the rule's application to persons who are subjected to a police search or interrogation can vary depending on their status and situation. For example, two persons in a vehicle subjected to the same improper search by the police may face different and unequal consequences. When the police unreasonably search a vehicle and find an illegal gun, the driver of the vehicle might go free while the passengers might not. This disparity results not from factors of guilt or innocence, but purely because of exclusionary rule technicalities. A driver with a proprietary interest in the vehicle can challenge the constitu-

---

1. *Mapp v. Ohio*, 367 U.S. 643 (1961).
2. *People v. Moore*, 6 N.Y.3d 496 (2006).

tionality of the search and might succeed in having the evidence excluded from use at his trial, while a passenger without a proprietary interest in the vehicle does not have standing to challenge the constitutionality of the search and thus cannot have the evidence excluded. The United States Supreme Court has held that a passenger does not have an expectation of privacy in the glove compartment, the area under the seat, or the trunk of a vehicle.[3] As a result, in the case of an improper search, a driver, who is more likely to be the actual owner of the gun, will avoid trial for unlawful possession of the gun while the passenger, who is less likely to be the owner of the gun, might have to stand trial and be convicted.

These kinds of results demonstrate the hyper-technicality, inconsistency, and unfairness that the exclusionary rule has wrought on our criminal justice system. Nevertheless, the American public has come to accept the rule as a constitutional imperative. They accept and believe that relevant and material evidence must be kept out of the courtroom to deter the police and the state from conducting unreasonable searches or seizures, and also that voluntary and truthful confessions must be kept out of the courtroom when the police conduct interrogations or questioning without adhering to the technical rules of criminal procedure. Misapplying the rationale for the proof-beyond-a-reasonable-doubt standard for convictions, they accept and believe that it is better that a hundred guilty defendants go free rather than one guilty defendant be convicted based on evidence obtained in violation of his constitutional rights.

Most Americans believe that the exclusionary rule was written in the Bill of Rights and has been the law of the land since the Constitution's ratification. They would be surprised to find that it was not. Contrary to popular belief, the exclusionary rule is not written in the Bill of Rights. The framers neither mentioned nor contemplated the imposition of such a rule. They intended the Bill of Rights as a check on the powers of the newly formed federal government, with no intention of interfering with the states' abilities to enforce local, traditional criminal laws. The Fourth Amendment of the Bill of Rights consists of two distinct clauses:

> The right of the people to be secure in their persons, houses, papers and effects, against unreasonable searches and seizures, shall not be violated, and no Warrants shall issue, but upon probable cause, supported by Oath or affirmation, and particularly describing the place to be searched, and the persons or things to be seized.

---

3. *Rakas v. Illinois*, 439 U.S. 128 (1978).

Particular remedies for violations of the Fourth Amendment, or any of the other Amendments, were not declared, and for 123 years, from the ratification of the Bill of Rights in 1791 to 1914, the exclusionary rule was essentially nonexistent. In the search-and-seizure context, it was first applied in the federal mail-fraud case of *United States v. Weeks*, 232 U.S. 383 (1914). In that case, a United States marshal entered the defendant's home without a warrant and seized letters and envelopes that were used as evidence to convict the defendant of mail fraud. Before the trial, the defendant filed a *replevin* action for return of his property on the grounds that it was seized illegally. His action was denied and the evidence was used at his trial. He appealed to the United States Supreme Court, and the Court ruled that entry into the home without a warrant was a violation of the Fourth Amendment and, consequently, the evidence obtained should have been returned to the defendant and not used against him at his trial. This was the birth of the exclusionary rule.

Six years later, in *Silverthorne Lumber Co. v. United States*, 251 U.S. 385 (1920), the Supreme Court decided a similar case in which federal agents had seized business records without a warrant. In this case, knowing they would have to return the documents, the agents copied the information from the records, returned the records, and subsequently subpoenaed them for use at the defendant's criminal trial. The Court excluded the use of the subpoenaed records and, as written in the majority opinion by Justice Oliver Wendell Holmes, the knowledge gained by the unlawful seizure of the records "shall not be used at all." This case was a forerunner of the "fruits of the poisonous tree" doctrine, which holds that evidence derived from constitutionally inadmissible evidence is likewise inadmissible. Not only evidence obtained directly from a constitutional violation, but also secondary evidence derived from the information obtained during the violation is tainted and may not be used against the person whose rights were violated.[4]

Both *Weeks* and *Silverthorne* involved personal property and records that citizens lawfully possessed. Neither case involved possession of unlawful contraband, such as narcotics, guns, counterfeit money, or stolen property. Obviously, the Court could not have ordered the return of unlawful contraband: later cases established the procedure that unlawful contraband would be excluded from evidence but not returned to the person from whom it was seized.[5]

The *Weeks* exclusionary remedy and the *Silverthorne* poisonous-tree doctrine were judge-made rules, and were far from universally approved. Neither

---

4. *Wong Sun v. United States*, 371 U.S. 471 (1963); *Brown v. Illinois*, 422 U.S. 590 (1975); *Dunaway v. New York*, 442 U.S. 200 (1979).

5. *United States v. Trupiano*, 334 U.S. 699 (1949); *United States v. Jeffers*, 342 U.S. 48 (1951).

English common law nor civil law nations recognized the exclusionary rule as a necessary legal device.[6]

After *Weeks*, the exclusionary rule was applied in federal courts, but it was not initially applied against state courts where most criminal cases are tried. Debate arose as to whether federal courts should mandate that the rule be applied against the states, and many of the greatest and most respected judges ruled against its imposition on the states. Benjamin Cardozo, in *People v. Defore*, 242 N.Y. 13 (1926), ruled against the exclusion of evidence as a remedy for search-and-seizure violations. He framed the issue for the upcoming debates:

> No doubt the protection of the statute would be greater from the point of view of the individual whose privacy had been invaded if the government were required to ignore what it had learned through the invasion. The question is whether protection for the individual would not be gained at a disproportionate loss of protection for society. On the one side is the social need that crime shall be repressed. On the other, the social need that law shall not be flouted by the insolence of office.

The continuing debate is not about whether the local police or government agents may violate the constitutional rights of citizens with impunity; rather, it is about what the remedy should be when such violations occur and what should be done to deter such violations. Those who support the exclusionary rule argue that it is the only effective deterrent to police misconduct while those who oppose the rule argue that the suppression of evidence is too much of a detriment to the truth-seeking process and it should never have been created.

The exclusionary rule developed during a century-long process. After the rule was applied in federal courts for violations of the Bill of Rights, two questions arose: first, did the Bill of Rights apply to the states, and, second, if so, did violations of the Bill of Rights by state agents require suppression of evidence obtained as a result.

Between 1925 and 1968, through the selective incorporation doctrine, almost every federal criminal procedure protection in the Bill of Rights was unequivocally applied to the states through the due process clause of the Fourteenth Amendment, but it was more debatable whether violations required evidence suppression.[7] In 1949, the United States Supreme Court, addressed the above issues in *Wolf v. Colorado*, 338 U.S. 25 (1949), a case involving intrusion into

---

6. *People v. Adams*, 176 N.Y. 351 (1903); *People v. Defore*, 242 N.Y. 13 (1926); *Wolf v. Colorado*, 338 U.S. 25 (1949).

7. *Gitlow v. New York*, 268 U.S. 652 (1925); *Powell v. Alabama*, 287 U.S. 45 (1932); *Brown v. Mississippi*, 297 U.S. 278 (1936); *Gideon v. Wainwright*, 372 U.S. 335 (1963); *Grif-*

a home without a warrant. The Court denounced such constitutional violations and held that they violated the Fourteenth Amendment. However, the Court debated what the remedy should be and ultimately rejected the extension of the federal exclusionary rule to the states. Justice Felix Frankfurter wrote the majority opinion.

> The knock at the door, whether by day or by night, as a prelude to a search, without authority of law but solely on the authority of the police, did not need the commentary of recent history to be condemned as inconsistent with the conception of human rights enshrined in the history and the basic constitutional documents of English-speaking peoples.
>
> Accordingly, we have no hesitation in saying that were a State affirmatively to sanction such police incursion into privacy it would run counter to the guaranty of the Fourteenth Amendment. But the ways of enforcing such a basic right raise questions of a different order. How such arbitrary conduct should be checked, what remedies against it should be afforded, the means by which the right should be made effective, are all questions that are not to be so dogmatically answered as to preclude the varying solutions which spring from an allowable range of judgment on issues not susceptible of quantitative solution....
>
> But the immediate question is whether the basic right to protection against arbitrary intrusion by the police demands the exclusion of logically relevant evidence obtained by an unreasonable search and seizure because, in a federal prosecution for a federal crime, it would be excluded. As a matter of inherent reason, one would suppose this to be an issue as to which men with complete devotion to the protection of the right of privacy might give different answers. When we find that in fact most of the English-speaking world does not regard as vital to such protection the exclusion of evidence thus obtained, we must hesitate to treat this remedy as an essential ingredient of the right.[8]

The Court recognized other available remedies that various states employed to rectify violations. Police who violated citizen rights could be sued in civil actions for trespass, battery, unlawful imprisonment, or other torts according to the circumstances. Violators who acted with the requisite criminal intent

---

fin v. California, 380 U.S. 609 (1965); *Duncan v. Louisiana*, 391 U.S. 145 (1968); *Benton v. Maryland*, 395 U.S. 784 (1969); et al.

8. *Wolf v. Colorado, supra.*

could be prosecuted. Violators could be subjected to discipline by their agencies, including termination of employment. In light of the variety of remedies available, the Court ruled that fashioning appropriate remedies should be left to the individual states rather than the federal courts.

In an important dissenting opinion in *Wolf v. Colorado, supra,* Justice Frank Murphy argued that suppression of evidence was the only effective means of deterring police from violating constitutional rights. He argued that the remedy of bringing a lawsuit against the police was ineffective because "even if the plaintiff hurdles all these obstacles, and gains a substantial verdict, the individual officer's finances may well make the judgment useless—for the municipality, of course, is not liable without its consent."9

Justice Murphy also argued that neither criminal prosecution nor administrative sanctioning of police was an effective deterrent, because district attorneys were reluctant to prosecute the officers whom they depend on and police agencies had not proven they could be trusted to engage in self-policing.

Twelve years later, the Court of Chief Justice Earl Warren, in *Mapp v. Ohio,* 367 U.S. 643 (1961), overruled the majority opinion in *Wolf,* and mandated that the exclusionary rule must be the remedy applied by all the states. The Court adopted Justice Murphy's dissent, finding that the remedies employed by states were "worthless and futile" and therefore the *Weeks* rule was the only effective remedy.

The Warren Court's *Mapp* decision opened the gates to a flood of search-and-seizure cases that expanded the rule, and the Court subsequently applied the rule against the states in cases involving custodial interrogation, lineups, access to counsel, and other procedural issues. The application to state courts, where most criminal charges are adjudicated, multiplied the rule's use. Considering that there were approximately 87,000 federal law-enforcement agents compared to approximately 800,000 sworn local and state law-enforcement officers, *Mapp* substantially expanded the reach of the exclusionary rule.

The Warren Court not only used the rule to enforce the Fourth Amendment but also to enforce the self-incrimination and due process clauses of the Fifth Amendment and the right to counsel clause of the Sixth Amendment.

The Fifth Amendment states: "No person shall … be compelled in any criminal case to be a witness against himself." It is a self-executing exclusion in that a defendant cannot be forced to testify in his or her criminal case. The Warren Court exclusionary rule goes beyond the self-executing requirements of the Fifth Amendment; it may exclude uncompelled out-of-court statements of a defendant that affect his or her criminal case.

---

9. *Id.* at 42, dissent.

The Fifth Amendment also states: "No person shall … be deprived of life, liberty, or property, without due process of law." The due process clause encompasses the independently developed common law rules prohibiting the use of coerced, involuntary confessions against a defendant. Applying these rules has been difficult. For more than a century, courts have struggled to define what degree of coercion makes a confession involuntary, and they have also struggled to explain the interrelations among the due process clause, the privilege against self-incrimination, and the prohibition against coerced, involuntary confessions.

The Sixth Amendment states: "In all criminal prosecutions, the accused shall enjoy the right … to have the Assistance of Counsel for his defense." It addresses the conduct of a criminal trial. The Warren Court exclusionary rule goes beyond the conduct of the trial; it extends the right to counsel to circumstances even before charges are filed, and it excludes statements elicited from a defendant outside of court in a manner that circumvents his or her right to counsel.

To safeguard Fifth and/or Sixth Amendments rights, the Warren Court established several prophylactic procedural rules, such as in *Mallory v. United States*, 354 U.S. 449 (1957),[10] *Malloy v. Hogan*, 378 U.S.1 (1964),[11] *Murphy v. Waterfront Commission*, 378 U.S. 52 (1964),[12] *Massiah v. United States*, 377 U.S. 201 (1964),[13] *Griffin v. California*, 380 U.S. 609 (1965),[14] and the most famous *Miranda v. Arizona*, 384 U.S. 436 (1966). Although these prophylactic rules were not expressly mandated by the language of the Constitution, the Court enforced them through the exclusionary rule.

In 1966, the Court shifted its main focus in criminal procedure matters from search-and-seizure cases to police custodial interrogation cases in order to safeguard the Fifth Amendment right that "No person … shall be compelled in any criminal case to be a witness against himself." In *Miranda v. Arizona*, 384 U.S. 436, (1966), the Court imposed a complex set of ground rules for law enforcement to follow during interviews and interrogations of suspects and defendants, extending the Fifth Amendment right against self-incrimination from the post-arraignment or post-indictment stage of a criminal prosecution

---

10. Undue delay between arrest and arraignment requires suppression of confession.

11. Fifth Amendment applicable against the states.

12. Despite immunity granted in one jurisdiction, Fifth Amendment can still be raised if possible incrimination in another jurisdiction.

13. Sixth Amendment right to counsel protects suspect against surreptitious contact by law enforcement agent.

14. Prosecutor may not comment on defendant's failure to testify.

to the arrest stage and even the pre-arrest stage: When a suspect is in police custody, whether formally charged with a crime or not, he must be read his rights before any questioning related to the crime.

The Court ruled that questioning in a police station is inherently coercive and that "the prosecution may not use statements, whether exculpatory or inculpatory, stemming from custodial interrogation of the defendant unless it demonstrates the use of procedural safeguards effective to secure the privilege against self-incrimination."

In *Miranda*, the Court suppressed the defendant's confession to the rape of a young woman and, in addition, went far beyond the requirements of the case. It imposed a nationwide requirement on all law enforcement agencies that before custodial interrogation a suspect must be given the following warnings:

1. You have the right to remain silent.
2. Anything you say can be used against you in court.
3. You have the right to have an attorney present and to consult with an attorney.
4. If you cannot afford an attorney, one will be appointed for you prior to any questioning if you so desire.

The Court summarized its extensive ruling:

To summarize, we hold that when an individual is taken into custody or otherwise deprived of his freedom by the authorities in any significant way and is subjected to questioning, the privilege against self-incrimination is jeopardized. Procedural safeguards must be employed to protect the privilege, and unless other fully effective means are adopted to notify the person of his right of silence and to assure that the exercise of the right will be scrupulously honored, the following measures are required. He must be warned prior to any questioning that he has the right to remain silent, that anything he says can be used against him in a court of law, that he has the right to the presence of an attorney, and that if he cannot afford an attorney one will be appointed for him prior to any questioning if he so desires. Opportunity to exercise these rights must be afforded to him throughout the interrogation. After such warnings have been given, and such opportunity afforded him, the individual may knowingly and intelligently waive these rights and agree to answer questions or make a statement. But unless and until such warnings and waiver are demonstrated by the prosecution at trial, no evidence obtained as a result of interrogation can be used against him.

Absent the above warnings, a voluntary confession by a defendant in custody would be deemed the equivalent of an involuntary confession and, therefore, inadmissible as evidence against the defendant. Furthermore, *Miranda* and a series of related decisions established the general rule that when the police question suspects in custody, either without completely or properly advising them of the Miranda warnings or by questioning them in violation of their right to counsel, any statements by the suspects or any evidence derived from their statements cannot be used in court against them.[15]

In addition to the institution of the prophylactic warnings that were designed to aid a suspect during custodial interrogation, the Court ruled that when a suspect requests to consult with a lawyer, all questioning must stop until a lawyer is present. By these rulings, the Court took an active legislative role, usually the province of Congress. Critics argued that instead of deciding whether Miranda's confession was voluntary or involuntary, or deciding the case on the basis of its facts and a just result for the particular case, the Court preemptively decided future confession cases without yet knowing the facts of those cases, without knowing whether the confessions in those cases were voluntary or not.

Miranda immediately caused a ground swell of criticism from police, politicians, and legal scholars. In 1969, Warren Burger, before he was appointed as Chief Justice of the Supreme Court, predicted that *Miranda* and its progeny would create an incomprehensible and contradictory set of rules:

> The seeming anxiety of judges to protect every accused person from every consequence of his voluntary utterances is giving rise to myriad rules, sub-rules, variations and exceptions which even the most alert and sophisticated lawyers and judges are taxed to follow. Each time judges add nuances to these "rules" we make it less likely that any police officer will be able to follow the guidelines we lay down. We are approaching the predicament of the centipede on the flypaper—each time one leg is placed to give support for relief of a leg already "stuck," another becomes captive and soon all are securely immobilized. Like the hapless centipede on the flypaper, our efforts to extricate ourselves from this self-imposed dilemma will, if we keep it up, soon have all of us immobilized. We are well on our way to forbidding any utterance of an accused to be used against him unless it is made in open

---

15. *Massiah v. United States*, 377 U.S. 201 (1964); *Brewer v. Williams*, 430 U.S. 387 (1977); *United States v. Henry*, 447 U.S. 264 (1980); *Arizona v. Roberson*, 486 U.S. 675 (1988).

court. Guilt or innocence becomes irrelevant in the criminal trial as we founder in a morass of artificial rules poorly conceived and often impossible of application.[16]

Justice Burger's prediction proved correct. After *Miranda*, an explosion of issues surfaced in cases across the nation dealing with related matters such as custody, waiver, rescinding waiver at a later time, the taint of an earlier confession on a later confession, attenuation of the fruits of the poisonous tree doctrine, and the need to administer the exact wording of the Miranda warnings. The Supreme Court itself has had to resolve more than sixty Miranda-related cases, and often the resolution of one issue spawned other issues that initiated new cycles of litigation and added new layers of complexity.

For every Supreme Court ruling that modified prior law, lawyers developed spin-off issues on which to base new arguments.

The complexities engendered by *Miranda* and related right to counsel cases have produced anomalous and inconsistent results. For example, in many states, two criminals who confess to a crime they committed together can face different and unequal consequences, depending on whether an attorney for one of them called the police station regarding his legal representation. When the attorney for the first defendant calls the police station to advise the police not to question his client, the confession of that defendant will be excluded from evidence, whereas the confession taken by the police from the second defendant who does not have an attorney will be admitted.[17]

The notification by the attorney need not be given to the specific police officers engaged in questioning the defendant, but rather it can be given to any member of the police agency. Therefore, the police who are questioning the defendant may not know of the attorney's notification, but they will be charged with the knowledge, and the confession will be inadmissible. In a case in which a confession determined guilt or innocence, the first defendant whose attorney called would be acquitted, and the second defendant would be convicted.[18]

In the above circumstances, additional chance occurrences can affect the outcome of a case. For example, were the attorney for the first defendant to call the right police department, which has custody of the defendant, the defendant's confession would be suppressed. However, were the attorney to call the wrong police department, which does not have custody of the defendant, the

---

16. *Frazier v. United States*, 419 F.2d 1161, 1176 (1969).

17. *People v. Arthur*, 22 N.Y.2d 325 (1968).

18. *People v. Pinzon*, 44 N.Y.2d 458 (1992); *Commonwealth v. Mavredakis*, 430 Mass. 849 (2000).

confession might be admissible.[19] Consequently, a defendant's acquittal or conviction can be based not on the voluntary and truthful nature of his confession, but on whether his lawyer knew which police department had custody of the defendant. A defendant's acquittal or conviction can result not from sound legal principles of justice, but wholly from chance and uncertain factors.

It has been said that justice delayed is justice denied. It may also be said that justice denied by the exclusionary rule fosters the belief that there is no such thing as justice. Benjamin Cardozo's facetious comment in 1926, "The criminal is to go free because the constable has blundered," resonates even more today.[20] Moreover, it is doubly disturbing when justice is dispensed on unequal terms. The ideal of equality before the law is affronted when one criminal goes free because one police officer felt it was necessary to take out a gun while another did not, or because one automobile occupant decided to drive while another decided to remain a passenger, or because one suspect had a lawyer on retainer when he was arrested while another who committed the same crime is convicted because he did not have a lawyer.

Without doubt, the exclusionary rule has definite consequences: it undermines the process of achieving satisfactory justice, thwarts the truth-seeking process, allows dangerous criminals to escape imprisonment, treats citizens unequally, encourages police perjury, encourages disrespect for the law, and engenders criminality. The theoretical purpose of the exclusionary rule is to deter the police from violating constitutional rights in the future. Whether such deterrence occurs has never been clearly demonstrated, and even if there is some level of deterrence, is it worth the considerable costs to society? We rationalize that we must accept the unjust results in a particular case in order to uphold the protections of the Constitution. However, when the unjust results reach a point of critical mass that topples the scales of justice, it is time for a reassessment. The elaborate reasoning that has been developed to support the rule is a masterpiece of intellectual creativity, but the reasoning begins with a fundamental misconception that the implementation of the rule will produce benefits greater than its detrimental consequences.

In light of these considerations and after almost a century of the expansion of the exclusionary rule, it is time to reexamine its history, purposes, and effects. It is time to identify and measure the rule's unintended consequences and to consider restricting or entirely eliminating the rule.

---

19. *People v. Carranza*, 3 N.Y.3d 719 (2004).
20. *People v. Defore*, 242 N.Y. 13 (1926).

Chapter Two

Justice Denied: Betrayal of the Victims

"Guilt or innocence becomes irrelevant in the criminal trial as we founder in a morass of artificial rules poorly conceived and often impossible of application."

— Justice Warren Burger

The exclusionary rule not only undermines the search for truth concerning the guilt or innocence of defendants, it also denies justice to victims of murder, rape, and other crimes. When a guilty criminal is released because of a legal technicality, a crime victim is denied justice. Releasing dangerous criminals is a failure by government to uphold its end of the social contract, and as government has increasingly endeavored to provide greater protections for criminal defendants, it has increasingly neglected to provide justice for crime victims.

Justice for the ultimate crime victim — the murder victim — has been sacrificed to protect the murderer. The exclusionary rule has been implemented in such an absolutist fashion that even the bodies of murder victims have been excluded from evidence. Judge Cardozo alluded to the possibility that the body of a murder victim could be inadmissible because of a police blunder:

> A room is searched against the law, and the body of a murdered man is found. If the place of discovery may not be proved, the other circumstances may be insufficient to connect the defendant with the crime. The privacy of the home has been infringed, and the murderer goes free.[1]

Cardozo's concerns were dismissed by advocates for the exclusionary rule, but his prediction came to pass — dead bodies, evidence that would establish the cause of death, and physical evidence that would connect a suspect to the murder scene have been suppressed.

---

1. *People v. Defore*, 242 N.Y. 13 (1926).

In 1977, the exclusionary rule led to the suppression of the body of a murder victim in one of the most egregious decisions ever issued by the Supreme Court: *Brewer v. Williams*, 430 U.S.387 (1977), often referred to as the Christian burial speech case. The facts in *Brewer* mirrored every parent's nightmare. On Christmas Eve, 1968, the Powers family attended a wrestling match in a YMCA in Des Moines, Iowa. While the parents watched their son's team, their 10-year-old daughter, Pamela, made a trip to the restroom. She never returned. Robert Williams, a former mental patient who had a room in the YMCA, raped and murdered the little girl.

After the crime, Williams was seen leaving the building and carrying a heavy object wrapped in a rug. The police immediately began searching for him and the girl, without success. Two days later, aided by an attorney, Williams surrendered to the police in Davenport, Iowa, where he was arraigned on the charge of abduction of a child. Davenport is 160 miles from Des Moines, and Williams had to be taken back to Des Moines for further investigation. His attorney advised the detectives not to question Williams on the automobile trip back. However, one of the officers, Detective Leaming, knowing Williams was a former mental patient and deeply religious, began a conversation with him, saying:

> I want to give you something to think about while we're traveling down the road. . . . They are predicting several inches of snow for tonight, and I feel that you yourself are the only person that knows where this little girl's body is . . . and if you get a snow on top of it you yourself may be unable to find it. And since we will be going right past the area where the body is on the way into Des Moines, I feel that we could stop and locate the body, that the parents of this little girl who was snatched away from them on Christmas Eve and murdered. . . . After a snow storm we may not be able to find it at all.

Although it did not contain direct questions, the religious overtones of the speech were clearly designed to induce Williams to show them where the little girl's body was dumped so that the parents could give her a Christian burial. The detective said, "I don't want you to answer me. I don't want to discuss it any further. Just think about it as we're riding down the road." Williams responded by agreeing to show the officers where he had left the body, and he directed them to the body.

Williams was tried for murder and convicted, but, on appeal, the case reached the Supreme Court, which ruled that the burial speech was an indirect form of questioning, equivalent to an unlawful interrogation in violation of the defendant's Fifth Amendment right against self-incrimination and Sixth

Amendment right to counsel. Since the unlawful interrogation led to the discovery of the body, under the poisonous-tree doctrine, the evidence of the body and any evidence on the body had to be excluded from evidence. Williams' conviction was reversed and a new trial was ordered.

It is questionable whether the judges in *Weeks* and *Silverthorne* who had suppressed business records, or the judges in *Mapp* who had suppressed pornographic materials, had contemplated that the rules they initiated would someday result in the suppression of the dead body of a murdered 10-year-old girl. Nevertheless, the *Brewer* court felt that the poisonous-tree doctrine required them to exclude the body from evidence.

Often when a new trial is ordered, the district attorney cannot proceed because the necessary evidence has been suppressed. However, Williams was retried, and at his second trial, although his admissions in response to the Christian burial speech were excluded from evidence, the victim's body was admitted under a new theory of admissibility: the inevitable discovery doctrine. Williams was convicted again, and he again appealed, contending that the body should have been suppressed.

The case, now entitled *Nix v. Williams*, 467 U.S. 431 (1984), again reached the Supreme Court. This time the Court upheld the conviction, reasoning that the evidence of the body was admissible because the police and citizens had mounted an extensive search party to look for the body and would have inevitably discovered it, even without the assistance of the defendant's confession. The Court explained the inevitable discovery doctrine as follows:

> The core rationale consistently advanced by this Court for extending the exclusionary rule to evidence that is the fruit of unlawful police conduct has been that this admittedly drastic and socially costly course is needed to deter police from violations of constitutional and statutory protections. This Court has accepted the argument that the way to ensure such protections is to exclude evidence seized as a result of such violations notwithstanding the high social cost of letting persons obviously guilty go unpunished for their crimes. On this rationale, the prosecution is not to be put in a better position than it would have been in if no illegality had transpired.
>
> By contrast, the derivative evidence analysis ensures that the prosecution is not put in a *worse* position simply because of some earlier police error or misconduct. The independent source doctrine allows admission of evidence that has been discovered by means wholly independent of any constitutional violation. That doctrine, although closely related to inevitable discovery doctrine, does not apply here;

Williams' statements to Leaming indeed led police to the child's body, but that is not the whole story. The independent source doctrine teaches us that the interests of society in deterring unlawful police conduct and the public interest in having juries receive all probative evidence of a crime are properly balanced by putting the police in the same, not a *worse*, position than they would have been in if no police error or misconduct had occurred. . . . When the challenged evidence has an independent source, exclusion of such evidence would put the police in a worse position than they would have been in absent any error or violation. There is a functional similarity between these two doctrines in that exclusion of evidence that would inevitably have been discovered would also put the government in a worse position, because the police would have obtained that evidence if no misconduct had taken place. Thus, while the independent source exception would not justify admission of evidence in this case, its rationale is wholly consistent with and justifies our adoption of the ultimate or inevitable discovery exception to the exclusionary rule.

If the prosecution can establish by a preponderance of the evidence that the information ultimately or inevitably would have been discovered by lawful means — here the volunteers' search — then the deterrence rationale has so little basis that the evidence should be received. Anything less would reject logic, experience and common sense.

Nix corrected the injustice perpetrated in *Brewer v. Williams*, though the ordeal for Pamela's family was exacerbated by the wait between the Supreme Court decisions. Not only had the parents suffered the loss of their 10-year-old daughter, they also endured Williams' first trial, the reversal of his conviction, a second trial, and the appeal to the Supreme Court of his second conviction. Finally, sixteen years after the murder, the courts and the lawyers had completed the discussion of the rights of Robert Williams.

The inevitable discovery doctrine of *Nix* provided a new path for prosecutors to avoid the fruits of the poisonous tree doctrine and the suppression of such evidence as the dead body of a murder victim, instruments of murder left with the body, marks and wounds on the victim, or the semen of a rapist/murderer left in the body of the victim.[2] However, it added more complexity to exclusionary rule determinations, and it has been difficult to apply. In *People v. Turriago*, 219 A.D. 2d 383 (1996), the inevitable discovery issue led to years of litigation over the admissibility of a dead body. Before discussing

---

2. *Nix v. Williams*, 467 U.S. 264 (1984).

Turriago, it is necessary to review two prior New York State inevitable discovery cases.

The New York Court of Appeals first applied inevitable discovery in *People v. Fitzpatrick*, 32 N.Y.2d 499 (1973), and admitted into evidence a gun that had been recovered after illegal questioning of a suspect. In *Fitzgerald*, the defendant, after robbing a gas station, shot and killed two police officers. Other officers traced the defendant to his house. They entered the house, and as they began searching for the defendant, he called from a closet in which he was hiding, "Don't shoot, I give up." The officers seized and handcuffed him. A few feet from the closet, they questioned him about the gun he had used. The defendant stated that it was on a shelf in the closet where they had found him. The police found the gun, with six empty shells in the cylinder.

Before his trial the defendant moved to suppress his statement and the gun. At the suppression hearing, the judge ruled that the prosecution did not provide sufficient information upon which he could find that "the Miranda requirement was complied with or that the defendant waived such rights." Accordingly, the judge suppressed the statement. However, he admitted the gun into evidence.

The defendant was convicted at a jury trial and sentenced to death. He appealed on the grounds that the gun should have been suppressed as the fruits of the poisonous tree related to the police questioning of the defendant without giving sufficient Miranda warnings. When the case reached the Court of Appeals, the Court upheld the conviction and the admission of the gun into evidence on the basis of the inevitable discovery doctrine, stating:

> It is quite unreal to suggest that, but for the defendant's admission, the police would not have looked for incriminating evidence in the closet where he had been hiding. The weapon, employed in a robbery and a shooting of two police officers, is a prime object of any investigation and, unless thrown away, was certain to be either on or near the defendant. If not found on him, the next most reasonable place to look for it was where he had been just before he was seized. Since, the, a search of the closet was inevitable regardless of the defendant's answers to questions put to him beyond its confines, it may not fairly be said that the police "exploited" the "illegality" "involved" in their interrogation.

The highest court of the state resolved the issue in favor of the prosecution, but to most citizens, it would seem astounding that in the circumstances of this case the courts had to even consider that the murder weapon could be kept from the jury.

Fourteen years later, and after several personnel changes on the Court of Appeals, the court declined to apply the inevitable discovery doctrine in *Peo-*

ple v. Stith, 69 N.Y.2d 313 (1987). In *Stith*, state troopers had stopped a truck driver for speeding. When the driver could not find the registration for the truck, a trooper went inside the cab himself to look for the registration and inadvertently found a gun. The driver was arrested, and further investigation disclosed that the truck had been stolen.

The court held that the search of the truck cab was unlawful, and even though the police unquestionably would have conducted an inventory search of the stolen truck and would have found the gun, it declined to apply inevitable discovery. In suppressing the gun found in the stolen truck, the court distinguished *Stith* from *Fitzgerald* and differentiated primary from secondary evidence. In *Stith*, the gun seized was the primary evidence obtained as a direct result of the unlawful search; in *Fitzgerald* the gun was secondary evidence, not derived directly from the unlawful interrogation of the defendant. Less subtle minds than those of our high court judges might have difficulty distinguishing these esoteric distinctions. Nevertheless, New York law now requires a distinction between primary and secondary evidence.

The inevitable discovery issue took on a more corporeal form in *People v. Turriago*, 219 A.D.2d 383, (1996), a case in which the New York courts faced an ultimatum: give a murderer immunity from prosecution by enforcing the exclusionary rule to the fullest, including the fruits of the poisonous tree, or apply the inevitable discovery doctrine in order to incarcerate a dangerous criminal and to achieve some justice for a murder victim.

The case involved State Troopers James Van Cura and John O'Leary, who were on patrol on November 24, 1990 in upstate New York on the second day of hunting season. The officers had been enforcing hunting regulations under the Environmental Conservation Law. It was standard practice for troopers to check hunters and their vehicles to ensure compliance with the law. Attention was given to unlicensed poachers who shot deer during the night and to hunters who might violate the regulations by transporting loaded rifles in their vehicles. The regulations require that rifles be unloaded and ammunition stored separately during vehicle transport. The purpose of this is to discourage hunters from stopping their vehicles on the roadway, jumping out, and shooting at a passing animal.

The Environmental Conservation Law, Section 71-0525 (1), (b), authorized the troopers to stop vehicles, to question the occupants, and, if they had cause to believe a violation of hunting laws was occurring, to search the vehicle without a warrant.

At 2:00 a.m., the troopers observed a U-haul truck speeding at 70mph in a 55mph zone. They stopped the truck. Leonardo Turriago was driving, and his associates, Edwin Sepulveda and Dennis Torres, were seated next to him. Trooper O'Leary asked Turriago for a license and registration, which he produced. The trooper then asked Turriago, "Do you mind if we see what's in the back of the truck?"

Turriago replied, "Sure, I'll show you."

The other trooper, Van Cura, also asked Turriago whether they could look in the back of the truck. Turriago replied, "Sure, no problem," and he began to open the cargo bay of the truck. The troopers did not know that thirteen hours earlier, during a narcotics transaction in an apartment in Manhattan, Turriago had killed Fernando Cuervo by shooting him five times in the head, and because Cuervo was still alive, striking him three times on the head with a hammer. Turriago, Sepulveda, and Torres wrapped Cuervo's body in cellophane and duct tape and put it inside a steamer trunk. They rented the U-haul van, and loaded the van with a cardboard box, a ladder, a toolbox, and the steamer trunk containing Cuervo's body. The men drove to West 125th Street and the Hudson River, where Turriago threw the gun he used into the river. They then drove upstate to burn and dispose of the corpse.

In the event that they were stopped, Turriago instructed his associates to tell the police he had hired them to help move construction materials. He went so far as to tell them how much they were allegedly making per hour, so that if questioned by the police their stories would be consistent.

When Trooper Van Cura entered the back of the truck with Turriago, the trooper observed the steamer trunk and the cardboard box. The defendant opened the cardboard box, which contained clothes and a hammer. Van Cura then asked Turriago if he would mind opening the trunk, to which Turriago replied, "Sure."

Turriago fumbled with the mechanism of the lock, and said he believed the lock was broken. Suddenly, there was an audible click, indicating the lock had sprung open by itself. Turriago promptly jumped from the truck and began to run. Van Cura opened the trunk and saw the body wrapped in the plastic and duct tape. He then chased and arrested Turriago, while Trooper O'Leary arrested Sepulveda and Torres.

The defendants were read Miranda rights and taken to the State Police barracks. As the Court noted, "Only then did Trooper O'Leary issue defendant summonses for speeding and failing to wear a seatbelt. Trooper Van Cura ran a computer check of defendant's license, which revealed that it was suspended, so he issued defendant a summons for aggravated unlicensed operation of a motor vehicle." Computer checks disclosed that neither of the other two men possessed a driver's license.

All three defendants gave statements to investigators, and based on those statements, search warrants were obtained for the apartment where the murder had been committed and for Turriago's residence. The searches recovered two .25 calibre bullet shell casings, cellophane and duct tape of the type consistent with that wrapped around the body, blood samples from a living room wall, eleven pounds of cocaine, three loaded firearms, sneakers and blue jeans with human blood stains consistent with the victim's blood type. A police scuba team recovered a .25 calibre Raven firearm from the Hudson River at West 125th Street where Turriago had said he disposed of the weapon.

Turriago was charged with murder and other crimes. He moved to suppress all the physical evidence recovered from the van, the apartments, and the river, as well as his statements subsequent to his arrest. The trial court denied the motion, and after a jury trial in 1991, Turriago was convicted.

On appeal, Turriago did not contest the legal sufficiency of the overwhelming evidence supporting his conviction, but he contended that the troopers had no right to ask him to consent to the search of the rental van. His argument was premised on *People v. Hollman*, 79 N.Y.2d 181 (1992), a New York Court of Appeals decision, which was decided after Turriago's arrest and conviction. *Hollman* held that police cannot request consent to search a vehicle unless they have a "founded suspicion that criminality is afoot." The *Hollman* "founded suspicion" requirement was unusual; neither federal courts nor most other states had this requirement. Generally, a person's voluntary consent was sufficient to authorize a police search.

In 1996, even though *Hollman* was decided after Turriago's arrest and conviction, the Appellate Division court agreed with Turriago's argument and reversed his conviction, ruling that the dead body, all the physical evidence connecting him to the murder, and his statements to the police should have been suppressed. The opinion of the judge who wrote the decision seemed less about logic and more about an exposition of his feelings:

> The scope of the constitutional problem is not immediately apparent from the circumstances of this particular case, in which a State Trooper's intuition seems to have been rewarded. . . . The constitutional ramifications are, however, much broader. When a motorist, stopped for some minor traffic infraction on a lonely stretch of road in the dead of night, is approached by two imposing State Troopers — the very personification of State authority on the highway — one of whom leans over the car and asks, "Mind if we look in the trunk?", can the forthcoming affirmative response truly be regarded as the product of free will? The courts have confronted this problem for 35 years, and the detailed criteria which have been formulated to balance the government's legitimate interest in law enforcement against the encroachment upon the individual's right to privacy and freedom of movement should not be lightly disregarded. The fruits of

the search of a detainee, undertaken without founded suspicion of criminal activity, are required to be suppressed under either the State or Federal Constitution.[3]

The picture painted by the court of the imposing State Troopers personifying oppressive authority versus the frightened citizen on a lonely road in the dead of night does not exactly characterize what occurred. Based on the record, Turriago was a cold-blooded criminal who with a preconceived strategy played the part of a cooperative citizen in an attempt to dispel any police suspicion. He consented to the police search as part of his ploy. Unfortunately for him, the lock on the steamer trunk sprung open at a very inopportune time.

The Appellate Division found that the troopers did not have a right to ask the defendant to consent to the search; therefore, the search was unreasonable and the evidence had to be suppressed. In addition, the court rejected the argument that the body of Fernando Cuervo would inevitably have been discovered. The prosecution had argued that when it was determined at the police barracks that none of the men had a valid driver's license, the van could not have been released to any of them but would have been held for pickup by the rental company. As standard police procedure, the contents of the van would be inventoried, and during the inventory the police would have found the body. This was a case in which the inevitable discovery exception could easily have been invoked. Nevertheless, the Appellate Division refused to apply inevitable discovery, noting: "The record indicates that they [the police] made no attempt to verify the documentation before proceeding to seek the defendant's permission to search it. This sequence of events only lends further support to the conclusion that the search 'was the product of an inseparable illegal detention.'"[4]

The court discounted the normal police procedure of running a computer check for a driver's license before letting a motorist proceed. The court noted that after the defendant was in custody at the police barracks, "Only then did Trooper O'Leary issue defendant summonses for speeding and failing to wear a seatbelt. Trooper Van Cura ran a computer check of defendant's license, which revealed that it was suspended, so he issued defendant a summons for aggravated unlicensed operation of a motor vehicle."

In other words, the constable blundered. The officers should have immediately begun the process of issuing the speeding ticket. During this process, they would have run a computer check of the defendant's license. It would have revealed the suspension. In accordance with regulations, they would have

---

3. *People v. Turriago*, 219 A.D.2d 383, at 389 (1996).
4. Id., at 387.

arrested Turriago, and they would have impounded and inventoried the truck. During the inventory, they would have found the body.

The putative legal "blunders" of these otherwise excellent troopers included reasonably believing that the Environmental Conservation Law gave them authority to ask for consent to look in the back of the van; believing Turriago's portrayal of himself as a law-abiding, cooperative citizen who was voluntarily consenting to the search rather than as a person in the process of committing a serious crime; patting Turriago's pocket as a safety precaution; and not immediately arresting him for speeding and aggravated unlicensed driving.

After the Appellate Division reversed Turriago's conviction, the district attorney appealed to the New York Court of Appeals, which modified the Appellate Division ruling. In *People v. Turriago*, 90 N.Y.2d 77 (1997), the high court held that the Appellate Division mistakenly rejected application of the inevitable discovery doctrine to the secondary evidence in this case. It instructed the lower courts: "Contrary to the view of the Appellate Division, our decision in *People v. Stith* (supra) . . . would not preclude the introduction of secondary evidence here under the inevitable discovery exception to the exclusion rules." This would mean that the secondary evidence could be admissible, including the defendant's statements, evidence from the apartments, and the gun from the river, but the primary evidence — the body — would not. Consequently, the Court of Appeals remitted the case to the trial court "for further proceedings in accordance with this opinion and, as so modified, affirmed."

The Court of Appeals reasoned that if at the trial court level the prosecution could establish that standard police procedures would have caused an inventory search of the van, "The suppression court could have further found the existence of a very high degree of probability that the body of Cuervo would have been discovered through that inventory search and that, following the discovery, incriminating secondary evidence, i.e., evidence not obtained during or as the immediate consequence of the invalid consent search, would also have been obtained by the police."

Apparently, the Court, expected the lower court to overlay a fiction upon a fiction, and adhering to its decisions in *Hollman* and *Stith*, directed the lower court to exclude the body but to consider admitting the secondary evidence, including the defendant's statements, the bullets, the duct tape, the bloodstains, and the gun. Fortunately, the secondary evidence against the defendant would be enough to obtain a conviction even without the body. However, in other cases with less evidence, the exclusion of a murder victim's body would likely preclude a successful prosecution.

What is so troubling about the Court of Appeals' resolution in *Turriago* is the simple fact that a slight change in circumstance would completely undermine the basis of their proposed solution. Had Turriago possessed a valid driver's license, the argument that an inventory search would have revealed the body loses its underlying premise. For a speeding violation by a licensed driver, an inventory search would not be required, and Turriago would have been issued a ticket and sent on his way with the vehicle. Furthermore, even if Turriago was arrested for driving with a suspended license, had one of the passengers possessed a valid license, normal police procedure would allow the passenger to take the van, also precluding the need for an inventory search. Justice for the victims of serious crimes should not rest on such chance irregularities and technicalities. Although Mr. Cuervo, the victim of this murder, may not have been the most sympathetic victim, he was, nonetheless, entitled to his life — and he and his family were entitled to justice.

The rationale offered by the proponents of the exclusionary rule for suppressing evidence of serious crimes even at the price of acquitting guilty defendants is that suppression protects citizens from coercive or intrusive police actions that violate constitutional rights. However, we cannot be protected from all police activity. Some levels of coercion and intrusion are inherent in the police to citizen relationship. The process by which police make inquiries of people or issue summonses to them is laden with various levels of inherent coercion, which is in the nature of encounters with police. When citizens, even the most law-abiding, see the turret lights of a police car flashing in their rearview mirror, it is a stressful experience. These encounters undoubtedly infringe on individual freedoms but are a necessary corollary to living in an orderly, regulated, and safe society.

In circumstances such as in *Turriago*, a police officer patting a person's pockets may be an unpleasant experience, but it is not the kind of conduct that the exclusionary rule was first designed to deter. It was not police busting down someone's door in the middle of the night without a warrant or justification. The conduct included a degree of coercion, but it should not have warranted excluding the corpse of the murder victim.

Turriago illustrates the complexities that the exclusionary rule generates. In addition, the Appellate Division opinion quoted above also illustrates the existence of the anti-police biases or unrealistic expectations that many judges hold. In another troubling case, one such judge in a dissenting opinion stated, in substance, that he would suppress three bodies because of the lack of speed of a police investigation. In *State v. Epperson*, 571 S.W.2d 260 (Mo. 1978), the defendant lived with his wife and two children. The mother-in-law of the defendant had become concerned that her daughter and two grandchildren had been missing for several days. She went to the defendant's house and noticed a smell of decomposing flesh coming from the house, so she went to a neighbor's house and called the police. From the neighbor's house, the police made several phone calls to the children's school and the parents' places of employment, and they learned that the defendant had been evasive about the whereabouts of his wife and two children.

About two-and-a-half hours after their initial arrival, the police and the defendant's father entered the house through a bedroom window and immediately discovered the dead bodies of the wife and children. Each body showed signs of violence. The children had plastic bags over their heads with chloroformed socks inside the bags, and one child had a Venetian blind cord around his neck. Other incriminating evidence was found in other rooms that the police searched.

The defendant was arrested and convicted for three counts of murder, but he appealed his conviction, not on the grounds that he was innocent of the murders, but on the grounds that the warrantless search of his home required the suppression of the bodies and the other evidence. The Supreme Court of Missouri denied the appeal and upheld the conviction, ruling that the entry into the home was justified under the emergency exception to the warrant requirement.

The dissenting judge, however, stated that the motion to suppress the bodies and the other incriminating evidence should have been granted. He opined that because the police were at the scene for two-and-a-half hours before entering the home, the emergency exception could not be applied. He wrote:

> I respectfully dissent. What the police did here was to break into a man's home. It is true that they did so rather politely, using the defendant's father as their arm, and not resorting to a sledge hammer, but the fact remains that they entered a man's home, a cherished and well nigh sacred place to most of us, by force, without first obtaining a search warrant to do so.

This judge appears not to have considered that it was also the home of the wife and two children, and were either of them by chance still alive, they would have wanted to be rescued. Moreover, no legal requirement exists that the police must always take action immediately; in fact, they are often criticized for acting too quickly. Would this judge have been satisfied had the officers entered within fifteen minutes or sixty minutes or some other time? Should a few minutes too long mean that the only evidence that could convict the defendant of the three murders had to be suppressed?

In circumstances such as in *Epperson*, the police are required to protect life and property. When an unexpected death occurs, the police are called to make an initial assessment of whether the death was natural, accidental, a suicide, or a homicide. They are unable to know beforehand what the outcome will be, and this occurs thousands of times per day. When the police enter a home without a warrant to investigate a death and it is determined that the death was natural, accidental, or a suicide, no penalty is imposed on the police for entering without a warrant. When, by chance, the death is determined to have been a homicide, no plausible reason exists to penalize the police for entering without a warrant.

The opinion of the dissenting judge in *Epperson* is not an uncommon representation of the viewpoints of many of our judges. The unnatural attachment of some judges to the exclusionary rule as a method of penalizing the police sometimes clouds their judgment and penalizes crime victims and society instead.

Chapter Three

Searching for Balance

Crime soared in the 1960s and was the primary reason for Richard Nixon's election to president in 1969. He had campaigned on a law-and-order platform and blamed the Warren Court for its "soft-on-crime" decisions. The Warren Court, between 1953 and 1969, had issued a host of decisions in favor of defendant's rights, many of which addressed the criminal trial process, including the right to counsel, to remain silent, to a speedy trial, an impartial jury, access to exculpatory evidence, and confrontation of accusers.[1] These decisions received some criticism, but they were not the main object of the complaints directed at the Court. It was the expansion of the exclusionary rule that received the harshest and most vitriolic criticism.

Despite Nixon's criticisms, the Warren Court decisions pertaining to the trial process were for the most part quickly accepted. Everyone believed that accused persons should receive a fair trial wherein both sides could present their own evidence and challenge the accuracy of the other side's evidence. Certainly, everyone believed defendants should not be prevented from introducing relevant evidence favorable to their position. However, no such consensus existed about the wisdom of excluding prosecution evidence, and the Court's decisions to suppress evidence incited calls for a change in direction. In addition to the well-known decisions in *Mapp v. Ohio, supra,* and *Miranda v. Arizona, supra,* the Warren Court suppressed evidence in the search and seizure cases of *Wong Sun v. United States,* 371 U.S. 471 (1963), *Aguilar v. Texas,* 378 U.S. 108 (1964), *Beck v. Ohio,* 379 U.S. 89 (1964), *Katz v. United States,* 389 U.S. 347 (1967), *Spinelli v. United States,* 393 U.S. 410 (1969), *Orozco v. Texas,* 394 U.S. 324 (1969), *Chimel v. California,* 395 U.S. 752 (1969), and in the interrogation cases of *Spano v. New York,* 360 U.S. 315 (1959), *Massiah v. United States,* 377 U.S. 201 (1964), *Escobedo v. Illinois,* 378 U.S. 478 (1964), among others.

---

1. *Gideon v. Wainwright,* 372 U.S. 335 (1963); *Griffin v. California,* 380 U.S. 609 (1965); *Klopfer v. North Carolina,* 386 U.S. 213 (1967); *Parker v. Gladden,* 385 U.S. 363 (1966); *Brady v. Maryland,* 373 U.S. 742 (1963); *Pointer v. Texas,* 380 U.S. 400 (1965).

When *Mapp v. Ohio, supra,* mandated that states apply the exclusionary rule for Fourth Amendment violations, the police found themselves in untenable circumstances. Lower federal courts and state courts quickly and expansively applied the *Mapp* rule from searches of residences to searches of individuals in public places. Although the police were required to deter and detect crime, they could no longer rely on the customary practices of stopping, questioning, and searching people. New and extraordinary restrictions were placed on their means to conduct investigations and to employ crime-prevention tactics. At the same time as these restrictions were being imposed, crime was increasing drastically, especially in large cities where much of the population was transient, and where the police generally did not know the identities of the people unless they stopped and questioned them. Nevertheless, courts held that the stop and detention of an individual for questioning constituted an arrest, and in order to arrest, the police needed probable cause.

The basic principles were relatively simple and straightforward. The term "arrest" was synonymous with those seizures governed by the Fourth Amendment. While warrants were not required in all circumstances, the requirement of probable cause, as elaborated in numerous precedents, was treated as absolute."[2]

Under the Fourth Amendment, police must have probable cause to arrest or seize a person, and probable cause exists when the "facts and circumstances within the officers' knowledge and of which they have reasonably trustworthy information are sufficient in themselves to warrant a man of reasonable caution to believe that an offense has been or is being committed" by a particular person.[3]

Were the police to seize and detain a person without probable cause for even a short period of time, any evidence obtained as a result of the seizure would be inadmissible at trial. Consequently, many police-citizen encounters that began as routine inquiries but evolved into searches or seizures resulted in the suppression of evidence, whether the evidence was a physical object or a verbal statement, and normal and proper police activities were adversely affected by concerns about evidence suppression. Asking questions of witnesses or possible suspects, making inquiries regarding possibly dangerous situations, or taking precautions against potential violence, all can quickly turn into arrest

---

2. *Dunaway v. New York,* 442 U.S. 200 (1979).
3. *Draper v. U.S.,* 358 U.S. 307 (1959); *Carroll v. U.S.,* 267 U.S. 132 (1925).

situations. However, without initial probable cause to detain the suspect, any evidence obtained had to be suppressed.

In 1968, because of the repercussions on police and prosecutors, Chief Justice Earl Warren pulled the Court back from the expansion of exclusionary rule and the absolutist interpretation of *Mapp*. Although Earl Warren's name is associated with the expansion of defendant's rights, he was never unmindful of the needs of law enforcement. Before becoming the Chief Justice, he had been a district attorney and California's Attorney General. In 1943, he was elected Governor of California as a republican, and in 1948, he ran for Vice President of the United States on the losing ticket with Thomas Dewey, another Governor and former district attorney. In the 1952 election, he supported President Dwight Eisenhower, which led to his appointment as Chief Justice in 1953. Surprisingly, the ex-prosecutor came to be known as the leading figure of the 1960s defendants' rights revolution.

In the landmark decision of *Terry v. Ohio*, 392 U.S. 1 (1968), Warren carved out the stop-and-frisk exception to the Fourth Amendment probable cause requirement—an intermediary procedure between a common law inquiry and an arrest that provided the police with a practical tool for crime-fighting and performing their routine functions.

In *Terry*, Martin McFadden, a Cleveland police detective, with 39 years experience, noticed Mr. Terry and a companion standing on a street corner. As McFadden put it, "They didn't look right to me at that time." McFadden observed the men take turns walking by and looking in a store window. They repeated this activity between five and six times each. A third man joined the first two men and conferred with them.

McFadden approached the three men, identified himself as a police officer and asked for their names . . . When the men "mumbled something" in response to his inquiries, Officer McFadden grabbed petitioner Terry, spun him around so that they were facing the other two, with Terry between McFadden and the others, and patted down the outside of his clothing. In the left breast pocket of Terry's overcoat Officer McFadden felt a pistol. He reached inside the overcoat pocket, but was unable to remove the gun. At this point, keeping Terry between himself and the others, the officer ordered all three men to enter Zucker's store. As they went in, he removed Terry's overcoat completely, removed a .38-caliber revolver from the pocket and ordered all three men to face the wall with their hands raised. Officer McFadden proceeded to pat down the outer clothing of the other two men and discovered another revolver.

The Supreme Court upheld the officer's actions and upheld Terry's conviction for possession of an unlawful weapon. Chief Justice Warren wrote the opinion for the court and stated:

We merely hold that where a police officer observes unusual conduct which leads him reasonably to conclude in light of his experience that criminal activity may be afoot and that the persons with whom he is dealing may be armed and presently dangerous, where in the course of investigating this behavior he identifies himself as a policeman and makes reasonable inquiries, and where nothing in the initial stages of the encounter serves to dispel his reasonable fear for his own or others' safety, he is entitled for the protection of himself and others in the area to conduct a carefully limited search of the outer clothing of such persons in an attempt to discover weapons which might be used to assault him. Such a search is a reasonable search under the Fourth Amendment, and any weapons seized may properly be introduced in evidence against the person from whom they were taken.

Although when Detective McFadden first approached the suspects, he did not have probable cause to arrest them, his conduct was reasonable and therefore not a violation of the Fourth Amendment. After the stop and frisk, the guns that were discovered provided sufficient probable cause to arrest the suspects; therefore, the guns need not be suppressed.

In his majority opinion, Chief Justice Warren recognized the difficulties of second-guessing the police in street encounters and wrote:

A rigid and unthinking application of the exclusionary rule, in futile protest against practices which it can never be used effectively to control, may exact a high toll on human injury and frustration of efforts to prevent crime. No judicial opinion can comprehend the protean variety of the street encounter.[4]

Terry does not mean that police officers can stop and frisk anyone who appears suspicious to them. They must have reasonable suspicion, which has been defined as specific facts and circumstances that would lead an officer to reasonably believe that "criminal activity is afoot."[5] The officer need not know a particular crime and the particular person who committed the crime, but he must reasonably believe that criminal activity has occurred, is occurring, or will occur.

An important purpose of stop, question, and frisk is to prevent crime. Reasonable suspicion that a crime will occur justifies police intervention short of an arrest. When the police stop and identify a person whom they suspect is

---

4. *Terry v. Ohio*, 392 U.S. 1 (1968).
5. *Id.*

preparing to commit a crime, the police action often does not result in an arrest but dissuades the person from committing the crime.

The frisk authorized by *Terry* is not a full-blown search. It is generally a pat-down search of a suspect's outer clothing to determine whether the suspect is armed with a weapon. Its purpose is for officer safety and public protection; it is not for the purpose of uncovering other evidence or contraband. Moreover, the authority to stop a person for questioning does not always carry with it the authority to frisk the person. To frisk, in addition to the grounds for making the stop, an officer must reasonably fear a danger of physical injury. In such case:

> He may search the person for a deadly weapon or any instrument, article, or substance readily capable of causing serious physical injury and of a sort not ordinarily carried in public places by law-abiding persons. If he finds such a weapon or instrument, or any other property, possession of which he reasonably believes may constitute the commission of a crime, he may take it and keep it until the completion of the questioning, at which time he shall either return it, if lawfully possessed, or arrest such person.[6]

In accordance with the law of unintended consequences, although Chief Justice Warren designed the *Terry* rules to clarify the lawful authority of police officers, they inevitably had the opposite effect—adding layers of complexity to the problem and creating new issues for courts and lawyers to debate. Even more than forty years since *Terry*, courts are still grappling with stop-and-frisk issues, and some recent decisions have been decided on the basis of infinitesimal differences, such as whether a police officer upon touching an object in a defendant's jacket recognized it immediately as a package of unlawful drugs or only after manipulating it with his fingers for a few seconds.[7]

In June of 1969, when Earl Warren resigned and Nixon appointed Warren Burger as Chief Justice to strengthen the "peace forces as against the criminal forces of the country," many court observers assumed that the pro-defendants' rights decisions of the Warren Court would be overturned in a short period of time and the exclusionary rule would be significantly cutback.

Most of the controversial defendants' rights decisions of the Warren Court had been decided by votes of five-to-four, so the addition of a "law-and-order" justice pointed towards a shift. However, the Burger Court did not abandon

---

6. New York State Criminal Procedure Law, Section 140.50 (3).
7. *Minnesota v. Dickerson*, 508 U.S. 366 (1993).

the Warren Court decisions, and only modified them at the margins, case by case. The influence of the Warren Court holdovers—Hugo Black, William Douglas, William Brennan, and Thurgood Marshall—remained strong for several years and prevented a wholesale eradication of their decisions. The struggle between the surviving liberal wing of the Court and the newly developing law-and-order Court was, in a sense, a life and death struggle. It was only impending death or severe illness that convinced the Warren Court justices to leave the bench.

In 1971, Hugo Black, after 34 years of service on the Court, retired at age 85 due to ill health.

In 1971, John Harlan II was gravely ill with spinal cancer when he retired. He died three months after his retirement.

In 1974, William Douglas suffered a stroke. Although seriously disabled, he refused to retire, saying, "Even if I'm only half alive, I can still cast a liberal vote." He held out for almost a year before retiring.

In 1981, Potter Stewart, after twenty-three years on the Court, retired relatively early at 66, but died just four years later.

In 1990, William Brennan suffered a mild stroke. He resigned after 34 years on the Court at the age of 84.

In 1991, Thurgood Marshall, after 24 years on the Court, retired at age 83 due to ill health.

The justices who replaced the Warren Court members were not counter-revolutionaries. Justices Burger, Harry Blackmun, Lewis Powell, William Rehnquist, John Paul Stevens, and Sandra Day O'Connor all shared a penchant for stability, and none advocated a sweeping reversal of prior decisions. They modified Warren Court precedents only to cure particularly egregious results. However, because of the increased complexities of search and seizure law, many of their decisions lacked consistency, either within decisions or with other decisions. *Coolidge v. New Hampshire*, 403 U.S. 443 (1971), demonstrated the Court's lack of uniformity and direction. In *Coolidge*, a 14-year-old girl, Pamela Mason, was found murdered. Pamela had been working as a babysitter and had left her home after receiving a call from an unknown male, apparently to baby sit. Eight days later, Pamela's frozen body was discovered in a snowdrift beside an interstate highway a few miles from her house. Her throat had been slashed, and she had been shot in the head.

After an intensive two-week investigation, the police arrested the defendant. Among other evidence, two witnesses reported that they had stopped to offer assistance to a man in a 1951 Pontiac automobile that had been parked near where the girl's dead body was later found, and the defendant owned a 1951 Pontiac. The police obtained a search warrant, which was signed by the New

Hampshire Attorney-General, for the defendant's Pontiac. Particles of forensic evidence found in the car matched particles on the victim's clothes, indicating that the girl had been in the car. The police obtained a gun belonging
to the defendant from his wife, and a ballistic examination concluded that it
was the gun used to murder the young girl.

Coolidge was tried and convicted. However, the Supreme Court, in a plu-
rality opinion, reversed the conviction on the grounds that forensic evidence
from the car should have been suppressed by the trial court because the
Attorney-General who had issued the warrant was not a neutral and detached
magistrate.

After rejecting the validity of the warrant, the Court examined and rejected
other possible justifications for the search of the car, including the exigent circumstances doctrine and the automobile and plain view exceptions to the
search warrant requirement. It is unnecessary to review the rulings here, since
they have been modified in several respects by subsequent cases. The significance of *Coolidge*, in addition to the reversal of the conviction, was the disagreement between the justices, and their failure to provide a cohesive opinion
that could provide direction for lower courts and law enforcement personnel.
The divergent votes of the justices said it all:

> Stewart, J., delivered the opinion of the Court, in which Burger, C.J.
> (as to Part III), and Harlan (as to Parts I, II-D, and III), Douglas,
> Brennan, and Marshall, JJ., joined. Harlan, J, filed a concurring opin-
> ion. Burger, C.J., filed a concurring and dissenting opinion. Black, J.,
> filed a concurring and dissenting opinion, in a portion of Part I and
> in Parts II and III of which Burger, C.J., and Blackmun, J., joined.
> White, J., filed a concurring and dissenting opinion, in which Burger,
> C.J., joined.

The confusion within the *Coolidge* decision raised additional calls for the
rule's elimination or modification; nevertheless, the Court continued to develop and expand the rule and its corollary fruit of the poisonous tree doctrine.

In *Dunaway v. New York*, 442 U.S. 200 (1979), police detectives had information that the defendant had participated in a robbery and murder. They
picked him up near his house and took him to a stationhouse for questioning.
After they gave him Miranda warnings, the defendant confessed to the crime,
and he was convicted. The Supreme Court reversed the conviction, ruling that
even though the defendant had been advised of his rights and had voluntarily
confessed, taking the defendant to the stationhouse was an arrest without probable cause and, consequently, the confession had to be suppressed. Justice
William Brennan wrote the majority opinion and devoted much of it to nar-

rowing the *Terry* stop-and-frisk authority of police. Brennan rejected the government's argument that the reasonable suspicion present in this case justified stopping the defendant and taking him to the stationhouse.

In *Payton v. New York*, 445 U.S. 573 (1980), the police had assembled evidence sufficient to establish probable cause to believe that the defendant had murdered the manager of a gas station two days earlier. They went to the defendant's Bronx apartment, and although light and music emanated from the apartment, no one answered their knock on the door. They used crowbars to break open the door and enter the apartment. No one was inside; however, in plain view was a .30-caliber shell casing that was seized and later admitted into evidence at the defendant's murder trial.

The Supreme Court reversed the defendant's murder conviction and ruled that the shell casing should have been suppressed. Acting in a legislative fashion similar to their actions in *Miranda v. Arizona, supra,* the Court mandated that for police to arrest suspects in their homes, an arrest warrant was required unless consent to enter the home was obtained or the police acted under emergency or exigent circumstances. Under prior law in most states, when police or other officials had probable cause to arrest a suspect, they could enter a home without a warrant to make the arrest. This has arguably been true under common law for hundreds of years and was not changed by the ratification of the Constitution.

During the twentieth century, to grant and clarify police authority, many states enacted statutes authorizing warrantless entries to make arrests. In some states, the arrests had to be for felonies; in other states, either felonies or misdemeanors. In 1971, New York State enacted Criminal Procedure Law 140.15 (4), which allowed:

> In order to effect such an arrest, a police officer may enter premises in which he reasonably believes such person to be present, under the same circumstances and in the same manner as would be authorized . . . if he were attempting to make such arrest pursuant to a warrant of arrest.

Payton struck down this statute as it applied to warrantless arrests of defendants inside their homes, but it did not declare the entire statute unconstitutional. The police may still enter without a warrant to effect arrests in "premises," which includes offices, work places, and the homes of other persons.

Violations of either *Dunaway* or *Payton* require the suppression of evidence obtained as a result of the violation. In both cases, the Court apparently intended to establish clear bright-line rules, but actually created more uncertainty and a myriad of new problematic issues, some of which have been debated for three decades.[8] Whether an arrest warrant was, in fact, valid, whether the police entered a home with consent, or whether they entered because of a genuine emergency or exigent circumstances became abundant areas for factual and legal dispute. The question of how stringently the poisonous-tree doctrine should be applied to derivative evidence that was obtained after a violation is still being litigated.

Clearly, when the justices of the Supreme Court cannot agree on the lawfulness of police actions during murder investigations, police officers and detectives in the field will be uncertain of the right course of action, and they will invariably do something wrong. In response to such criticism, the Court gradually attempted to shape a more uniform and balanced approach to the exclusionary rule.

The Supreme Court will grant a *writ of certiorari* to hear cases of its choosing, and political considerations influence its choices. In the area of criminal justice, the Court takes only a handful of cases each year. During periods when the majority of the Court wishes to limit or constrain police and prosecutorial conduct, as during the Warren years, they will accept cases in which the police or prosecutors clearly abused their authority and unfairly mistreated individuals. When the majority of the Court wishes to maintain or enhance the capabilities of law enforcement, as during the Burger and Rehnquist years,[9] they will accept cases in which the police or prosecutors may have made a mistake or misjudgment but had acted in good faith to accomplish a reasonable law enforcement objective.

In 1981, Justice Potter Stewart, the author of the majority opinion in *Coolidge v. New Hampshire, supra,* retired. He was replaced by Justice Sandra Day O'-Connor, the first woman to serve on the Court. This change shifted the balance on the Court to the right, and during the 1980s, the Court granted *writs of certiorari* to a high number of exclusionary rule cases, apparently for the purpose of curing some of the legal technicalities that they thought were undermining public confidence in the courts.

Justice Byron White was not the Chief Justice, but he was a leading figure during this time. He had been appointed to the Warren Court by President John F. Kennedy in 1962 and could not be characterized as either a liberal or conservative. He consistently voted to uphold anti-discrimination laws, voted

---

8. *Minnesota v. Olson*, 495 U.S. 91 (1990); *New York v. Harris*, 495 U.S. 14 (1990); *Minnesota v. Carter*, 525 U.S. 83 (1998).

9. Justice William Rehnquist was appointed to the Court in 1971 and became Chief Justice in 1986 when Warren Burger retired. Rehnquist served until 2005, the year in which he died.

against the discriminatory application of the death penalty, yet voted to uphold the death penalty when applied in a fair and objective manner.[10] In the area of defendants' rights, he had consistently been in the dissent during the Warren years, and he had dissented in *Coolidge v. New Hampshire, supra.* Then, with the addition of Justice O'Connor, he was able to effectively advocate for modifying the more extreme pro-defendant decisions and cutting back expansive applications of the exclusionary rule.

In 1983, Justice White, in his concurring opinion in *Illinois v. Gates,* 462 U.S. 213, articulated the position that the exclusionary rule was not a constitutional mandate but a practical tool to deter police misconduct that should be applied only when the benefits outweigh the costs.

> These cases reflect that the exclusion of evidence is not a personal constitutional right but a remedy, which, like all remedies, must be sensitive to the costs and benefits of its imposition. The trend and direction of our exclusionary rule decisions indicate not a lesser concern with safeguarding the Fourth Amendment but a fuller appreciation of the high costs incurred when probative, reliable evidence is barred because of investigative error. The primary cost, of course, is that the exclusionary rule interferes with the truth seeking function of a criminal trial by barring relevant and trustworthy evidence. We will never know how many guilty defendants go free as a result of the rule's operation. But any rule of evidence that denies the jury access to clearly probative and reliable evidence must bear a heavy burden of justification, and must be carefully limited to the circumstances in which it will pay its way by deterring official lawlessness. I do not presume that modification of the exclusionary rule will, by itself, significantly reduce the crime rate—but that is no excuse for indiscriminate application of the rule.
>
> The suppression doctrine entails other costs as well. It would be surprising if the suppression of evidence garnered in good faith, but by means later found to violate the Fourth Amendment, did not deter legitimate, as well as unlawful, police activities. To the extent the rule operates to discourage police from reasonable and proper investigative actions, it hinders the solution and even the prevention of crime. . . . The rule also exacts a heavy price in undermining public confi-

---

10. *Regents of the University of California v. Bakke,* 478 U.S. 265 (1978); *Furman v. Georgia,* 408 U.S. 238 (1972); *Gregg v. Georgia,* 438 U.S. 153 (1976).

dence in the reasonableness of the standards that govern the criminal justice system.[11]

During the following years, Justice White's concurring opinion that a costs/benefits analysis must be applied before imposing the exclusionary rule became the accepted position of the Court.

The majority opinion in *Gates* also changed earlier exclusionary rule doctrine by establishing the totality of the circumstances test for evaluating probable cause. This was a modification of the prior Warren Court decisions in *Aguilar v. Texas*, 378 U.S. 108 (1964), and *Spinelli v. United States*, 393 U.S. 410 (1969).

Gates reversed the Illinois state court's suppression of evidence and rejected the hyper-technical, Aguilar/Spinelli two-pronged test that required a confidential informant to demonstrate both a basis of knowledge and prior reliability before his information could be sufficient for probable cause.[12] In *Gates*, the police received an anonymous letter that detailed the operations of an interstate drug smuggling ring. After the police conducted surveillances that confirmed most of the detailed information in the letter, they executed search warrants, recovered illegal narcotics, and made arrests. The defendant appealed his conviction on the grounds that the prior reliability of the writer of the anonymous letter had not been established.

The Court rejected that argument. As it would be impossible to establish the prior reliability of an anonymous person, the Court held that a lack in one part of the two-pronged test could be compensated for by strength in the other part of the test. Here, the confirmed details of the letter established a strong basis of knowledge and, therefore, under a totality of circumstances analysis, the issuance of the search warrant was reasonable.

In 1984, the movement to modify the exclusionary rule accelerated, and the Court ratified several exceptions to the rule. To establish the good-faith exception, the Court decided two cases on the same day, *Massachusetts v. Sheppard*, 468 U.S. 981, and *United States v. Leon*, 468 U.S. 897.

In *Sheppard*, the defendant was convicted of the murder of a woman after a trial in which evidence obtained pursuant to a search warrant was admitted against the defendant. The evidence included a pair of bloodstained boots, bloodstains on a concrete floor, a woman's earring with bloodstains on it, a bloodstained envelope, a pair of men's jockey shorts, a woman's bloodstained leotard, three types of wire, and a woman's hairpiece.

---

11. *Illinois v. Gates*, 462 U.S. 213 (1983).
12. *Aguilar v. Texas*, 378 U.S. 108 (1964); *Spinelli v. U.S.*, 393 U.S. 410 (1969).

The Massachusetts appellate court reversed the conviction and suppressed the evidence because the warrant was technically defective. The warrant application and the accompanying affidavit had been inadvertently filled out in error. The wrong form was used, and instead of listing the items to be seized in the application, the items were listed in the affidavit.

The Supreme Court reversed the Massachusetts court, holding that the officers acted in good faith and no legitimate purpose would be served by excluding the evidence because of a clerical error.

In *United States v. Leon, supra,* Justice White wrote the majority opinion, which applied the good faith exception to a search based on a warrant that was later deemed insufficient. In *Leon,* police officers had conducted an extensive investigation into the activities of a drug-dealing ring. The officers obtained a search warrant and during its execution, recovered quantities of unlawful drugs. After the indictments of the ring members, the defendants challenged the validity of the search warrant. The district court held an evidentiary hearing and, while recognizing that the case was a close one, concluded that the affidavit for the search warrant was insufficient to establish probable cause. As a result, the district court suppressed the evidence.

The prosecution appealed the ruling to the United States Supreme Court and the Court reversed the lower court ruling. Justice White stated, "Our evaluation of the costs and benefits of suppressing reliable physical evidence seized by officers reasonably relying on a warrant issued by a detached and neutral magistrate leads to the conclusion that such evidence should be admissible in the prosecution's case in chief."

He explained that the purpose of the exclusionary rule was to deter the police from committing constitutional violations. In this case, the officers acted in objective good faith, obtained a search warrant, and acted within its scope. "There is no police illegality and thus nothing to deter. . . . We conclude that the marginal or nonexistent benefits produced by suppressing evidence obtained in objectively reasonable reliance on a subsequently invalidated search warrant cannot justify the substantial costs of exclusion."

Leon has made clear that in cases wherein the rule does not have the effect of deterring future police violations, the imposition of the rule serves no purpose. In cases wherein the rule may have a minimal, indirect effect of deterring future police violations, the rule must be weighed against the costs of withholding reliable evidence from the truth-seeking process. It must be weighed against the costs to crime-prevention, and it must be weighed against the costs to crime victims and their families.

The good-faith exception has become an established argument for prosecutors. One could argue that were *Coolidge v. New Hampshire, supra,* decided today, it might be decided differently since the police officers acted in good faith on the warrant issued by the New Hampshire Attorney-General and would not have known that a court would subsequently invalidate the warrant. The good faith exception has produced beneficial results; however, like the inevitable discovery exception, it has limited application, and while it has saved some prosecutions, it has done little to reverse the overall detrimental effects of the exclusionary rule.

Saving a few cases here and there by judicial legerdemain does not resolve the overarching problem; it does not cure the injustice caused by the rule. The Court has continued on the path of modifying and limiting the rule at the margins, but the jurisprudence behind the rule remains in place and continues to subvert the truth-seeking process.

Since 1984, the balance on the Court has shifted, perhaps temporarily, in favor of those who would modify and limit the rule as against those who would absolutely maintain and even expand the rule. Nonetheless, an acrimonious division still persists, with both sides feeling strongly about their positions. In *Segura et al. v. United States*, 468 U.S. 796 (1984), a bitterly divided Court, in a five-to-four decision written by Chief Justice Burger, joined by justices White, Powell, Rehnquist, and O'Connor, applied the independent source exception to the fruits of the poisonous tree doctrine and ruled that some of the evidence should not have been suppressed.

In *Segura*, agents of the federal Drug Enforcement Administration were conducting a surveillance of a drug ring and had compiled information about the ring's operations. After observing a drug sale, they arrested two participants, and then followed another participant, Segura, to an apartment. They arrested Segura outside the apartment, and then entered the apartment. Inside, several persons were present and the agents observed and recovered drug paraphernalia and a gun. To secure the apartment and prevent the destruction of other evidence, the agents remained in the apartment while other agents obtained a search warrant. For various reasons, mainly delay by the United States Attorney's Office, it took between eighteen and twenty hours for the other agents to return with the warrant. When they executed the search warrant, they found a substantial amount of packaged cocaine and $50,000 in cash.

Lower federal courts suppressed all the evidence that had been recovered; however, the Supreme Court held that although the evidence obtained during the initial illegal entry into the apartment (the drug paraphernalia and the gun) must be suppressed, the evidence obtained as a result of the search warrant (the packaged cocaine and the $50,000) was admissible. The Court ruled that the agents had independent sources of information to establish the probable cause necessary to obtain the search warrant and the issuance of the warrant was based on an independent source of information obtained prior to the initial entry into the apartment.

Chief Justice Burger wrote, "We decline to extend the exclusionary rule, which already exacts an enormous price from society and our system of justice, to further 'protect' criminal activity, as the dissent would have us do."

Referring to the dissenting opinion that the agents should not have remained in the apartment, Burger wrote, "The essence of the dissent is that there is some 'constitutional right' to destroy evidence. This concept defies logic and common sense."[13]

The dissent written by Justice Stevens and joined by Justices Brennan, Marshall, and Blackmun contained equally disparaging remarks directed at the Chief Justice. Stevens wrote:

> Petitioners' privacy rights were unreasonably infringed by the agents' prolonged occupation of their home. The CHIEF JUSTICE simply ignores this point, assuming that there is no constitutional distinction between surveillance of a home from the outside and police occupation from the inside. The CHIEF JUSTICE'S assumption is, of course, untenable. . . . Nevertheless, in what I can only characterize as an astonishing holding, the CHIEF JUSTICE . . . concluded that the 18- to 20-hour seizure of the apartment was not unreasonable.

The above kinds of disparaging personal comments demonstrated how wide the philosophical divide was between the justices. Resistance by the minority justices made the majority's effort to change direction frustrating and difficult. Justices Brennan and Marshall were the most visible proponents for resisting the new direction of the Court, and their absolute adherence to the rule and their resistance to any modifications never wavered. Brennan, finding himself on the losing side of exclusionary rule cases, took up the "state constitutionalism" movement. He gave life and authority to that movement in his 1977 seminal article, "State Constitutions and the Protection of Individual Rights," calling for states to rely on their own constitutions as a counterweight to the new leadership on the Supreme Court.[14] Under the theory of "state constitutionalism," which propounds that although a state must grant its citizens at least the minimum rights guaranteed by the United States Constitution, a state may grant greater rights and protections to its citizens.[15] With Brennan's sup-

---

13. *Segura v. U.S.,* 468 U.S. 796 (1984).
14. *90 Harvard L. Rev. 489* (1977).
15. *Commonwealth v. Upton,* 394 Mass. 363 (1985); *People v. Elwell,* 50 N.Y.2d 231 (1980).

port, state courts that could not logically fit their view of the law within the parameters of the newer Supreme Court majority decisions simply disregarded those decisions and employed their own state constitutions as a basis for their nonconforming decisions.

Since 1980, state courts have increasingly exercised their prerogative to apply the exclusionary rule in more expansive ways than the Supreme Court required. These state courts, at trial and appellate levels, are where tens of thousands of exclusionary rule cases are decided, and many of the decisions rendered in these courts have not followed the Supreme Court path to moderation but instead have applied the rule in absolutist terms. Consequently, in those states, the exclusionary rule is employed today as much as or more than ever, and it continues to undermine the goals of the criminal justice system.

An example of a state court utilizing the exclusionary rule to the fullest regardless of the consequences is *People v. Breazil*, 52 A.D.3d 523, 860 N.Y.S.2d 137 (2008). In that case, the crime occurred thirteen years earlier on May 22, 1995. Terrance Breazil had been out of prison for a year when he allegedly saw another man, Michael Kinard, talking to his girlfriend outside the Farragut Housing Development in Brooklyn, New York. Breazil shot Kinard in the genitals, and Kinard subsequently died from his injuries. Breazil also seriously injured another man during the shooting.

Breazil fled, but the police identified him and issued a wanted bulletin to apprehend him in connection with the shootings. Then, about two months later, on July 17, 1995, in an unrelated incident, police officers responded to an anonymous 911 call of a robbery in progress at Franklin Avenue and Fulton Street in Brooklyn. The description given was "six males robbing one male—one male with a gun wearing all white, a second male wearing number three jersey on a bike in front of a 24-hour deli store." The officers arrived on the scene within minutes and observed Breazil on a bicycle, wearing all white clothing and heading eastbound on Fulton Street. They placed him against the wall, frisked him, and found a 9mm. handgun and 21 vials of crack-cocaine.

Breazil was not identified as one of the robbers, and he was not charged; however, he was arrested for possession of the gun and the drugs. A ballistics examination proved that the gun was the one used to kill Kinard. The police then put Breazil in a lineup, where a witness identified him as the person who had shot Kinard. He was convicted of murder, attempted murder, and possession of a weapon, and he was sentenced to 45 years in prison.

Several years later, in 2000, the United States Supreme Court issued its opinion in *Florida v. J.L.*, 529 U.S. 266, ruling that an uncorroborated anonymous tip, such as a 911 call, cannot be used as the sole basis for a stop-and-frisk.

Breazil, while reading in the library in Attica prison, learned of the ruling and filed a *pro se* motion to vacate his convictions on the grounds that according to *Florida v. J.L.* his stop-and-frisk was unconstitutional He argued that all the evidence obtained, including the gun and the witness' identification, had to be suppressed.

The New York Appellate Division agreed, vacated the convictions, and ordered a new trial without the use of the gun. Unfortunately for district attorneys, an order for a new trial for many cases is the equivalent of a dismissal or a reduced charge. In this case, the shooting occurred in 1995, and it is highly unlikely that the witness would still be around and willing to testify or would remember details sufficiently to convince a jury without the gun as corroboration.

Also problematic was the appellate court's application of *Florida v. J.L., supra,* to the facts in *Breazil.* In *Florida v. J.L.,* the juvenile defendant was arrested when the police received a call that a young man, wearing a plaid shirt and standing at a bus stop, was carrying a concealed gun. The police immediately drove to the bus stop where they saw three young men, including J.L. who was wearing a plaid shirt. They frisked him and found a gun.

The Supreme Court ruled that the gun must be suppressed, stating:

> The anonymous call concerning J.L. provided no predictive information and therefore left the police without means to test the informant's knowledge or credibility. That the allegation about the gun turned out to be correct does not suggest that the officers, prior to the frisks, had a reasonable basis for suspecting J.L. of engaging in unlawful conduct. The reasonableness of official suspicion must be measured by what the officers knew before they conducted their search. All the police had to go on in this case was the bare report of an unknown, unaccountable informant who neither explained how he knew about the gun nor supplied any basis for believing he had inside information about J.L.

The Court made it clear that an anonymous tip, such as that in *Florida v. J.L.,* must be corroborated before police may act upon it. The corroboration may come from additional factors indicating criminal activity or from verifying the predictive information contained within the tip itself.[16]

Breazil was an entirely different matter than *Florida v. J.L.* The police were responding to a robbery in progress at one of the most notorious locations in the city for robberies. For years, the area around Franklin Avenue and Fulton

---

16. *Alabama v. White,* 496 U.S. 325 (1990).

Street had been recognized as a known location for the sale of heroin and cocaine and also where drug-related robberies constantly occurred. Such factors must be considered when judging the appropriateness of a police response. When police respond to robberies in progress, it is standard and proper procedure to look for possible suspects fleeing from the area of the robbery. Obviously, by the time a description of the robbers is called into the police and broadcasted over the police radio, the robbers have fled the site of the robbery. When responding police officers observe a possible suspect, who matches the description given of one of the robbers, leaving the site of the robbery, close in time to the robbery, the police would be derelict in their duty not to stop him. Carrying the court's rationale to its full extent, police officers would have to give up the tried-and-true practice of stopping suspects from leaving the area of just committed robberies, burglaries, and assaults.

In *Florida v. J.L.*, the Supreme Court noted that the report "does not show that the tipster has knowledge of concealed criminal activity."[17] The tipster did not state that he saw a gun. In *Breazil*, the caller did not report concealed criminal activity. Instead, he reported an unconcealed robbery in progress at a specific location and gave a detailed description of the robbers. No need existed for the caller to explain any basis of his possession of inside information; he was simply reporting an ongoing crime. It is not uncommon for citizens to hurriedly call 911 to report crimes in progress and then hang up; nonetheless, the police must respond to such calls.

In addition, robberies are inherently violent crimes that incite a reasonable fear for safety and may justify a frisk of the suspect. Here, the suspect himself, Breazil, was a career criminal, wanted for a recent murder and assault with a gun that he was still carrying. Surely, these facts were reflected in his demeanor and movements. Under the totality of the circumstances, the officers should have been allowed to conduct a safety frisk, the gun should have been admissible evidence, and the conviction should have been upheld.

While Breazil's story of learning how to do legal research while in prison, filing an appeal, and successfully invoking the exclusionary rule may be interesting, it should not be forgotten that he committed a senseless and vicious crime and that the victim suffered greatly and died from the wounds inflicted on him.

It also should not be forgotten that the police are required to intercept crimes in progress and persons fleeing from such crimes, and they need the authority to protect themselves by conducting frisks when necessary.

---

17. *Florida v. J.L.*, 529 U.S. 266, at 271 (2000).

It seems absurd that in balancing the right to privacy against the need for enforcement of the criminal laws in this case, the court sided with the wanted criminal. Breazil had already forfeited his right to privacy when he shot and killed Kinard and then traveled the streets with a loaded gun. Had the police recognized him, they could have arrested him on the spot. Constructing a wall of protection around a fugitive who was on the run and carrying the loaded semiautomatic gun that he had used to commit a murder is not required by the Constitution. As has been often repeated—the Constitution is not a suicide pact. Furthermore, it should not be used as a tool to deprive crime victims of their right to justice. As the technicalities of suppression law have grown, nothing has been added that helps achieve truth and justice. Rather, the opposite has been the result, and the criminal justice system has thus been diminished. Perhaps one of life's most disheartening experiences is to be victimized by a false and unjust court decision, whether rendered by a judge or a jury. Because of human fallibility, this happens all too often. However, it should not occur on purpose. When the evidence and truth are purposely suppressed, when falsehood is allowed to flourish in our courtrooms, the morality on which society is built is severely undermined. Unfortunately, as long as the exclusionary rule remains in force, efforts by the Supreme Court in such cases as *Terry v. Ohio, supra, Illinois v. Gates,* and *United States v. Leon, supra,* to alleviate the rule's most damaging consequences will be contravened by courts misapplying the law or rejecting the more balanced approach.

Chapter Four

Suppressing
Voluntary Confessions

Confessions constitute the highest and most satisfactory species of evidence. This is for the reason that no innocent man, in full possession of his faculties, can be supposed ordinarily to be willing to risk his life, liberty, or property voluntarily by a false confession.[1]

Before the advent of fingerprints, DNA, and other forensic evidence, law enforcement relied on interrogations as the primary means to investigate serious crime and prove guilt. Under Anglo-American common law, convictions required proof beyond a reasonable doubt, and confessions in many cases were the only viable means of meeting that high standard. As Lord Patrick Devlin noted:

> The least criticism of police methods of interrogation deserves to be most carefully weighed because the evidence which such interrogation produces is often decisive; the high degree of proof which the English law requires—proof beyond a reasonable doubt—often could not be achieved by the prosecution without the assistance of the accused's own statement.[2]

In many cases, suspects confess almost willingly—they simply respond to the pressure of being accused and confronted with evidence. Some are "glad to get it off their chests." Other suspects resist, but through the art of interrogation, the police ultimately persuade many of them to confess. Sometimes they confess as the result of a rational decision that admitting their crime will be in their best interests; more often they confess because of emotional stress.

---

1. *Richardson on Evidence*, Prince, 10th Ed., Brooklyn, NY: Brooklyn Law School, Section 556; *People v. Bennett*, 37 N.Y. 117 (1867); *People v. Joyce*, 233 N.Y. 61(1922).
2. Patrick Devlin, *The Criminal Prosecution in England*, New Haven, Ct: Yale University Press, (1958), 58.

There is a need to confess that springs from the moral, religious, and psychological foundations of human experience. For the individual involved in a serious criminal matter, confession can be cathartic: it can be a healthy release from overbearing layers of psychological constraint or an attempt to set matters right.

Of course, confessions must be voluntary and truthful, and during the past century, courts have excluded many confessions on the grounds that the confessions were involuntary, unreliable, or unfair. However, courts have not ruled that custodial police interrogations are *per se* unlawful, and they have distinctly recognized that police interrogation is a necessary crime-fighting tactic. In *Culombe v. Connecticut*, 367 U.S. 568 (1961), Justice Felix Frankfurter described their necessity:

> Despite modern advances in the technology of crime detection, offenses frequently occur about which things cannot be made to speak. And where there cannot be found innocent human witnesses to such offenses, nothing remains—if police investigation is not to be balked before it has fairly begun—but to seek out possibly guilty witnesses and ask them questions, witnesses, that is, who are suspected of knowing something about the offense precisely because they are suspected of implication in it.
>
> The questions which these suspected witnesses are asked may serve to clear them. They may serve, directly or indirectly, to lead the police to other suspects than the persons questioned. Or they may become the means by which the persons questioned are themselves made to furnish proofs which will eventually send them to prison or death. In any event, whatever its outcome, such questioning is often indispensable to crime detection. Its compelling necessity has been judicially recognized as its sufficient justification, even in a society which, like ours, stands strongly and constitutionally committed to the principle that persons accused of crime cannot be made to convict themselves out of their own mouths.

Even the Warren Court in *Miranda v. Arizona*, 384 U.S. 436 (1966), the case that has done so much to discourage confessions, recognized their value:

> Confessions remain a proper element in law enforcement. Any statement given freely and voluntarily without any compelling influence is, of course, admissible in evidence.… There is no requirement that the police stop a person who enters a police station and states that he wishes to confess to a crime, or a person who calls the police to offer

a confession or any other statement he desires to make. Volunteered statements of any kind are not barred by the Fifth Amendment and their admissibility is not affected by our holding today.[3]

A voluntary, truthful confession not only solidifies the case against a defendant but also reduces the chances of convicting innocent persons on the basis of circumstantial evidence. Solving a case satisfactorily by obtaining a truthful confession reduces the practice of enlisting informants to testify against a defendant in exchange for lesser charges or reduced prison time. It lessens the need to rely on the eyewitness testimony of strangers, which has been shown to be substantially unreliable and which has led to many wrongful convictions. It reduces the possibility of misapplying or misinterpreting physical evidence.

Confessions and admissions obtained from suspects when the police first confront them are of high evidentiary value since the suspects often impart information not already known to the police. Verifying the information after the suspect offers it or finding evidence where a suspect directs the police to find it lends a high degree of reliability to the truthfulness of the suspect's statements. Such confessions are viewed as more trustworthy than confessions obtained after the police have collected other evidence and developed a theory of the case. When the police already have detailed facts of a case, a subsequent confession may be tainted by the possibility that the details were suggested to the suspect.

Cases without confessions and based solely on circumstantial evidence usually contain an element of doubt, and to prevent injustices in such cases, courts have employed the inconsistent-with-innocence standard for circumstantial evidence convictions:

> Unless there be a confession or direct testimony by observers of the act, dependence must be upon circumstances attending the event and then the question, in a capital case, which is presented to us for our consideration is whether the guilt of the accused has been established to a moral certainty by circumstances which not only point to the guilt of the accused but are inconsistent with his innocence.[4]

Direct evidence cases, either with testimony from an eyewitness who knew the defendant or a confession from the defendant, are generally stronger than purely circumstantial cases. Advocates for strong law enforcement believe police interrogations are essential to obtain the necessary evidence for accurate

---

3. *Miranda v. Arizona*, 384, U.S. 436 (1966).
4. *People v. Feldman*, 299 N.Y. 153 (1949).

convictions because a complete and voluntary confession to a crime provides the best and most satisfactory evidence that a defendant, in fact, committed the crime alleged. Some advocates maintain that the human need to confess should be encouraged, even exploited, for the purposes of solving crimes, resolving doubts about suspects, and convicting the right person. Confessions not only provide direct evidence of the guilt of the accused person but also provide leads to additional evidence against others who may have been involved in the crime.

On the contrary, many defense attorneys and judges with defense-minded orientations reject almost any confession obtained through police interrogation. For them, the total elimination of police-station interrogations is a reasonable policy. They distrust the police and prosecutors, and they advocate that protection for suspects is more important than criminal convictions. They oppose the use of police interrogation, and argue that unless suspects are accompanied by an attorney, their confessions given in the inherently coercive atmosphere of a police station should not be admitted into evidence.

In furtherance of their views, they strictly adhere to hyper-technical interpretations of the exclusionary rule. They have abandoned the traditional common law demarcation between admissible voluntary confessions and inadmissible involuntary confessions in favor of the technicalities of *Miranda v. Arizona*, 384 U.S. 436 (1966), and its progeny.

While *Miranda* is often thought of as the case that prevents the use of confessions, *Miranda* is only part of a vast and complex set of rules related to the use of confessions and incriminating statements. Fourth, Fifth, and Sixth Amendment doctrines applied in combinations to police-citizen encounters create an endless permutation of possible outcomes: depending on how legal doctrines are combined, a defendant's truthful confession may or may not be suppressed. Under the poisonous-tree doctrine, a Fourth Amendment violation might lead to the suppression of a defendant's subsequent incriminatory statements even though the statements were not obtained by violations of the Fifth or Sixth Amendment. Conversely, Fifth and Sixth Amendment violations might lead to the suppression of physical evidence derived from statements unlawfully obtained from a defendant.

The doctrines pronounced in *United States v. Massiah*, 377 U.S.201 (1964), *Wong Sun v. United States*, 371 U.S. 471 (1963), *Michigan v. Mosley*, 423 U.S. 96 (1975), *Dunaway v. New York*, 442 U.S. 200 (1979), *Payton v. New York*, 445 U.S. 573 (1980), *Edwards v. Arizona*, 451 U.S. 477 (1981), and many others cases, add layers of complexity to decisions about confessions, statement admissibility, and derivative evidence.

Miranda initially pertained to custodial interrogations; it was designed to counteract the inherently coercive atmosphere of the police station. However, it quickly found application outside of police stations, and new issues arose, such as whether the police must give the warnings verbatim, whether suspects who assert their rights may be questioned at a later time, or whether a suspect who asserts his rights regarding one case may be questioned regarding another case.

The Supreme Court addressed the verbatim question in *Michigan v. Tucker*, 417 U.S. 433 (1974). In the case, the defendant confessed to the rape and beating of a 43-year-old woman. Before questioning the defendant, the police had asked him whether he wanted an attorney and whether he knew his constitutional rights. The defendant replied that he did not want an attorney and he understood his rights. The police then advised him further that any statements he might make could be used against him in court; however, they did not advise him that he could be assigned an attorney if he could not afford one. For the defendant's trial, his confession was suppressed, and the Supreme Court affirmed the suppression because the warnings given by the police did not completely meet the requirements of *Miranda*. The Court ruled that even though the defendant stated he did not want an attorney, the police nevertheless should have completed the warnings and advised him of his right to have an attorney appointed for him if he could not afford one.

Suppressing the voluntary and truthful confession that might have been essential to the conviction of a violent rapist was a high price to pay for the police neglecting to recite all the words of the Miranda warnings, particularly when it was abundantly clear that the defendant understood his rights and knowingly waived them.

Subsequent Waivers

In *Michigan v. Mosley*, 423 U.S. 96 (1975), the Court dealt with subsequent questioning of suspects who had invoked their right to remain silent. The defendant, Mosley, while in custody for a series of robberies, and after receiving Miranda warnings, indicated that he did not want to answer questions about the robberies. Two hours later, other detectives questioned him about an unrelated murder. They gave him fresh Miranda warnings, told him about the evidence against him, and within fifteen minutes he confessed to the murder. The Supreme Court allowed the statements into evidence, holding that the exercise of the right to remain silent in one case does not forever prevent the police from questioning the defendant regarding other cases. As long as the suspect is given fresh Miranda warnings and he then waives his right to remain silent, he may be questioned.

Edwards v. Arizona, 451 U.S. 477 (1981), also dealt with subsequent questioning but in the context of a request for counsel. Defendant Edwards was arrested for robbery. After detectives advised Edwards of his rights, they questioned him, and during the course of the questioning, he stated, "I want an attorney before making a deal." This statement invoked the right to counsel before any further questioning, as opposed to the defendant in *Mosley*, who invoked only the right to remain silent.

When Edwards asked for an attorney, the detectives ceased questioning him, but the following night, two other detectives visited the defendant in jail. They gave him Miranda warnings, and he said he was willing to talk, but he first wanted to hear a taped statement of an accomplice who had implicated him in the crime. After listening to the tape for several minutes, he then confessed to the crime. The Supreme Court ruled that the confession should have been suppressed, stating:

> Although we have held that after initially being advised of his Miranda rights, the accused may himself validly waive his rights and respond to interrogation … the Court has strongly indicated that additional safeguards are necessary when the accused asks for counsel; and we now hold that when an accused has invoked his right to have counsel present during custodial interrogation, a valid waiver of that right cannot be established by showing only that he responded to further police-initiated custodial interrogation even if he has been advised of his rights. We further hold that an accused, such as Edwards, having expressed his desire to deal with the police only through counsel, is not subject to further interrogation by the authorities until counsel has been made available to him, unless the accused himself initiates further communication, exchanges, or conversations with the police.

The Court's statement that an accused can waive the presence of an attorney when "the accused himself initiates further communications, exchanges, or conversations with the police" was surely made in contemplation of situations in which defendants, after thinking about their situations, voluntarily decide to cooperate or make a deal with the police.[5] However, in *Edwards*, the detectives initiated the further communications, which precluded further questioning without the presence of the defendant's attorney.

Edwards differs from *Mosley* because Edwards said, "I want an attorney before making a deal," and Mosley said, "I don't want to talk about the robberies." When each defendant was approached again by the police, they were given Miranda warnings, and they made full and voluntary confessions to their crimes.

---

5. *Oregon v. Bradshaw*, 462 U.S. 1039 (1983).

Edwards' confession was suppressed; Mosley's was admitted. It is a shame (for Mosley's sake, not the robbery victims) that he did not utter the word "attorney" as Edwards did; if he had, he may have escaped his long prison sentence.

In addition to protection against any further questioning on the charge for which the defendant requested an attorney, a defendant's affirmative request for an attorney also protects against further questioning about unrelated crimes.[6] In contrast, a defendant who does not affirmatively ask for an attorney may be questioned about unrelated crimes.[7] The *Mosley-Edwards* dichotomy illustrates again how the exclusionary rule produces unequal results and unequal justice, not on the basis of guilt or innocence, but on a choice of words.

The implied Fifth Amendment right to counsel established by *Miranda* and *Edwards* is contingent on a suspect asking for counsel. This quasi-right does not apply automatically and may be waived even in the absence of counsel.[8] To the contrary, the Sixth Amendment right to counsel, once it attaches either by request or at arraignment, cannot be waived in the absence of counsel, unless the defendant initiates contact with the police.[9] This automatic attachment of the right to counsel has often operated as a mechanical technicality resulting in the suppression of voluntary confessions and other important evidence. Once the right to counsel has attached, further investigation by law enforcement is severely hampered. Not only are the police constrained from questioning suspects about newly developed evidence, but they are also precluded from utilizing private citizens to engage suspects in conversations for the purpose of obtaining corroboration. For example, in sex abuse cases where the parties are known to one another, a standard investigative tactic is to have the alleged victims telephone the suspects and ask them to explain their actions or apologize. If a suspect does so, it may amount to an admission of guilt that corroborates the allegations and provides the necessary proof to obtain a conviction. These kinds of standard investigative tactics have been thwarted by the extension of the right to counsel to venues outside courtrooms and police stations.

Ubiquitous Right to Counsel

Two years before *Miranda* was decided, the Court, in *Massiah v. United States*, 377 U.S. 201 (1964), established the landmark precedent that the explicit Sixth

---

6. *Arizona v. Roberson*, 486 U.S. 675 (1988).
7. *McNeil v. Wisconsin*, 501 U.S. 171 (1991).
8. *Patterson v. Illinois*, 487 U.S. 285 (1988).
9. *Massiah v. United States*, 377 U.S. 201 (1964).

Amendment right to counsel applies to post-arraignment and post-indictment critical stages of a criminal proceeding, in addition to the trial. Just as defendants are accorded counsel at trial unless they waive the right, an indicted defendant must be afforded the right to counsel during any questioning by the police, including indirect questioning by undercover officers or informants acting as agents of the police. This rule applies to any location and any circumstance in which the government comes into contact with the defendant.

In *Massiah*, the defendant, a merchant seaman and a member of the crew of the *S.S. Santa Maria*, was arrested for smuggling three and a half pounds of cocaine aboard that ship from South America to the United States. He and several others were indicted for violating federal drug laws. Massiah retained an attorney and was arraigned. After Massiah's release on bail, one of the other codefendants, Colson, agreed to cooperate with the government agents. The agents installed a radio transmitter in Colson's car and sent him to engage the defendant in conversations about the crimes. During the conversations, Massiah made incriminating statements, which the agents overheard and which they used at trial to convict him.

The Warren Court suppressed the incriminating statements and reversed the conviction, ruling that an indicted defendant's right to counsel is violated when government agents deliberately elicit statements from the defendant in the absence of counsel.

Additionally, *Massiah* raised several contentious legal questions:

1. When the police elicit information from a represented defendant by indirect communications, under what circumstances will a court deem the communications to be the equivalent of direct questioning in violation of the right to counsel?
2. May the police through undercover agents or jailhouse informants continue to gather evidence against a represented defendant?
3. When a suspect has counsel in a particular case, does the representation last indefinitely, and are the police forever precluded from approaching or questioning the suspect?
4. May the police question a suspect in one case who is represented by counsel in another case?

Massiah was a foundation for the Court's decision in *Brewer v. Williams*, 430 U.S.387, (1977), the Christian burial speech case. *Brewer*, as discussed in chapter two, ignited debate regarding the propriety of questioning or deliberately eliciting information from defendants after an arraignment and the attachment of the right to counsel. In that case, the Court ruled that the detective's Christian burial speech was a deliberate elicitation and the equivalent of questioning, and since counsel had been retained, the questioning was a Sixth Amendment violation. Therefore, the defendant's confession and the evidence derived from the confession had to be suppressed.

In *United States v. Henry*, 447 U.S. 264 (1980), the Court addressed the issue of indirect questioning of represented defendants not by police officers but by government informants. In *Henry*, federal agents used a prison inmate, who was a paid informant, to covertly elicit incriminating statements from the defendant about a murder. The cellmate was successful, and Henry told him about the murder he had committed. The Court reinforced the deliberate elicitation rules espoused in *Massiah v. United States, supra,* and *Brewer v. Williams, supra,* holding that the statements had to be suppressed because the agents intentionally created a situation likely to induce the represented defendant to make incriminating statements without the assistance of counsel.

Police do not easily forego effective tactics for gathering evidence, and they typically adjust their tactics to circumvent court rulings. In *Kuhlman v. Wilson*, 477 U.S. 436 (1986), detectives investigating a murder placed a paid jailhouse informant in the defendant's cell; however, to avoid the *Henry* ruling, they instructed the informant not to ask questions and to listen only passively to the defendant's unsolicited statements. They told him to "keep his ears open." The defendant eventually talked about the murder, and his statements were used to convict him. This time, the Court ruled that deliberate elicitation had not occurred and the defendant's overheard incriminating statements were admissible.

Henry and *Kuhlman* show again that under the exclusionary rule slight differences in conversation and word choices can determine whether a murderer will be brought to justice or go free, and, certainly, testimony about conversations occurring over a period of time between an informant and a defendant is a thin reed on which to base such crucial determinations.

Interminable Right to Counsel

Perhaps the most problematic issue raised by the *Miranda-Massiah* line of cases is the "interminable right to counsel" question that has arisen in state courts. The New York Court of Appeals addressed this and related issues in *People v. West*, 81 N.Y.2d 370 (1993). Should an attorney's admonition to the police not to question his client last forever? What if the attorney dies? Is disbarred? Resigns from the case? What if the discovery of new evidence initiates a new police investigation? Are the police forever barred from instituting a follow-up investigation?

People v. West was an offspring of *Massiah* but went much further. It was a murder case in which Kenneth West was convicted by a jury for the execution-style shooting of Sylvester Coleman, a stranger to him, outside a New York City apartment on West 116th Street in Manhattan. Mr. West, in the presence of his associates, "shot Coleman in the head in a fit of anger because Coleman had parked on the street in a place West had "reserved" for his own use to sell drugs."

In 1982, shortly after the murder, the police apprehended West and placed him in a lineup. West's attorney appeared at the lineup and told the police not to question his client. The lineup was inconclusive, and West was released.

Three years later, one of West's associates, Michael Davenport, was arrested for unrelated charges. In exchange for a lesser sentence, he agreed to provide information about the Coleman shooting. He admitted that he was with West during the shooting, and agreed to testify against him. However, since a defendant cannot be convicted on the uncorroborated testimony of an accomplice, the police needed additional evidence before they could make an arrest.

Mark Davenport, Michael's brother, was also an associate of West. In order to help his brother, Mark agreed to surreptitiously tape-record conversations with West to obtain incriminating and corroborating statements.

The strategy was successful, and while being tape-recorded, West made incriminating statements about the shooting. The taped statements figured prominently in West's trial, and he was convicted. However, the Court of Appeals reversed the conviction, holding that because the taped conversations were the equivalent of police questioning and three years earlier West's attorney had advised the police not to question his client, the surreptitiously taped statements were taken in violation of the defendant's right to counsel. Therefore, the taped statements had to be suppressed.

The court stated:

> We do not hold that the right to counsel is interminable. This is not a case where the police, at the time they arranged for the secret tape recordings, had any reason to believe that a known attorney-client relationship in the matter had ceased. If indeed it had been shown that defendant's lawyer had died, been disbarred, withdrawn, or terminated the relationship because of a conflict of interest, the case would be a different one.

Although West had not been charged with a crime at the time of the telephone contacts, the court indicated that the police had the burden to determine whether the attorney-client relationship had been terminated. How they would go about doing so, the court did not make clear. Should the police have asked

Mr. West whether he still had counsel on the case? Doing so surely would have alerted him that the investigation had been renewed and would have put him on guard. Should the police have asked the lawyer? The same result would likely follow.

The *West* decision has created another circumstance of unequal citizenship: Persons who once retain an attorney in connection with a case are, in effect, immune from further police efforts to obtain additional evidence to prove the case; in contrast, persons without an attorney can be subjected to police overt or covert efforts to obtain additional evidence.

West extended the right to counsel to situations where uncharged criminals voluntarily reminisce with their cohorts about the glories of their past crimes. It is not clear why the New York court believed it is justice that one person would be acquitted because he had the good fortune of having an attorney who was still alive when the police "questioned" him while another person would be convicted because he had the misfortune that his attorney had died. As George Orwell once wrote, "One has to belong to the intelligentsia to believe things like that: no ordinary man could be such a fool."

The *West* decision occasioned a gross injustice. The murdered victim and the victim's family have been denied justice. They have been denied justice in order to support a right to counsel doctrine that was contemplated neither by the Fifth nor Sixth Amendments. *West* went beyond *Miranda* or *Massiah*, extending the right to counsel from situations in which a charged defendant is face-to-face with the power of government in courts or police stations to persons who are not yet charged with a crime and who at any time and place voluntarily disclose the details of their crimes. A conversation with an undercover informant is not the same as interrogation by detectives in the back of a station house or compulsion to testify at a trial. Nowhere in the Constitution does it say that a defendant is entitled to the protection of an attorney as he goes about his daily life and has conversations with people he believes are his friends. Nowhere in the Constitution does it say that because a defendant hires an attorney, he has a shield against any further police investigation of his criminal activities.

That a suspect has hired an attorney should not prevent the police from enlisting the aid of people to whom the suspect might normally confide. Just as the hiring of an attorney should not prevent the police from conducting lawful searches to recover physical evidence, they should not be prevented from asking people to report evidence against a suspect. Incriminating statements freely made to friends or relatives about a crime are generally admissible evidence. Friends, acquaintances, and relatives can be subpoenaed to testify regarding conversations with a defendant, irrespective of whether the conversations occurred before or after the crime. The defendant's right to counsel does not preclude compelling other persons to testify to his incriminating statements. The same statements made to informants should also be admissible. They should not be excluded simply because the police encouraged them to obtain evidence from a suspect.

Using undercover agents, whether law enforcement personnel, paid informants, or an individual with a personal interest in the case, has been long recognized as a necessary tool of criminal investigation. Judge Learned Hand wrote:

> Courts have countenanced the use of informers from time immemorial; in cases of conspiracy, or in other cases when the crime consists of preparing for another crime, it is usually necessary to rely upon them or upon accomplices because the criminals will almost certainly proceed covertly.[10]

The Sixth Amendment was not meant to address how and where the government obtained evidence; the right to counsel was for legal advice and strategy during the critical stages of criminal proceedings. *Massiah, Henry, West*, and other cases have imprudently extended the reach of the amendment.

Massiah opened the door to extravagant levels of complexity and widely inconsistent court rulings. The conviction or acquittal of a murderer might depend on such nuances as whether a police informant's conversation with a suspect is interpreted as having tended to elicit information or merely involved passive listening to a suspect's admissions. A convicted murderer might be set free depending on whether his attorney hired many years before the murderer's confession was still practicing law or had retired or died. Such nuances and chance factors should not be the stuff of which justice is constructed.

Massiah bars relevant, reliable, and highly probative evidence of whether the defendant committed the act with which he is charged. A defendant's confession obtained as a result of his voluntary confidences to a "friend" might be more reliable and probative than a confession obtained as a result of pre-arrest custodial interrogations by detectives; nevertheless, *Massiah* makes it inadmissible. Suppression of such confessions or incriminating statements seriously impedes the search for truth that a criminal trial seeks. Suppression of such crucial evidence creates a new privilege, unrecognized at common law, and unwarranted by constitutional law. Admitting into evidence the voluntary statements of such criminals as Massiah, Henry, and West interfered with their right to counsel no more so than the statements of Kuhlman interfered with his right to counsel. None of these defendants were prevented from meeting

---

10. *United States v. Dennis*, 183 F.2d 201 (1950), at 224.

and consulting with counsel. No meetings were disturbed or spied upon, and preparation for trial was not obstructed. Their right to counsel was not violated; the only thing violated was the trust between them and those they perceived as their partners in crime.

Offense-Specific Right to Counsel Problems

Although the American public would not stand for the elimination of police interrogations and such legislation could not be passed, several state courts have attempted to eliminate *de facto* the ability of law enforcement to conduct interrogations in certain circumstances. New York State, for example, has used its constitution to provide a far stronger right to counsel to its citizens than required by the United States Constitution. In *People v. Bartolomeo*, 53 N.Y.2d 225 (1981), the New York Court of Appeals suppressed a defendant's Mirandized, voluntary confession to a murder because the defendant had been arrested eleven days earlier for an unrelated arson and had an attorney in the arson matter. *Bartolomeo* held that even though the defendant waived his right to counsel and even though the police officers were unaware of the prior charge, the attachment of counsel to the prior arson case carried over to the subsequent unrelated murder case and, therefore, questioning the defendant without the presence of counsel was impermissible.

Nine years later, *Bartolomeo* was overruled by *People v. Bing*, 76 N.Y.2d 331 (1990), because it was "unworkable" and riddled with exceptions. The *Bing* court, assuming first-time offenders would less likely have an attorney and repeat-offenders would more likely have an attorney, stated that the *Bartolomeo* rule created an inequality:

> The first-time arrestee, with no criminal experience, may waive his rights and be questioned without the presence of counsel. *Miranda v. Arizona* ... requires only a warning of the right to counsel, not the actual presence of counsel ... Why then should the second-time offender, who presumably has received prior advice on how to deal with the authorities and has voluntarily chosen a different course of action on the new charge, be foreclosed from waiving his rights on the matter for which he was detained? As the dissenters (in *Bartolomeo*) noted, the court, without apparent reason, had provided "a dispensation" for persistent offenders for it is the common criminal, not the first-time offender, who will nearly always have representation on a pending charge and thus be immunized from questioning in subsequent investigations.

The back-and-forth between the advocates for and against the use of confessions obtained by police interrogation has been ongoing. In 1990, the same year the New York Court of Appeals overturned *Bartolomeo*, the Supreme Court **attempted to** limit the reach of the *Massiah* rule. In *Illinois v. Perkins*, 496 U.S. 292 (1990), Perkins was incarcerated on a charge of aggravated battery for which he had counsel. He shared a cell with a cellmate, who informed the police that Perkins had told him that he had murdered Richard Stephenson in 1984. At that point, the Stephenson murder had remained unsolved, and Perkins had not been charged and did not have counsel in connection with the Stephenson murder.

The police decided they would need more evidence than just the cellmate's testimony before they could arrest Perkins. To obtain such evidence, a police undercover officer, posing as an inmate, was placed in the jail cell with the defendant and the informant. While in the cell, the three men talked about escaping, and the undercover officer asked Perkins whether he had ever killed anyone. Perkins said he had killed Stephenson and described the murder in detail.

Perkins was charged with the murder, and his confession was used to convict him. He appealed on the grounds that he should have received Miranda warnings and the police were prohibited from undercover contacts with incarcerated suspects that are reasonably likely to elicit an incriminating response.

The Supreme Court rejected the appeal and held that the defendant's incriminating statements regarding the murder were admissible in that his right to counsel had not yet attached to that charge. Also, the Court rejected the argument that Miranda warnings were required because the "questioning" did not occur in a "police-dominated atmosphere." Warnings were "not required when a suspect is unaware that he is speaking to a law enforcement officer and gives a voluntary statement … *Miranda* was not meant to protect suspects from boasting about their criminal activities in front of persons whom they believe to be their cellmates."

One might ask: if *Miranda* was not meant to protect suspects from boasting to their friends about their crimes, why does *Massiah* protect them from their boasts?

Factually-Related Cases

Although the Supreme Court in *Perkins* and the New York court in *Bing* attempted to limit the reach of *Massiah* and *Bartolomeo*, these rulings left uncertain whether legal representation in a prior case that was separate but factually related to a new charge carried over to the new charge and protected a suspect against any interrogation relating to that charge.[11] In 1997, that issue reached the New York Court of Appeals in *People v. Cohen*, 90 N.Y.2d 632 (1997), and the court, applying New York's stronger right to counsel protections, held that legal representation in one case should be automatically applied to a factually-related case.

In *Cohen*, the defendant was a suspect in the burglary of Thompson's Garage in Lake George, New York. Three guns had been stolen in the burglary. Cohen retained counsel in that matter, and the counsel advised the police not to question his client. A few weeks after the burglary, an unrelated robbery and murder took place at a Citgo gas station mini-mart on the Northway in the Town of Lake George. In the robbery, a Citgo employee was shot and killed with a .22 caliber gun. Subsequently, the police received information from an informant implicating Cohen in both crimes. They executed a search warrant at Cohen's residence, and they recovered the three guns taken in the Thompson's Garage burglary, including a .22 caliber revolver that was a ballistic match to the bullet that killed the Citgo employee. They asked Cohen to come with them to the police station, advised him of his Miranda rights, and interrogated him without his counsel present. Cohen confessed, and he was arrested and convicted for the Citgo murder and robbery. However, the New York Court of Appeals suppressed the confession and reversed the conviction, holding that Cohen's legal representation in the Thompson burglary investigation applied to the Citgo murder case, and the interrogation violated Cohen's right to counsel.

The Court of Appeals justified their holding somewhat by pointing out that the detectives interrogating Cohen about the Citgo murder asked him questions about guns stolen in the Thompson burglary. However, the court disregarded the essential fact that the trial was for the Citgo murder, not the Thompson burglary, and his statements were not used to convict him of the Thompson burglary.

At his retrial in which his confession was not admissible, Cohen was acquitted of all charges. Although the United States Supreme Court could do nothing about Cohen's acquittal, the Court obviously had paid close attention to the case and granted a *Writ of Certiorari* to another case with similar legal issues, *Texas v. Cobb*, 532 U.S. 162 (2001), in which the Court clarified its offense-specific rule that a defendant's right to counsel invoked in one case does not attach to other offenses, even offenses "closely related factually."

In *Cobb*, in December 1993, a complainant, Lindsey Owings, reported that his home had been burglarized and his wife, Margaret, and their 16-month-

---

11. *People v. Vella*, 21 N.Y.2d 249 (1967); *People v. Ermo*, 47 N.Y.2d 863 (1979).

old daughter, Kori Rae, were missing. The defendant, Raymond Levi Cobb, lived across the street, and in July 1994, he was charged with the burglary. At his arraignment, an attorney was appointed for him, and he was released on bail.

In November 1995 after Cobb told his father that he had committed the murders, the father turned him in to the police. The defendant was arrested on a warrant for the murders of Margaret and Kori Rae. He was given Miranda rights, and after questioning for a short time, confessed to killing them both. He explained that while he was committing the burglary, Margaret caught him stealing a stereo, and he stabbed her in the stomach with a knife. He dragged her body to a wooded area a few hundred yards from the house. He stated:

> I went back to her house and I saw the baby lying on its bed. I took the baby out there and it was sleeping the whole time. I laid the baby down on the ground four or five feet away from its mother. I went back to my house and got a flat edge shovel. That's all I could find. Then I went back over to where they were and I started digging a hole between them. After I got the hole dug, the baby was awake. It started going toward its mom and it fell in the hole. I put the lady in the hole and I covered them up. I remember stabbing a different knife I had in the ground where they were. I was crying right then.

After his confession, the defendant led the police to the location where he had buried the victims' bodies. A jury convicted him of murder and sentenced him to death.

Cobb appealed, and the Texas Court of Criminal Appeals reversed his conviction on the grounds that he had asserted his right to counsel at the burglary arraignment, and since the murders were "factually interwoven with the burglary," the right to counsel had attached to the murder charges. The Texas Court held that the right attached even though Cobb had not yet been charged with the murders, and, therefore, the police were precluded from questioning Cobb without his counsel.

The Supreme Court reversed the Texas Court of Criminal Appeals, rejected that court's "factually interwoven" analysis, and reinstated Cobb's conviction. The Supreme Court held that the right to counsel is offense-specific. It cannot be invoked once for all future prosecutions. At the time the defendant confessed, he had been charged with the burglary but not with the murders. Burglary and murder are not the same offense; therefore, the police were not barred from questioning the defendant regarding the murders, and the defendant's confession was admissible. The Court emphasized, "It is critical to recognize that the Constitution does not negate society's interest in the ability of police to talk to witnesses and suspects, even those who have been charged with other offenses." This was, perhaps, the Court's strongest endorsement of the institution of police interrogations since *Culombe v. Connecticut, supra.*

Of note in *Cobb* was the Court's discussion of *Brewer v. Williams*, 430 U.S.387 (1977), the Christian burial speech case, in which the defendant's confession was suppressed because the police violated his right to counsel by questioning him while they were transporting him from Davenport to Des Moines, Iowa. The Court in *Cobb* clearly indicated that under its more recent interpretation that the right to counsel is offense specific, *Brewer v. Williams* might have been decided differently. Since the defendant in *Brewer v. Williams* had been arraigned only on the charge of abduction of a child and had not yet been charged with the murder, his right to counsel had attached only to the abduction charge and not the murder charge. Since questioning by the police would not have infringed the defendant's right to counsel regarding the murder charge, the confession would have been admissible.

A review of the cases noted above shows that each of the defendants made truthful and voluntary incriminating statements that supported their convictions, yet some of the convictions were reversed while others were not, purely for reasons unrelated to the achievement of justice. As these cases show, the ever-changing rules and interpretations of the right to counsel as they pertain to out-of-court confessions have proved unworkable, and the deep division within the courts has made it clear that it is time to abandon the exclusionary rule as a penalty for technical violations. Truthfulness, reliability, and voluntariness should be the standards for admissibility.

Chapter Five

Terrorism and the Rule

The acquittal of the Al Qaeda terrorist, Ahmed Khalfan Ghailani, of 284 of 285 charges in connection with the 1998 terrorist bombings of the United States embassies in Kenya and Tanzania has demonstrated again the catastrophic effects of the exclusionary rule. The bombings killed 224 people and injured more than 4,000. However, at Ghailani's trial, because the testimony of a key witness against him was suppressed, the jury was deprived of the evidence that Ghailani had purchased the bomb-making materials used to destroy the buildings and so many lives.

The Ghailani acquittals in 2010 also highlight the exclusionary rule's part in the September 11, 2001 terrorist attacks that destroyed the Twin Towers in New York, part of the Pentagon in Washington, D.C., and four commercial airliners with all their passengers. The exclusionary rule was a major factor in the failure to prevent the 9/11 attacks. It was the justification for the construction of "the wall" between the CIA and FBI counter-terrorism units on one side and FBI criminal investigation units and Justice Department prosecutors on the other. This wall prevented necessary intelligence sharing, and the 9/11 Commission[1] identified it as one of the major causes of the failure to prevent the attack. As the 9/11 Commission noted, a wall had been built between those agencies to prevent extra-judicial actions of the CIA from "tainting" evidence used by the FBI and U.S. prosecutors in criminal cases. The Justice Department had faced the dilemma that the failure to turn over the sources of evidence to defense counsel resulted in suppression of evidence and other sanctions, yet if the source were revealed to have come from the CIA, defense counsel could examine the CIA activities, and in many cases would most likely find that the evidence was not obtained in accordance with the rules of our criminal justice system. To avoid this no-win dilemma, the Justice Department built the wall. The consequence was that critical information in

---

1. Final Report of the National Commission on Terrorist Attacks Upon the United States, W.W. Norton & Co, New York.

the possession of the CIA and the FBI counter-terrorism units was not forwarded to FBI criminal investigation units or Justice Department prosecutors, thus severely limiting any chance of apprehending the terrorists before they struck.

The 9/11 Commission found that in 1995 Attorney General Janet Reno issued formal procedures aimed at managing information sharing between law-enforcement agencies. Then through a series of missteps, such as an FBI Deputy Director informing agents that "too much information sharing could be a career stopper," the practice developed that foreign security intelligence could not be shared with domestic criminal investigators. Adding to the problem, a presidential executive order restricted the commingling of foreign intelligence with domestic information, and the National Security Agency issued orders that prior approval was required before sharing terrorism-related reports with criminal investigators and prosecutors.

With day-to-day intelligence sharing thus severely constrained, opportunities to apprehend the 9/11 hijackers before they struck were lost. The 9/11 Commission recounted the failure to share information about Khalid al Mihdhar, one of the hijackers who had entered the United States with a fraudulent visa, as a lost opportunity to prevent the attacks. Mihdhar had been identified as a suspect in the October 12, 2000 bombing of the U.S.S. Cole in Yemen. The Commission report recounted the communications between FBI agents regarding a lead about Mihdhar's activities:

> One of the *Cole* case agents read the lead with interest, and contacted "Jane" to obtain more information. "Jane" argued, however, that because the agent was designated a "criminal" FBI agent, not an intelligence FBI agent, the wall kept him from participating in any search for Mihdhar. In fact, she felt he had to destroy his copy of the lead because it contained NSA [National Security Agency] information from reports that included caveats ordering that the information not be shared without OIPR's [Office of Intelligence Policy Review] permission. The agent asked "Jane" to get an opinion from the FBI's National Security Law Unit (NSLU) on whether he could open a criminal case on Mihdhar.
>
> "Jane" sent an email to the *Cole* case agent explaining that according to the NSLU, the case could be opened only as an intelligence matter, and that if Mihdhar were found, only designated intelligence agents could conduct or even be present at any interview.…
>
> The FBI agent angrily responded:
>> Whatever has happened to this—someday someone will
>> die—and wall or not—the public will not understand why

we were not more effective and throwing every resource we had at certain "problems."

Let's hope the National Security Law Unit will stand behind their decisions then, especially since the biggest threat on us now, UBL [Usama bin Laden], is getting the most "protection."[2]

The agent was right: Almost 3000 people died on 9/11, and in the aftermath, the public learned about the wall and the failure to share intelligence. However, it was not made clear to the public that a major underlying reason for the wall and a significant cause of the intelligence failure was the fear of the exclusionary rule.

Two months after 9/11, Congress passed the U.S.A. Patriot Act,[3] which included provisions dismantling the wall between foreign intelligence investigators and domestic criminal investigators. Intelligence sharing between the CIA and the FBI improved, and the capture of important members of Al Qaeda followed. That is exactly what happened in the Ghailani case.

Shortly after the embassy bombings, Ghailani became a prime suspect and his photograph was circulated throughout the media. He was eventually captured in 2004 by Pakistani intelligence and transferred to CIA custody. The CIA held him in custody for two years and placed him in the Rendition, Detention and Interrogation Program, which was designed to obtain information for use in defending the United States against additional terrorist attacks. The program was authorized as part of the President's power to conduct the war on terrorism, and the program included the use of enhanced interrogation techniques that were coercive. Some critics have characterized these techniques as torture; others have defended them as lawful tools in the war on terror. In any case, as a result of the interrogation, the CIA obtained information from Ghailani confirming his connection to the bombings. Of great importance, they learned that Ghailani had purchased the bomb materials (TNT) and detonator caps from Hussein Abebe in Tanzania. The CIA passed that information to the FBI who passed the information to the Tanzanian government.

In 2006, Tanzanian authorities arrested Mr. Abebe, questioned him, and then allowed the FBI to question him. Abebe admitted that he sold the TNT and detonator caps to Ghailani, and he agreed to testify against him.

In 2009, the U.S. government indicted Ghailani in the U.S. Southern District of New York on 285 criminal counts, including charges of murder, de-

---

2. Id. Section 8.2, p. 271.
3. 50 U.S.C. 1801 et seq.

stroying U.S. government buildings, and conspiracy to destroy U.S. buildings and property. However, prior to trial, the defense moved, first, to suppress the statements that Ghailani made during his CIA interrogations on the grounds that his statements were coerced and taken in violation of his Fifth Amendment right against compelled self-incrimination, and, second, to exclude the use of any information derived from the interrogations, specifically any potential testimony from Abebe. The defense contended that Abebe's identity was the fruit of the poisonous tree of Ghailani's illegal interrogation.

The admissibility of Ghailani's coerced statements was not the most crucial issue of the case, and that issue was not even an exclusionary rule matter. Coerced statements have always been inadmissible from long before the creation of the exclusionary rule. In Anglo-American criminal justice systems, coerced or involuntary confessions have been inadmissible primarily because of their unreliability and the increased probability that such confessions might be false. As noted in 1831 in *King v. Parratt*, 4 Car. & P. 570:

> A free and voluntary confession is deserving of the highest credit, because it is presumed to flow from the strongest sense of guilt ... but a confession forced from the mind by flattery of hope, or by the torture of fear, comes in so questionable a shape ... that no credit ought to be given to it; and therefore it is rejected.

Judges generally avoid the ultimate issue of whether a confession was truthful or false, as that is the province of the jury. Judges confine themselves to hearing evidence to determine whether a confession was given freely and voluntarily by a competent person and under circumstances indicating reliability; if it was not, it will not be admitted into evidence. Justice Felix Frankfurter summarized the practice in *Culombe v. Connecticut*, 367 U.S. 568 (1961):

> The ultimate test remains that which has been the only clearly established test in Anglo-American courts for two hundred years: the test of voluntariness. Is the confession the product of an essentially free and unconstrained choice by its maker? If it is, if he has willed to confess, it may be used against him. If it is not, if his will has been overborne and his capacity for self-determination critically impaired, the use of his confession offends due process. The line of distinction is that at which governing self-direction is lost and compulsion, of whatever nature or however infused, propels or helps to propel the confession.

The government conceded that Ghailani's statements were coerced and, therefore, inadmissible. Nevertheless, the government argued that Abebe's testimony should be admissible because he was an independent witness and his willingness to testify was not the direct and close result of Ghailani's interrogation. This was a crucial issue that had to be decided before the trial.

The trial and preliminary proceedings were conducted by U.S. District Court Judge Lewis A. Kaplan. The judge acknowledged that prior case law held that fruits of illegally obtained evidence can be admissible when the government proves that the connection between the illegal government action and the evidence offered at trial is so attenuated, or so thinly connected, as to dissipate the taint. To decide the issue, he conducted a hearing and examined the government's proof using the criteria from *United States v. Ceccolini*, 435 U.S. 268 (1978), and *United States v. Leonardi*, 623 F.2d 746 (2nd Cir. 1980), which required consideration of (1) the stated willingness of the witness to testify, (2) the role played by the illegally obtained evidence in gaining cooperation, (3) the proximity of the illegal behavior to the decision to cooperate and the actual testimony at trial, and (4) the police motivation for engaging in the illegal activity.

After taking testimony from representatives of the FBI, CIA, Tanzanian National Police, and Abebe, and after reviewing the evidence, Judge Kaplan excluded Abebe's testimony from the trial because his identity was learned from Ghailani's coerced statement and thus fell within the "fruits of the poisonous tree" doctrine, which precludes the use of such derivative evidence. In his opinion, the government failed to prove that Abebe's testimony was sufficiently attenuated from Ghailani's coerced statement to permit its reception in evidence.

Of course, that was one judge's opinion; another judge might have evaluated the facts differently. Moreover, had the Attorney General's Office appealed to the Circuit Court of Appeals or the Supreme Court, either of those courts might have reversed the judge's ruling on the basis of ample case law that supports the admissibility of live-witness testimony derived from an earlier illegality. In both *Ceccolini* and *Leonardi*, *supra*, the courts upheld the admissibility of the live-witness testimony that had been derived from Fourth Amendment violations. In addition, in *Michigan v. Tucker*, 417 U.S. 433 (1974), a Fifth Amendment case, the Supreme Court upheld the admission of testimony of a witness whose identity had been learned from the questioning of the defendant who had not been given full Miranda warnings. In *Tucker*, even though the defendant's confession was excluded, the witness, whose identity was learned during the questioning, and who was later contacted by the authorities, was allowed to give incriminating testimony against the defendant.

While it is true that *Tucker* involved a relatively minor Miranda nonconstitutional violation, even more serious Fifth Amendment violations have not automatically barred derivative live-witness testimony. In *United States v. Sweets*, 526 F.3d 122 (4th Cir. 2007), the Fourth Circuit Court of Appeals allowed the testimony of a witness whose identity was derived from a Fifth Amendment violation. In *Sweets*, the police had coerced the defendant to lead them to the location of a witness, and the witness subsequently cooperated and testified against the defendant.

Judge Kaplan was not required to follow *Sweets* as that case was not within the Second Circuit in which he served. Nonetheless, *Sweets* provided a significant argument for appeal, and the Attorney General could also have made several other appellant arguments on the basis of widely recognized exceptions to the exclusionary rule, such as the attenuation, inevitable discovery, independent source, and public safety doctrines. However, the Attorney General's Office, in what can only be described as an enormous tactical blunder, did not appeal the judge's pretrial ruling but proceeded to trial while knowing they could not use Abebe's testimony. Clearly, his testimony would have been powerful, but the U.S. attorneys believed that even without it, they had enough evidence to convict on the main charges. They were mistaken.

At the trial, the prosecution presented substantial circumstantial evidence showing that Ghailani engaged in activities in preparation for the bombings, including renting an apartment where bomb materials were found and buying one of the trucks used in the bombings as well as the acetylene and oxygen gas cylinders used to remodel the truck interior. The defense did not dispute that Ghailani had performed many of the specific acts attributed to him, but they maintained that he had been duped into performing them and believed they were for a different purpose. They maintained that he had no awareness of the conspiracy or its objective to bomb the embassies. The jury, evidently believing the defense or having a reasonable doubt of guilt, acquitted Ghailani of 284 of the 285 counts. He was only convicted of one count of conspiracy to destroy buildings and property of the United States.

In all probability the verdict would have been different had Abebe been allowed to testify that Ghailani bought the TNT and detonators used in the bombings. With such testimony before the jury, Ghailani could not have credibly claimed that he did not have knowledge of the plan to explode the bombs.

For the Attorney General, the one-count conviction blunted potential embarrassment over the prosecution's tactics. It also avoided sparking a new round of public outrage about the exclusionary rule and the fruits of the poisonous tree doctrine, which might have ensued had Ghailani been acquitted of all counts. The minimal outrage that surfaced died down quickly; it should not have. The Ghailani case should have ignited debate, not only about the Attorney General's tactics and concessions, but also about the broader issue of applying the exclusionary rule in the context of the war on terror.

To aid the war on terror, the Attorney General's Office should have litigated the fundamental question as to whether Ghailani had constitutional rights when he was outside the United States. Several Supreme Court precedents have held against extending American constitutional rights to noncitizens in foreign countries. When Ghailani was questioned, he was not an American citizen or on American soil. In *United States v. Verdugo-Urquidez*, 494 U.S. 259 (1990), the Supreme Court analyzed the historical record and concluded, "The purpose of the Fourth Amendment was to protect the people of the United States against arbitrary action by their own Government; it was never suggested that the provision was intended to restrain the actions of the Federal Government against aliens outside of the United States territory." Furthermore, the Court ruled, "aliens outside the United States who lack a substantial connection to this country do not enjoy the protection of the Fourth Amendment because they are not 'the people' whose protection was contemplated by the framers of the Fourth Amendment."

As for the Fifth Amendment applying to aliens outside the United States, it would indeed seem odd that foreign enemies, engaged in a terroristic war against the United States, acting in violation of the laws of war, should automatically gain American constitutional rights by murdering American citizens on foreign soil. In 1950, the Supreme Court rejected just such a proposition. In *Johnson v. Eisentrager*, 339 U.S. 763 (1950), the Court held that enemy aliens arrested in China and imprisoned in Germany after World War II could not obtain *writs of habeas corpus* in our federal courts on the grounds that their convictions for war crimes had violated the Fifth Amendment and other constitutional provisions.

More recently, in 2010, the D.C. Circuit Court of Appeals, in *Maqaleh v. Gates*, 605 F.3d 84 (2010), specifically ruled that enemy combatants held in foreign countries do not possess the constitutional right of *habeas corpus*. The court ruled that enemy combatants held in the Bagram Airfield base in Afghanistan did not have the right to petition for a *writ of habeas corpus* in an American court.

Maqaleh differed from *Boumediene v. Bush*, 553 U.S. 723 (2008), the case in which the Supreme Court allowed *habeas corpus* rights to enemy combatants held in Guantanamo Bay, Cuba. The difference was that *Boumediene* rested on the determination that Guantanamo was a *de facto* American territory, essentially the same as if the defendant were held in an American prison. The Court clearly indicated that if Guantanamo were not an American territory, the defendant would not have the right of *habeas corpus*. Because Bagram Airfield was the sovereign territory of another nation outside the jurisdiction of United States courts, Maqaleh did not have the right of *habeas corpus*.

Once it is determined that enemy combatants outside United States territory do not have *habeas corpus* rights, it follows that they do not have other constitutional rights. Furthermore, where no constitutional rights exist, no violations can occur, and it was illogical for the court to suppress evidence as a penalty for a nonexistent violation.

As a practical matter, if constitutional rights are given to enemy combatants, the American military and the CIA will have the impossible task of attempting to capture terrorists while having to operate within the rules of the American criminal justice system. Terrorism is neither a criminal matter nor a conventional war; it is an ongoing attack in progress that must be thwarted. Stealth and surprise attacks are the terrorists' most lethal weapons, and the CIA must obtain timely intelligence to defend national security.

The CIA anti-terrorism branch, by its nature, cannot act as if it were a law-enforcement agency; it is a *de facto* arm of our military forces. It acts under authority granted by Congress in the 2001 Authorization for Use of Military Force Act, 50 U.S.C.S. 1541, which promulgated:

> The President is authorized to use all necessary and appropriate force against those nations, organizations, or persons he determines planned, authorized, committed, or aided the terrorist attacks that occurred on September 11, 2001, or harbored such organizations or persons, in order to prevent any future acts of international terrorism against the United States by such nations, organizations or persons.

Acting in its capacity as a quasi-military agency, the CIA identified Ghailani as a member of Al Qaeda and interrogated him under its authority to "use all necessary and appropriate force" against that organization. The CIA was motivated by intelligence objectives, not the prosecution of Ghailani; and irrespective of any law enforcement interest in a subsequent prosecution, the CIA would have conducted the same interrogation.

At the trial, for reasons hard to understand, the Attorney General's Office conceded the existence of extraterritorial constitutional rights to enemy combatants. Consequently, Judge Kaplan had to decide the case under the supposition that Ghailani's Fifth and Sixth Amendment rights had been violated. However, hypothetically, even if Ghailani's rights actually had been violated, the suppression of Abebe's testimony was not required. The Supreme Court, in case after case, has reiterated that the purpose of the exclusionary rule is to deter the police or other government agents from committing constitutional violations. If suppressing particular evidence does not result in appreciable deterrence, the suppression serves no purpose and should not be imposed. See *United States v. Calandra*, 414 U.S. 338 (1974), *United States v. Janis*, 428 U.S.

433 (1976), *Illinois v Gates*, 462 U.S. 213 (1983) J. White concurrence, *United States v. Leon*, 468 U.S. 897 (1984), *Arizona v. Evans*, 514 U.S. 1 (1995), and *Herring v. United States*, 555 U.S. 135 (2009). In the *Ghailani* case, suppressing Abebe's testimony would not have the effect of deterring the CIA from performing its functions; therefore, the testimony should not have been suppressed.

The administrations of President Bush and President Obama have approached the terrorism threat substantially from a warfare perspective. They have maintained that the terrorist organizations that have emerged are as dangerous and formidable as a foreign military, perhaps more so, and their intention is to prevent attacks by whatever means necessary, including drone missile strikes to kill suspected terrorists in Afghanistan and Pakistan. It would seem rather incongruous to maintain that the subjects of the missile strikes possess constitutional rights.

To the contrary, the defense bar and other advocates, with the acquiescence of the Attorney General's office, have argued to apply the exclusionary rule and the poisonous-tree doctrine to the capture and detention of overseas enemy combatants. They approach the war on terror from a criminal justice perspective, and they maintain that full constitutional protections should be applied to suspected terrorists captured on foreign soil. They argue that the investigative methods used to build cases against suspected terrorists must comport with constitutional protections. To dispense with constitutional protections even for terrorists, they argue, will lead to a diminishment of due process protections for all citizens: Arbitrary arrests, indefinite detentions, harsh interrogations, and torture might be applied against innocent persons. However, a clear line separates citizens and other persons in United States territory from noncitizen enemy combatants on foreign soil.

When noncitizen enemy combatants are brought into United States territory, their constitutional rights begin, including the protections of *habeas corpus*, the right to counsel, the right to a fair trial, etc., but they should not be granted such rights *nunc pro tunc*, now for then, and their prosecutions should not be hampered by events that occurred in overseas war zones prior to their arrival in the United States. Their prosecutions should not be hampered because of necessary actions taken in connection with military operations. Judicial tools designed to deter domestic law enforcement agencies from violating the rights of Americans should not be transferred to foreign enemy combatants on overseas battlefields.

In *Ghailani*, applying the exclusionary rule and the poisonous-tree doctrine to Abebe's testimony served no legitimate purpose and was an unwarranted judicial intrusion into the President's authority to conduct the war on terror by all necessary and appropriate means.

Chapter Six

State Rebellions

The United States Supreme Court has ameliorated some of the more im-practical and unjust results of the exclusionary rule by modifying prior deci-sions and establishing limited exceptions to the rule. However, several state courts have mounted a judicial resistance to the modifications and have failed to adopt the exceptions. Instead, under the authority of their state constitutions, the rule's application has continued to expand.[1]

The concept of "state constitutionalism" was given life by Justice William Brennan. As he slipped from the majority into the minority on the Supreme Court, Brennan led the call for states to rely on their own constitutions as a coun-terweight to the new leadership on the Court. He provided the authoritative voice for the state constitutionalism movement.[2]

Tens of thousands of exclusionary rule cases are decided at state trial and ap-pellate court levels, and many of the decisions rendered in these courts have not only rejected Supreme Court precedents, they have also greatly extended the exclusionary rule to a point that unjustifiably diminishes public safety in favor of expansive protections for criminal defendants. For example, several state courts, including courts in Massachusetts, Arizona, Florida, Illinois, and New York, have declined to apply the Supreme Court's inevitable discovery excep-tion to the fruits of the poisonous tree doctrine.[3]

The Arizona Supreme Court, in *State v. Ault*, 150 Ariz. 459 (1986), sup-pressed the introduction into evidence of tennis shoes that connected the de-fendant to a series of burglaries and sexual assaults. The police recovered the tennis shoes during the arrest of the suspect in his apartment. After the arrest, they obtained a search warrant to return to the defendant's apartment to find other clothing he wore while committing the alleged crimes. During a pre-

---

1. *Commonwealth v. Upton*, 394 Mass. 363 (1985); *People v. Elwell*, 50 N.Y.2d 231 (1980).
2. *90 Harvard L. Rev.* 489 (1977).
3. *Commonwealth v. Balicki*, 436 Mass. 1 (1982); *State v. Ault*, 150 Ariz. 459 (1986); *Moody v. Florida*, 842 So.2d 754 (2003); *People v. Harris*, 207 Ill.2d 515 (2003); *People v. Stith*, 69 N.Y.2d 313 (1987).

trial suppression hearing, the defense argued that the initial arrest of the defendant was unlawful and, therefore, the tennis shoes had to be suppressed, while the prosecution argued that the tennis shoes would have been inevitably discovered during the later execution of the search warrant. The court sided with the defense, stating:

We are unpersuaded that the shoes would have been inevitably discovered during the legal afternoon search. Appellant's roommate had plenty of time between the unlawful search and the lawful search during which he could have hidden, removed, or destroyed the shoes. The fact that the roommate did not tamper with clothing, which he knew appellant had worn during his alleged criminal activities suggest that the shoes may have remained untouched by him. This is reasoning in retrospect, however. The mere fact that the appellant's roommate had easy access to the shoes during the day precludes us from concluding that the shoes would have been *inevitably* discovered during the legal afternoon search.[4]

The Arizona court's speculation about what the suspect's roommate might or might not have done shows how courts sometimes stretch to find reasons outside the record to continue applying the exclusionary rule.

In *Moody v. State of Florida*, 842 So.2d 754 (2003), the Florida court declined to apply the inevitable discovery doctrine to two murder weapons recovered after a defendant had been illegally arrested for a traffic violation. The prosecution argued that after the discovery of the first murder weapon in the defendant's car, the police would have initiated an investigation leading to the discovery of the second murder weapon. The court rejected the argument, stating that inevitable discovery cannot be based on speculation that the police would have investigated the defendant.

State courts have declined to follow several other Supreme Court exceptions or modifications. Regarding the Supreme Court's decision in *Moran v. Burbine*, 475 U.S. 412 (1986), which allowed a suspect's confession despite the failure of the police to notify him that an attorney had been retained for him, states have divided on whether or not to follow the ruling. Connecticut, Delaware, Florida, Illinois, Kentucky, Michigan, New Jersey, Oregon, and Massachusetts have rejected the Court's decision.[5] On the other hand, Arkansas,

---

4. *State v. Ault*, 150 Ariz. 459.

5. *State v. Stoddard*, 206 Conn. 157 (1988); *Bryan v. State*, 571 A.3d 170 (Del. 1990); *Halliburton v. State*, 514 So.2d 1088 (Fla. 1987); *People v. McCauley*, 163 Ill. 2d 414 (1994); *West v. Commonwealth*, 887 S.W.2d 338 (Ky. 1994); *People v. Bender*, 452 Mich. 594 (1996); *State v. Reed*, 133 N.J. 237 (1993); *State v. Simonsen*, 319 Ore. 510 (1994).

Indiana, Maryland, South Carolina, Tennessee, Washington, and Wisconsin are among the states that have followed the Supreme Court.[6]

In the Massachusetts case of *Commonwealth v. Mavredakis*, 430 Mass. 848 (2000), the facts were similar to *Moran v. Burbine, supra*, yet the Massachusetts court declined to follow the Supreme Court and came to an entirely different conclusion. In *Mavredakis*, the defendant and a male named John, using the keys of a store employee, were burglarizing a Kentucky Fried Chicken restaurant when the store manager, Thomas Henson, returned to the store after making a night deposit. The defendants shot Henson three times. Despite being shot, Henson made it to the front of the restaurant and collapsed. After he fell to the floor, he was shot twice more. "The defendant and John took approximately $1,000 in bills and rolled coins from three cash register drawers that were in the safe. They also took receipts, a police scanner, and a white towel. They wiped off the surfaces that they had touched and placed the drawers in water-filled sinks in an attempt to remove their fingerprints."

Henson's body was found in the morning. That evening, Mavredakis voluntarily accompanied the police to the station house to give a statement. Though not initially in custody, he was given Miranda warnings. He waived his rights and confessed to the murder. While he was being questioned, his father and an attorney had attempted to speak to him, and a second attorney had appeared at the station house, but the police did not inform the defendant of this information.

On the basis of its own constitution, the Massachusetts court suppressed the confession and granted a new trial, holding that "a suspect's knowledge of an attorney's efforts to render assistance was necessary to effect a knowing and intelligent waiver of a suspect's Miranda rights, and that if a suspect were not so informed, any waiver obtained from the defendant was inoperative."

In *Moran v. Burbine, supra*, the Supreme Court had said just the opposite:

> Events occurring outside the presence of the suspect and entirely unknown to him surely can have no bearing on the capacity to comprehend and knowingly relinquish a constitutional right … [T]he same defendant, armed with the same information and confronted with precisely the same police conduct, would have knowingly waived his *Miranda* rights had a lawyer not telephoned the police station.

---

6. *Mitchell v. State*, 306 Ark. 464 (1991); *McClaskey v. State*, 540 N.E.2d 41 (Ind. 1989); *Lodowski v. State*, 307 Md. 233 (1986); *State v. Drayton*, 293 S.C. 417 (1987); *State v. Stephenson*, 878 S.W.2d 530 (Tenn. 1994); *State v. Earls*, 116 Wn.2d 364 (1991); *State v. Hanson*, 126 Wis.2d 195 (1987).

The outcome of the diverse rulings on this issue is that defendants in-volved in almost identical situations receive opposite judicial results de-pending on the state in which they commit their crimes or the court deciding the issue.

California's Counter-Rebellion

California had adopted the exclusionary rule even before *Mapp v. Ohio, supra,* was decided. In *People v. Cahan,* 44 Cal. 2d 434 (1955), the California Supreme Court, using its own constitution as authority, adopted the rule six years before *Mapp,* and in line with that judicial approach, California courts, for more than three decades until 1982, consistently provided greater protec-tions for defendants than required by the Supreme Court. Moreover, Califor-nia not only adopted the exclusionary rule, but enhanced it by establishing the "vicarious exclusionary rule," which allowed the automatic standing of defen-dants to challenge the admissibility of evidence illegally seized from a third party.[7] Vicarious standing is a major departure from traditional standing re-quirements to bring a court action. Civil law has generally disallowed vicarious-standing lawsuits because, as an illustration, they would allow A to file a lawsuit against B because B injured C, and would allow A to collect the proceeds from a favorable judgment. Furthermore, in the event of an unfavorable judgment, the injured B would be precluded from obtaining a recovery from C because the case had already been adjudicated in A's lawsuit.

In the exclusionary rule context, the vicarious-standing doctrine lets a de-fendant challenge the admissibility against him of evidence uncovered during the search of another person's house. It does so even though the defendant's privacy was not violated by the search. Also, the vicarious-standing doctrine lets a defendant challenge the constitutionality of statements taken from another person that implicate or lead to evidence against the defendant, even though the defendant was not questioned.

The Supreme Court has rejected the vicarious-standing doctrine. In a series of decisions, *Rakas v. Illinois,* 439 U.S. 128 (1978), *United States v. Salvucci,* 448 U.S. 83 (1980), and *Rawlings v. Kentucky,* 448 U.S. 98 (1980), the Court reiterated the requirement of standing to challenge the legality of a search. For standing, a defendant must have an expectation of privacy in the place searched by the police, such as a proprietary interest in a vehicle or home that was

---

7. *People v. Martin,* 45 Cal.2d 755 (1955).

searched. If the police find evidence that could be used against the defendant in the vehicle or home of a third party, the defendant has no standing to challenge the constitutionality of the search of that vehicle or home, and the evidence obtained could be admissible against him. Nevertheless, despite the Supreme Court rulings, California courts continued to employ the vicarious-standing doctrine on the authority of its state constitution, and also declined to follow most of the other Supreme Court modifications and exceptions to the exclusionary rule.

For example, California courts, in *People v. Pettingill*, 21 Cal.3d 231 (1978), declined to follow the Supreme Court's precedent in *Michigan v. Mosley*, 423 U.S. 96 (1975). The defendant, Pettingill, had been arrested for burglary. He was given Miranda warnings and expressed his wish to remain silent. Three days later, after detectives obtained evidence connecting Pettingill to a series of other burglaries, they gave him new Miranda warnings and questioned him. He confessed to the series of burglaries. However, California suppressed the confession under the authority of its constitution, holding that once a defendant expresses a desire not to talk to the police, he or she may not be approached for questioning by the police, even about other crimes.

A series of such decisions favorable to criminal defendants made the California Supreme Court the subject of much criticism from politicians and commentators. Then, after Governor Jerry Brown appointed Justice Rose Bird as Chief Justice of the California Supreme Court (1977–1986), the criticism increased dramatically as her court issued numerous rulings that favored defendants, including a ruling against the constitutionality of the death penalty.

Coincidentally, during the tenure of the Bird court, crime increased in California at a pace faster than most other sections of the country, and when public pressure to do something about the rising crime rate failed to achieve results from the California courts or the state legislature, a movement to curtail the actions of the courts through the referendum process gained momentum. In 1982, a direct voter anticrime referendum, Proposition 8, was passed overwhelmingly. Proposition 8 amended the California Constitution to include Article I, Section 28(d), and provided as follows:

> *Right to Truth in Evidence.* Except as provided by statute hereafter enacted by a two-thirds vote of the membership in each house of the Legislature, relevant evidence shall not be excluded in any criminal proceeding, including pretrial and post conviction motions and hearings, or in any trial or hearing of a juvenile for a criminal offense, whether heard in juvenile or adult court. Nothing in this section shall affect any existing statutory rule of evidence relating to privilege or

hearsay, or Evidence Code, Sections 352, 782 or 1103. Nothing in this section shall affect any existing statutory or constitutional right of the press.

The purpose of Section 28(d) was to prevent the California courts, without legislative approval, from creating independent state grounds for exclusion of relevant evidence. Violations of the federal Constitution, as interpreted by controlling federal decisions, were to remain the necessary predicate for invocation of the exclusionary rule. Consequently, broader interpretations, such as the California vicarious exclusionary rule, were no longer viable, and could not be imposed in the future unless the California legislature enacted the exclusion into statutory law by means of a two-thirds vote.

The voters did not stop there. Judges to the California Supreme Court are appointed for 10-year terms by the Governor, but their re-appointments are subject to voter approval. When Justice Bird and two other judges appointed by Governor Brown came up for re-appointment, the same voters who passed Proposition 8 rejected the judges' re-appointments and voted them off the court—a highly unusual occurrence.

California courts are now supposed to invoke the exclusionary rule based only on the United States Constitution and interpretations thereof by the Supreme Court or other federal courts.[8] It would seem that suppression issues would be simplified by this approach; however, California is covered by the Ninth Circuit of the U.S. Circuit Court of Appeals, a court that has been notorious for its continuous conflict with the U.S. Supreme Court.[9] As a result, since California State courts have to follow the Ninth Circuit's interpretations of the United States Constitution, exclusionary rule issues in California remain problematic, and the California courts have to wait for the U.S. Supreme Court to overrule Ninth Circuit court opinions before the law is clarified.

An example of Ninth Circuit thinking is illustrated by its ruling in *United States v. Padilla*, 960 F.2d 854 (1992). Although the Ninth Circuit could not invoke the vicarious-standing doctrine that had been rejected by the Supreme Court, it created a substitute in what it termed a "coconspirator exception" to the rule regarding who may challenge the constitutionality of a search or seizure. Under its reasoning, a coconspirator obtains a legitimate expectation of pri-

---

8. *People v. Daan*, 161 Cal.App.3d 22 (1984).

9. In 2008, the Supreme Court granted *writs of certiorari* to 16 petitions appealing Ninth Circuit opinions, more than granted for any other Circuit. The Supreme Court reversed 13 of the 16 Ninth Circuit opinions, and fully affirmed only 1 opinion. Two opinions were partly affirmed and partly reversed.

vacy for Fourth Amendment purposes if he has either a supervisory role in the conspiracy or joint control over the place or property involved in the search or seizure. The facts in *Padilla* were as follows:

A police officer spotted a Cadillac traveling westbound on a highway at approximately 65 miles per hour. The officer followed the Cadillac for several miles because he thought the driver acted suspiciously as he passed the patrol car. Ultimately the officer stopped the Cadillac because it was going too slowly. Luis Arciniega, the driver and sole occupant of the car, gave the officer his driver's license and an insurance card demonstrating that respondent Donald Simpson, a United States customs agent, owned the Cadillac. The officer believed that Arciniega matched the drug courier profile. Acting on this belief, he requested and received Arciniega's permission to search the vehicle. The officer found 560 pounds of cocaine in the trunk and immediately arrested Arciniega.

After agreeing to make a controlled delivery of the cocaine, Arciniega made a telephone call to his contact from a motel in Tempe, Arizona. Jorge and Maria Padilla drove to the motel in response to the telephone call, but were arrested as they attempted to drive away in the Cadillac. Like Arciniega, Maria Padilla agreed to cooperate with law enforcement officials. She led them to the house in which her husband, Xavier Padilla, was staying.

The defendants were charged with conspiracy to distribute and possess with intent to distribute cocaine, in violation of 21 U.S.C., Section 846, and possession of cocaine with intent to distribute, in violation of §841(a)(1). Xavier Padilla was also charged with engaging in a continuing criminal enterprise, in violation of 21 U.S.C., Section 848. Defendants moved to suppress all evidence discovered in the course of the investigation, claiming that the evidence was the fruit of the unlawful investigatory stop of Arciniega's vehicle.

The district attorney objected to the suppression motion on the grounds that Xavier Padilla and the others had no standing to challenge the stop or search of the car. However, the Ninth Circuit ruled that the defendants had standing, holding that "A coconspirator's participation in an operation or arrangement that indicates joint control and supervision of the place searched establishes standing," and "because Xavier Padilla [and others] have demonstrated joint control and supervision over the drugs and vehicle and engaged in an active participation in a formalized business arrangement, they have standing to claim a legitimate expectation of privacy in the property searched and the items seized." Xavier Padilla established an expectation of privacy because he "exhibited substantial control and oversight with respect to the purchase [and] the transportation of drugs from Mexico into Arizona." The court expressly stated that it did not matter that Padilla was not present during the stop.

The Ninth Circuit's opinion creates the anomalous result that while a passenger in a vehicle in which cocaine is found in the trunk cannot challenge a search of the trunk,[10] a co-conspirator of the driver, though not present at the search, can challenge the constitutionality of the search. In a sense, the Ninth Circuit rewards those who participate in a conspiracy to distribute illegal drugs. According to their opinion, a drug kingpin in a foreign country who sends a shipment of illegal drugs into the United States could challenge the seizure of the drugs from one of his transporters.

Within a year, in *United States v. Padilla*, 508 U.S. 77 (1993), the Supreme Court reversed the Ninth Circuit, stating:

> The Ninth Circuit appears to stand alone in embracing the "coconspirator exception." We granted certiorari to resolve the conflict, and now reverse. It has long been the rule that a defendant can urge the suppression of evidence obtained in violation of the Fourth Amendment only if that defendant demonstrates that his Fourth Amendment rights were violated by the challenged search or seizure. We applied this principle to the case of co-conspirators in *Alderman*, in which we said: "The established principle is that suppression of the product of a Fourth Amendment violation can be successfully urged only by those whose rights were violated by the search itself, not by those who are aggrieved solely by the introduction of damaging evidence. Coconspirators and codefendants have been accorded no special standing."[11] The "coconspirator exception" developed by the Ninth Circuit is, therefore, not only contrary to the holding of *Alderman*, but at odds with the principle discussed above. Expectations of privacy and property interests govern the analysis of Fourth Amendment search and seizure claims. Participants in a criminal conspiracy may have such expectations or interests, but the conspiracy itself neither adds to nor detracts from them.

While the Supreme Court has closed the co-conspirator loophole, the Ninth Circuit still creates new exclusionary rule loopholes that the California courts must follow unless or until the Supreme Court overrules the Ninth Circuit.

------

10. *Rakas v. Illinois*, 430 U.S. 128 (1978).
11. *Alderman v. United States*, 394 U.S. 165 (1969).

Since federal judges are appointed for life, and little prospect exists that the mindset of the Ninth Circuit is likely to change, the exclusionary rule will continue as a problem for the voters of California. As a result, this confused state of the law allows defendants lawfully convicted in California to file *habeas corpus* petitions in federal district courts under the supervision of the Ninth Circuit and to have their convictions overturned on the basis of a contradictory set of legal interpretations.

The exclusionary rule has generated conflict among voters, legislatures, and courts. In California, where the voters enacted limits on what they considered to be judicial activism by their state courts, the federal Ninth Circuit has vitiated the prohibition, and in other states, the judicial branches have opposed the constitutional jurisprudence of the Supreme Court by adopting state constitutionalism as a substitute. In New York, the judicial branch has most strongly opposed Supreme Court jurisprudence and has arguably acted illegally in violation of its own constitution.

Chapter Seven

New York's False Foundation

In 1980, the New York Court of Appeals began using the New York State constitution as authority to issue search and seizure rulings contrary to the Supreme Court rulings.[1] New York's rationale was that New York State should provide greater levels of protection against governmental infringements than the minimum protections required by the United States Constitution. However, the Court's reliance on the New York State constitution as a mandate for the exclusionary rule is unsupported by the document and its historical underpinnings. The use of the exclusionary rule was rejected at the New York Constitutional Convention of 1938.

New York's original constitution, written in 1777, did not expressly include a right against unreasonable searches and seizures. The writers could be excused for this omission since they wrote the document while fleeing from the British army during the Revolutionary War.[2] It was not until 1828 that the state legislature enacted Civil Rights Law, Section 8, which used the same language as the Fourth Amendment of the U.S. Constitution:

> The right of the people to be secure in their persons, houses, papers, and effects, against unreasonable searches and seizures, shall not be violated, and no warrants shall issue, but upon probable cause, supported by Oath or affirmation, and particularly describing the place to be searched, and the persons or things to be seized.

During the remainder of the nineteenth century and for most of the twentieth century, violations of the Civil Rights Law were addressed by civil lawsuits. The exclusionary rule was unrecognized.

---

1. In *People v Elwell*, 50 N.Y.2d 231 (1980), the New York Court of Appeals rejected the U.S. Supreme Court totality of the circumstances standard for corroborating the information of confidential informants.

2. Pitler, Robert M., "Independent State Search and Seizure Constitutionalism: The New York State Court of Appeals' Quest for Principled Decision-making," *62 Brooklyn Law R. 1* (1996).

In 1914, the Supreme Court in *United States v. Weeks*, 232 U.S. 383, began applying the exclusionary rule in federal courts, and in 1926 the New York Court of Appeals in *People v. Defore*, 242 N.Y. 13, was petitioned to apply the rule in New York. In *Defore*, Justice Benjamin Cardozo wrote his famous opinion rejecting the application of the rule. He wrote:

> No doubt the protection of the statute would be greater from the point of view of the individual whose privacy had been invaded if the government were required to ignore what it had learned through the invasion. The question is whether protection for the individual would not be gained at a disproportionate loss of protection for society. On the one side is the social need that crime shall be repressed. On the other, the social need that law shall not be flouted by the insolence of office.

His answer took the side of protection for society, and his opinion has been well remembered for his comment:

> The criminal is to go free because the constable has blundered.... A room is searched against the law, and the body of a murdered man is found. If the place of discovery may not be proved, the other circumstances may be insufficient to connect the defendant with the crime. The privacy of the home has been infringed, and the murderer goes free.

In 1938, the issue arose again at the Constitutional Convention in which the New York constitution was revised and amended. New York's constitution has the same force and effect in New York as the United States Constitution has for the nation. Each sentence in the New York constitution serves as a foundation for New York statutory and common law, and great care was taken regarding what would be put in and what would be left out.

1938 was in the depression era, and crime during that period had reached high and dangerous levels. Prohibition had been rescinded in 1933, but the organized crime gangs created by Prohibition continued and expanded their criminal endeavors and were a threat to public safety. Consequently, crime and law enforcement procedures were major topics debated at the convention.

Two proposals were put before the convention delegates. The first proposal was to incorporate Civil Rights Law, Section 8, into the new constitution. The second proposal was to do the same, but to also include an exclusionary rule mandate. Delegates and advocates engaged in extensive debate on the convention floor, in other forums, and in the media over the inclusion of the proposals. The first proposal was accepted, but the second with the exclusionary rule was rejected.

The citizens of New York, through their representatives, transferred Civil Rights Law, Section 8, into Article I, Section 12, of the New York constitution, without the proposed exclusionary rule.[3] New York did by omission in 1938 what the citizens of California did expressly in Proposition 8 in 1982: They rejected a state exclusionary rule.

Without a constitutional mandate, New York courts did not employ an exclusionary rule as some other states had done. But in 1961, *Mapp v. Ohio, supra,* mandated that New York courts had to follow the rule on the basis the United States Constitution and federal precedents, and it did so.[4] However, in later years, when the leadership of the Supreme Court shifted and the Court began curtailing the expansion of the rule, New York did not follow suit; instead, it continued the rule's expansion. New York courts adopted the state constitutionalism concept and expressly rejected several of the Supreme Court's modifications and exceptions to the exclusionary rule. New York courts suppressed evidence that the Supreme Court had ruled should be admissible.

As a matter of purported state constitutional law, the New York Court of Appeals in *People v. Bigelow,* 66 N.Y.2d 451 (1985), declined to adopt the Supreme Court's *United States v. Leon* good faith exception. In *People v. Bethea,* 67 N.Y.2d 364 (1986), the court declined to follow the *Michigan v. Mosley* voluntary waiver exception to the right to remain silent. In *People v. Stith,* 69 N.Y.2d 313 (1987), the court refused to apply the inevitable discovery rule. In *People v. Griminger,* 71 N.Y.2d 635 (1988), the court rejected the *Illinois v. Gates* totality of the circumstances approach to determining probable cause.

In *People v. Gokey,* 60 N.Y.2d 309 (1983), a search after arrest case, the New York court declined to follow the Supreme Court ruling in *New York v. Belton,* 453 U.S. 454 (1981), that allowed police to search containers in the immediate control or reachable area of a suspect being placed under arrest. Referring to *Belton,* the New York Court stated, "This court has declined to interpret the State constitutional protection against unreasonable searches and seizures so narrowly.... Under the State Constitution, an individual's right of privacy in his or her effects dictates that a warrantless search incident to arrest be deemed unreasonable unless justified by the presence of exigent circumstances."

New York courts have also created a much broader right to counsel than required by federal courts. In New York, once criminal actions are commenced by the filing of an accusatory instrument, defendants may not be questioned or waive their right to remain silent without a lawyer present.[5] To the contrary,

---

3. Ibid.
4. *Mapp v. Ohio,* 367 U.S. 643 (1961).
5. *People v. Samuels,* 49 N.Y.2d 218 (1980).

under federal law, a defendant, without a lawyer present, may make a voluntary, knowing, and intelligent waiver of the right to remain silent.[6]

Certainly, New York courts can interpret the New York constitution to give broader protections against unreasonable searches and seizures and broader rights to counsel, since these rights are written in the document. If it so chose to do, the state could impose strong criminal or civil sanctions for violations of these rights. However, the exclusionary rule is not written in the state constitution, and the Convention purposely withheld the authority to employ such a rule. Therefore, by suppressing evidence that the Supreme Court has ruled should be legally admissible, the New York courts not only violated the spirit of the United States Constitution, they violated their own constitution.

New York's interpretation of search and seizure law unnecessarily deprives crime victims of justice. *People v. Johnson*, 66 N.Y.2d 398 (1985), is an example of how New York's flawed jurisprudence denies justice. Although the language of the Fourth Amendment of the U.S. Constitution and the language of the New York State Constitution, Article I, Section 12, regarding unreasonable searches and seizures are identical, in *Johnson*, the New York court's use of the two-pronged test for information from confidential informants resulted in the exclusion of the defendant's confession to murder, whereas the Supreme Court's totality of the circumstances standard would have allowed the confession into evidence.

In *Johnson*, on March 3, 1982, a man named Raymundo Alcantara, who was working in his grocery store, was shot and killed during a robbery. After the murder, the police questioned Bolivar Abreu as a possible accomplice in the murder. Abreu implicated Joseph DiProspro and the defendant, Melvin Johnson, as the murderers. Abreu related conversations that he heard between them in his girlfriend's apartment before and after the two men went out to commit the robbery. When they came back to the apartment, Johnson had a gun (which Abreu described in detail) and Johnson dumped six spent bullet shells on the floor. Johnson repeatedly described the robbery and how he had killed Alcantara.

Based on Abreu's information, the police arrested DiProspro and Johnson. Within an hour and a half of his arrest, Johnson confessed that he and DiProspro entered the grocery to commit a robbery. He said that DiProspro pulled out a gun, Mr. Alcantara grabbed for it, and during the struggle DiProspro shot Alcantara.

A jury convicted Johnson of murder, attempted robbery, criminal use of a firearm, and criminal possession of a weapon. During the trial, his confession

---

6. *Patterson v. Illinois*, 487 U.S. 285 (1988).

was admitted into evidence. He appealed on the grounds that when the police arrested him they did not have probable cause to arrest him and, therefore, his confession was obtained illegally and should have been suppressed. The New York Court of Appeals agreed, suppressed his confession, and reversed his conviction.

The court decided that the probable cause to arrest him was insufficient because although Abreu had a basis of knowledge for his information, his reliability had not been established. Therefore, the police information did not satisfy the required two-part test of a basis of knowledge and reliability. The court discussed the Supreme Court's *Illinois v. Gates* totality of the circumstances test and declined to apply it. They stuck to the position that both parts of the two-pronged test must be fully satisfied and that strength in one part cannot compensate for weakness in another. They concluded that the police had no authority to arrest and question Johnson.

What may be puzzling to citizens about this ruling is that when a murder has been committed and a witness who observed all or part of the crime reports it to the police, (here, Abreu's observed the end of the crime when Johnson came back to the apartment and unloaded the spent shells), the police will make an arrest before the criminal can escape or destroy evidence. They do not have to check the background of every eyewitness before they can act. Examining the witness can be left for trial and cross-examination. The police job is to apprehend dangerous criminals as soon as possible and before they can destroy evidence or commit additional crimes. They did not arrest Johnson on a whim. They had detailed information from an eyewitness. When such information comes from someone deemed a reputable citizen and not someone labeled a confidential informant, the police are presumed to have probable cause to make an arrest.

Apprehending a suspect sooner rather than later after a crime has been committed increases the chances of a confession, and Johnson confessed. A voluntary confession is by far the best and most direct evidence of guilt, and the drastic step of voiding a confession of guilt should not be taken lightly and should not rest on labels. This case showed why the Supreme Court had good reason to abandon the two-pronged hyper-technical test and to adopt the totality of the circumstances test.

Moreover, the New York court applied the two-pronged test that is usually applied to search warrant applications in drug cases or other organized crime cases. In such cases a confidential informant works with the police and provides information that is often based on indirect or hearsay evidence regarding an ongoing criminal operation. The police then submit an application for a search warrant without providing the identity of the confidential informant.

The judge reviews the past reliability of the informant and the basis of knowledge of his assertions. If the judge deems these elements sufficient, he will issue a warrant without knowing the identity of the informant. Here, Abreu was not going to be a confidential informant, whose identify would be kept secret, but a testifying witness to a crime of which he observed the beginning and end. His primary testimony would not be based on indirect information but on the same type of direct observation that any eyewitness to a crime provides.

It is reasonable to assume that the dead man, Raymundo Alcantara, the man who was working long, hard hours in the grocery store to support his family when he was suddenly murdered, would not understand why Johnson's confession had to be suppressed. To Mr. Alcantara, classifying Abreu as a confidential informant rather than an eyewitness to the crime would seem nonsensical. The place to ascertain whether Abreu was telling the truth should be during cross-examination at trial.

The refusal of New York courts to follow U.S. Supreme Court jurisprudence when adjudicating state cases is one level of conflict between the courts. A more extreme conflict arises when the Supreme Court remands an exclusionary rule case back to the state court with directions as to how it should be decided, but the state court nevertheless refuses to follow the directions. These refusals seem almost like insubordination; however, New York courts claim they have authority to do so on the basis of their own constitution. As noted above, this claim contravenes the proclamation made by the 1936 Constitutional Convention that rejected the exclusionary rule; the public is largely unaware of this contravention, and citizens are often puzzled by the inconsistent rulings that result.

Thelma Staton, were she alive, would not understand why the New York court, in *People v. Harris*, 72 N.Y.2d 614 (1988), voided the conviction of the man who freely and voluntarily confessed to cutting her throat, nearly decapitating her. On January 11, 1984, the police found the body of Mrs. Staton. She had been murdered in her apartment. The police developed information that her ex-boyfriend, Bernard Harris, had killed her, and three detectives then went to Harris' apartment. They did not obtain an arrest warrant.

Inside the apartment, the detectives advised Harris of his Miranda rights. After sipping some wine, he told them, "I am glad you came for me." He confessed to cutting Mrs. Staton's throat, saying he did it because "she was a bad mother."

Harris was arrested and taken to the station house. After being advised of his Miranda rights again, he confessed a second time. A detective took down the confession, and Harris signed it. Later, when an assistant district attorney arrived to take a videotaped confession, he asked Harris whether he wanted to speak about the death of Thelma Staton. Harris answered, "Well, I really don't know what to say right now … I have said all I can say." Nevertheless, he gave a third videotaped confession.

During the state trial proceedings, the first and third confessions were suppressed. The first was suppressed because the police had entered Harris' apartment without an arrest warrant, exigent circumstances, or consent to enter, and under *Payton v. New York*, 445 U.S. 574 (1980), their action requires the suppression of any evidence obtained while in the home, including any incriminating statements.

The third confession was suppressed because Harris had indicated by his statement "I have said all I can say" that he wanted to stop. Therefore, any further questioning violated his right to remain silent.

The second confession became the issue of extensive litigation. It was admitted into evidence at Harris' trial, and he was convicted of the murder. Harris appealed his conviction to the New York Appellate Division, where four of the five Appellate judges agreed with the trial judge that the second confession was admissible.[7]

Harris then appealed to the New York Court of Appeals, and the court reversed the Appellate Division, overturning the murder conviction and ordering a new trial. The court ruled that the second confession should have been suppressed because it violated the Supreme Court's ruling in *Payton v. New York, supra,* and there was insufficient attenuation (breaking the chain of causation) between the *Payton* violation and the interrogation at the station house.[8]

The New York District Attorney appealed the ruling of the state's highest court to the United States Supreme Court, arguing that the New York court misinterpreted the Supreme Court's ruling in *Payton.*

The Supreme Court, in *New York v. Harris*, 495 U.S. 14 (1990), agreed with the district attorney, ruling that despite the *Payton* violation, the second confession was admissible. Obtaining the confession did not violate the United States Constitution. "We decline to apply the exclusionary rule in this context because the rule in *Payton* was designed to protect the physical integrity of the home; it was not intended to grant criminal suspects, like Harris, protection for statements made outside their premises where the police have probable cause to arrest the suspect for committing a crime."[9]

---

7. *People v. Harris*, 124 A.D.2d 472.
8. *People v. Harris*, 72 N.Y.2d 614 (1988).
9. *New York v. Harris*, 495 U.S. 14 (1990).

The Supreme Court reversed the New York Court of Appeals, reinstated the conviction, and remanded the case back to New York.

In February 1991, seven years after Thelma Staton's murder, the New York Court of Appeals, in *People v. Harris*, 77 N.Y.2d 434 (1991), again suppressed the second confession. In something like an act of rebellion, the court circumvented the Supreme Court's decision by replacing the United States Constitution with the New York constitution. The court ruled, " … the Supreme Court's rule does not adequately protect the search and seizure rights of citizens of New York. Accordingly, we hold that our State Constitution requires that statements obtained from an accused following a *Payton* violation must be suppressed unless the taint from the violation has been attenuated."[10]

The New York Court upheld its reversal of Harris' conviction and ordered a new trial. Of course, ordering a new trial seven years after the murder is problematic for the prosecution. Witnesses and evidence are difficult to marshal after so many years, and often the district attorney is forced to offer a plea bargain to a lesser charge rather than attempt to retry the case without the suppressed evidence. If a retrial goes forward, the probabilities of acquittal of the guilty murderer are greatly increased.

There is irony in New York's reliance on its state constitution in its final *Harris* decision (77 N.Y.2d 434). It was a *Payton* violation that New York proposed to remedy by suppressing the confessions. However, New York had never established a *Payton*-type violation under its constitution. In fact, New York found the underlying conduct in *Payton* constitutional,[11] but its decision was reversed by the United States Supreme Court in *Payton v. New York*, 445 U.S. 573 (1980). The Supreme Court mandated that for police to arrest a suspect in his home, an arrest warrant was generally required. Under prior law in most states, when police had probable cause to arrest a suspect, they could enter a home without a warrant to make the arrest, and New York statutory law authorized entry into homes to make an arrest. New York Criminal Procedure Law 140.15 (4), states:

> In order to effect such an arrest, a police officer may enter premises in which he reasonably believes such person to be present, under the same circumstances and in the same manner as would be authorized … if he were attempting to make such arrest pursuant to a warrant of arrest.

---

10. *People v. Harris*, 77 N.Y.2d 434 (1991).
11. *People v. Harris*, 45 N.Y.2d 300 (1978).

Payton struck down this statute as it applied to warrantless arrests of defendants inside their homes, but it did not declare the entire statute unconstitutional. The police may still enter without a warrant to effect arrests in "premises," which includes offices, work places, and the homes of other persons.

The irony is that after the Supreme Court ruled in *Harris* that suppression of the confession was not required to remedy a warrantless arrest inside the house, the New York court ruled that the New York constitution required the suppression of the confession in order to remedy a violation that it had previously ruled did not exist.

Putting aside legal ironies, the New York court's ruling created further practical problems for homicide detectives. According to the court, since the detective's had probable cause, they should have obtained an arrest warrant before going to Harris' apartment. The Court surmised that the detective's motivation for not obtaining an arrest warrant was for the underhanded purpose of questioning Harris without an attorney present. In New York, once an arrest warrant is obtained, the subject has an indelible right to an attorney, and the police could not question him in the absence of his attorney. The Court believed, "They have every reason to violate *Payton* … because doing so enables them to circumvent the accused's indelible right to counsel. Indeed, the evidence indicated that the police were motivated by just such considerations in this case. Even though they had developed probable cause early in their investigation, they did not secure a warrant but arrested the defendant in his apartment, then questioned him in the absence of an attorney."

Contrary to what the New York court suggested was the devious motivation of the detectives, the detectives' primary motivation was surely and simply to apprehend the murderer of Thelma Staton. One could fairly surmise that the Court's pique at being overruled by the Supreme Court led them to stretch their logic and to shift the blame for its decision to the detectives. The blame is misplaced. Were the detectives motivated by a desire to question Harris without his attorney, it would be a simple matter of arresting him outside his apartment. They could have put the apartment under surveillance and waited for him to come out. They could have knocked on his door and asked him to come outside to talk. They could have called on the telephone and asked him to come down to the station house.

The New York Court connected the first confession inside the apartment with the second confession at the station house, and they assumed that suppressing the second confession would deter the police from violating *Payton* and obtaining confessions such as the first confession. However, as the Supreme Court said, suppressing the second confession has little deterrent value. The detectives already knew that a *Payton* violation would result in suppression of evidence obtained inside the house. "Given that the police have probable cause to arrest a suspect in Harris' position, they need not violate *Payton* in order to interrogate the suspect."[12]

The detectives were not acting in an arrest mode but in an investigative mode. In homicide investigations, detectives want to question relatives and associates of the victim as soon as possible after the crime. Sometimes these persons know something about the crime or are potential suspects, and the police want to see their reactions and obtain information and explanations from them. This is an essential part of the investigative process. This is part of a continuing process of developing probable cause, part of the process of obtaining necessary evidence, and part of the process of assuring that they do not arrest the wrong person.

The New York ruling forces detectives to desist from visiting potential suspects at their homes. Although the detective's intention may be to gain consent to enter the suspects' home to interview them, they do not know how events will develop at the scene and they cannot rely on later convincing the court that they gained entry by consent. The court might find that they did not have consent to enter the premises and should have obtained a warrant.

Probable cause is not the end of a complete and accurate investigation; ultimately, the state needs to prove a criminal case beyond a reasonable doubt. No requirement exists in any constitutional ruling or statute that the police must stop investigating and commence criminal charges by obtaining an arrest warrant when they first develop enough evidence for probable cause. They can wait until they have a stronger case, and they should wait until they are sure they are arresting the right person and have enough evidence for a conviction.

It often occurs that when the police visit a potential suspect to conduct an interview, the suspect talks to the police and convinces them that he or she was not involved in the crime. The suspect might have a truthful alibi, might not have any physical wounds that the real criminal would surely have had, or might provide information that is helpful and points to the real criminal. Requiring the police to obtain an arrest warrant before attempting to interview a suspect substantially hampers the investigation of crime.

Furthermore, police investigations generate evidence that courts and juries have traditionally used in making their determinations. When the police come around to investigate and a suspect reacts by fleeing, concealing evidence, or providing false information, such actions are appropriate subjects for consideration and are indicative of consciousness of guilt. "The demeanor of a pris-

---

12. *New York v. Harris*, 495 U.S. 14 (1990).

oner at the time of his arrest, or soon after the commission of the crime, or upon being charged with the offense, is a proper subject of consideration in determining the question of guilt."[13] The New York Court's ruling in *Harris* closes an opportunity to obtain potentially crucial information of the kind that judges and juries need when making decisions of guilt or innocence.

As a punitive measure against the police, the exclusionary rule exacts a heavy penalty on society. The list of criminals released outright or released early and the list of victims denied justice is far too long. Cases such as those noted above are examples of the difficulties resulting from ill-considered New York court decisions, first, disregarding the clear intent of the 1938 New York Constitutional Convention, which voted against implementing an exclusionary rule, and, second, diverging from the path of the more well-considered United States Supreme Court jurisprudence.

---

13. *Greenfield v. New York*, 85 N.Y. 75 (1881).

Chapter Eight

Disarming the Police

New York courts have not only placed restraints on police investigative procedures, but they have also attempted to dictate how and when police officers may utilize their weapons as a safety precaution. The intent of the courts may have been to protect the rights of citizens to be free of unreasonable government intrusion, but the actual effect has been to place police officers in a dilemma in which they must decide whether they should draw their weapons and risk causing the suppression of crucial evidence or not draw their weapons and leave themselves more vulnerable to a sudden assault.

In one of many such cases, *People v. Hampton*, 606 N.Y.S.2d 628, (1994), a New York Appellate Division court reversed two murder convictions because a police officer had drawn his gun when he approached a suspect. The incident that led to the court ruling occurred after midnight on May 30, 1990, in the Bronx, New York. At that time, crime had been escalating and there had been a rash of gunpoint robberies of taxicab drivers. Many of the victims were shot and left for dead. In the preceding year, fifty New York City taxicab drivers had been robbed and murdered. To address the problem, an association of Bronx taxicab drivers entered into an agreement with the police wherein the police would conduct safety checks of taxicabs carrying passengers, especially in areas prone to robberies.

Two police officers, Kevin McGarvey and John Kennedy, were on patrol and assigned to conduct the taxicab checks when they observed a cab with three male passengers in the back seat. McGarvey testified at a suppression hearing that the cab was being driven in an "erratic manner ... stopping in the middle of the block, starting to make turns, and then just kept going like he was lost." Suspecting a robbery, the officers followed the cab until it stopped at a corner. Hampton, the suspect, emerged from the rear passenger door, carrying a thin, white plastic bag that appeared "weighed" down by a heavy object. The officers left their vehicle and drew their guns. They told Hampton to stop. McGarvey approached him and saw the outline of an Uzi-type machine-gun through the plastic bag. He directed Hampton to put the bag down. When Hampton complied, the bag fell open, exposing the gun. The two other passengers fled, leaving two more guns on the floor of the cab.

The officers arrested Hampton. In addition to the Uzi machine-gun and 29 live rounds of ammunition found in the bag, narcotics were found in Hampton's jacket. At the station house, a further search of the defendant revealed $4,701 in cash, and vehicle registration and insurance cards in the name of a woman whom Hampton initially claimed was his girlfriend. After investigation, it was discovered that the woman was not his girlfriend, but the documents belonged to a woman who had been murdered during a robbery.

When questioned about the documents, Hampton waived his Miranda rights and gave incriminating statements regarding the murder of the woman and also regarding another woman murdered during a different robbery. Lineups were conducted and Hampton was identified in connection with the two murders.

During criminal proceedings in which Hampton was charged with two counts of murder in addition to the machine-gun charge, his attorney made a motion to suppress the evidence, claiming the stop of Hampton was an unreasonable search and seizure in violation of the Fourth Amendment. He claimed that the Uzi should be excluded from evidence, and under the fruits of the poisonous tree doctrine, all subsequent evidence obtained as a result of the unlawful arrest also should be suppressed.

The trial judge denied the motion, and Hampton plea-bargained to two counts of attempted murder, robbery first degree, and possession of unlawful narcotics. He was sentenced as a second-time felony offender to imprisonment from ten years minimum to twenty years maximum.

Not satisfied with the plea-bargain deal, Hampton appealed the denial of his motion to suppress all the evidence. His appeal was granted. The Appellate Division of the New York Supreme Court, First Department, reversed the trial court ruling and held that the evidence should have been suppressed. The Court ruled that the "conduct of the police officers in this case constitutes an impermissible intrusion upon the privacy and security of the defendant ... requiring exclusion of the evidence seized."[1] Therefore, the gun, ammunition, narcotics, jewelry, documents and money, together with Hampton's incriminating statements and the lineup identification were all suppressed. The court reasoned that by drawing their weapons, the police escalated the situation from an investigative inquiry to a forcible stop. According to the New York State Criminal Procedure Law, a police officer may forcibly stop a person only "when he reasonably suspects that such person is committing, has committed or is about to commit ... a crime."[2] The Court felt that the actions of the taxicab driver

---

1. *People v. Hampton*, 606 N.Y.S.2d 628, 629 (1994).
2. *NY Criminal Procedure Law*, section 140.50.

and the defendant were "susceptible of an innocent interpretation" and did not constitute reasonable suspicion. The Court did concede that "the circumstances in this case were sufficient to arouse interest and justify a request for information...."[3] Therefore the officers were justified in approaching the cab and the defendant, but were not justified in taking out their guns. Had they kept their guns in their holsters until they actually observed the Uzi machine-gun, the arrest and search would have been valid. Had they kept their guns in their holsters, Hampton's convictions for the robberies and murders of the two women could have been upheld.

Certainly, it could be surmised that had the officers kept their guns in their holsters, Hampton or his accomplices might have shot and killed the officers. Speculation aside, the consequence of the court's decision was that Hampton got away with murdering two women.

The decision raised other questions. If the officers had drawn their weapons, but kept them pointed down and out of sight, would that have been allowable? What if they had kept their weapons in the holsters, but loosened them and kept their hands on the handles? What if one of the officers had taken out his gun, without the defendant knowing it? Should any of these possible actions have made any difference in the murder cases against Hampton?

Neither the legislature nor the New York City Police Department has ever tried to mandate when officers should or should not take out their guns—there are too many variables. Experiences, feelings, instincts all play a part in the decision to take out a gun. Checking out prowler calls, responding to crime incidents, approaching suspicious persons, all may cause an officer to take the precaution of readying a weapon. When an officer stops a suspicious person, the eye movements, body language, and hand movements of the person might signal danger and trigger an instinctual response. With a competent and experience officer, such natural reactions are often the most accurate assessments of the situation. In *Hampton*, the criminal whom the officers encountered had recently killed two women, was in possession of incriminating evidence, and was carrying an illegal machine-gun. Such criminals give off signals, and police officers develop radar for such signals. The signals may be hard to articulate; nonetheless, they are real.

After the initial shock of the *Hampton* case dissipated, many in New York law enforcement disregarded it. They thought it was an aberration, just another one of those bad cases that come along, a case that is generally not followed by other courts, and one that is often overruled by wiser judges or judges having a better day. They disregarded the ruling because they believed it was

---

3. *People v. Hampton*, 606 N.Y.S.2d 628, 629 (1994).

their decision whether or not to take out their guns. No court could tell an officer who senses danger as he approaches a potentially dangerous criminal that he could not take out his gun. The officers in *Hampton* were dealing with a situation involving the cold-blooded murder of fifty taxicab drivers in one year. They observed a taxi being driven erratically with three males in the backseat who fit the descriptions and profiles of the suspected murderers. They were right in their assessment, because Hampton, indeed, was carrying an Uzi. These experienced officers knew that they should take out their guns.[4]

They also knew the case of Detective Louis Miller. Detective Miller was a 34-year veteran of the New York City Police Department. Although he was a uniformed officer, he was promoted to detective because he was regarded as one of the best training officers in the department. The "rookies" he trained in the 70th Precinct affectionately called him "The Commander." He was known for his gift of calming stressful situations, for gentle persuasion, and for helping people in need. He trained his rookies to believe that the most effective police officers are courteous, understanding, and friendly, rather than curt or abrasive. He trained them in the latest court rulings involving reasonable suspicion, probable cause, and the restrictions on police. He prided himself on never having to use his weapon during his 34-year career.

On March 11, 1987, Detective Miller responded with two of his rookies to a 911 call of a burglary in progress in an apartment building in Brooklyn, New York. On the fourth floor of the building, he came upon two young men and asked them for identification. He had not drawn his gun. One of the young men pulled a gun and shot Miller in the chest and the stomach. Miller died on the way to the hospital. This tragedy might have been prevented had Miller trained his gun on the young men as he questioned them.[5]

---

4. In 2002 in *People v. Abad*, 98 N.Y.2d 12, the New York Court of Appeals, in a small concession to the dangerous circumstances that New York police and New York taxi-drivers confront, approved the police department's Taxi/Livery Robbery Inspection Program (TRIP). This program was instituted after the *Hampton* decision in 1994 and in response to the ongoing murders and robberies of taxi-drivers, including two murders in one weekend. In 1992 alone, there were 3600 reported robberies of taxi-drivers in New York City. TRIP is a voluntary program to which owners of taxis and livery cars consent, allowing the police to stop and visually inspect taxis and livery cars to ensure the driver's safety. A decal is displayed in the vehicle to notify passengers of the program. However, the protocol of the program does not grant the police any more authority regarding the passengers than they have under the reasonable suspicion and probable cause standards of criminal procedure law. Therefore, TRIP would not have altered the exclusion of evidence in *Hampton*.

5. Todd S. Purdum, "Detective Dies and Officer Is Wounded in Brooklyn Shootout," *New York Times*, 3/12/87.

Detective Miller's death was one of many that may be attributable to officers not drawing their weapons. Of the 594 police officers feloniously killed in the line of duty between 1995 and 2004, only 126 of the victim officers fired their weapons.[6] It may be inferred from this that 468 of the victim officers who did not fire their weapons were unprepared to fire when they were assaulted. Although definitive information is not readily available, it may be inferred further that of the 468 victim officers, most had failed to draw their weapons before they were killed.

Two years after Detective Miller's death, the New York Court of Appeals in *People v. Torres*, 74 N.Y.2d 224 (1989), ignored his death and issued another ruling that restricting police officers during street-encounter search and seizure incidents. In *Torres*, the Court overruled the decisions of the trial court and the Appellate Division court. The case began on October 25, 1985, at 11:00 a.m. when the police at the 25th Precinct in New York City received a telephone tip from an anonymous caller that "Poppo," a man wanted for a homicide, was having his hair cut at a barbershop located at East 116th Street and Third Avenue in the East Harlem section of Manhattan. The caller described Poppo as a large, six-foot tall Hispanic male, wearing a white sweater and carrying a gun in a shoulder bag. Poppo drove a black Cadillac Eldorado.

Two detectives went to the location and observed Poppo, later identified as Miguel Torres, leaving the barbershop with another man. Torres was wearing a white sweater and carrying a green nylon shoulder bag. He and the other man entered a black Cadillac Eldorado that was parked at the curb. The detectives quickly approached the car with their guns drawn, identified themselves, and ordered the two men out of the car. As one of the detectives frisked Torres, the other detective reached into the car and took the shoulder bag from the front seat. The detective felt the outside of the bag, discerned the shape of a gun, unzipped the bag, and found a revolver. The revolver was loaded with five live rounds of ammunition.

Torres was arrested and charged with criminal possession of a weapon. His attorney made a motion to suppress the gun, but the trial court denied the motion, holding that the anonymous tip coupled with the confirmatory observations of the detectives on the scene was sufficient to justify seizing the shoulder bag. Torres pled guilty, but appealed the denial of his motion to suppress the gun.

The Appellate Division, First Department, agreed with the trial court's ruling and denied the appeal. The Court ruled, "While the immediate frisk may not have been permissible given the facts, including that there was no showing that the caller was reliable or the source of his information, it was reason-

---

6. Uniform Crime Reports, U.S. Department of Justice, FBI, Officers Killed or Assaulted, 2004.

able for the police officer to remove the bag from the car for his own protection."

Torres, however, appealed to the Court of Appeals, and in July 1989, that court came to diametrically opposite conclusions than the lower courts. It assented to the "reasonableness of the detectives' conduct in ordering the suspects out of the car and conducting a protective pat-down," but ruled that reaching into the car for the bag was unlawful. Ordering the gun suppressed and the indictment against the defendant dismissed, the Court stated, " … we conclude that the detective's conduct in reaching into the car and removing the bag, conduct which revealed the presence of a gun, was not reasonable related to the need to protect the officers' safety in this street encounter."

Apparently the court believed that it was constitutionally significant that Torres was able to sit in the car before the police were able to approach him. If they had stopped him before he got into the car, their frisk would have lawfully included the shoulder bag. Whether the suspect sat down or stood up, sat on a park bench or in a car, kept his bag on his shoulder or placed it next to him seems insignificant compared with the detectives' obligation to investigate a detailed and substantially confirmed tip that a person wanted for homicide was present at a specific location and was carrying a gun in a bag.

The actions on the street by the detectives generated three different rulings by three reviewing New York courts:

Court	Stop & Frisk of Suspect	Removal of Bag from Car
Trial Court	Lawful	Lawful
Appellate Division	Unlawful	Lawful
Court of Appeals	Lawful	Unlawful

In view of the difficulties that the courts experienced while deliberating what the detectives should or should not have done while confronting this homicide suspect, it seems unfair for the Court of Appeals to have condemned the detectives' necessarily quick decisions. In addition, the Court of Appeals decision was in contravention of the United States Supreme Court decision in *Michigan v. Long*, 463 U.S. 1032 (1983), which had been decided differently on the basis of similar facts. In an effort to justify distinguishing *Torres* from *Long*, the Court of Appeals explained:

> There was nothing to prevent these two armed detectives from questioning the two suspects with complete safety to themselves, since the suspects had been isolated from the interior of the car, where the nylon bag that supposedly contained the gun was located. Any residual fear

that the detectives might have had about the suspects' ability to break away and retrieve the bag could have been eliminated by taking the far less intrusive step of asking the suspects to move away from the vicinity of the car. Finally, it is unrealistic to assume, as the Supreme Court did in *Michigan v. Long*, that having been stopped and questioned without incident, a suspect who is about to be released and permitted to proceed on his way would, upon reentry into his vehicle, reach for a concealed weapon and threaten the departing police officer's safety. Certainly, such a far-fetched scenario is an insufficient basis upon which to predicate the substantial intrusion that occurred here.

The Court of Appeals made several assumptions about what could have happened next. It assumed that the detectives were going to release Torres and his companion and that Torres and his companion knew or believed the detectives were going to release them. It assumed the police inquiry had been completed and the detectives were not going to arrest Torres. It assumed the detectives were not going to ask Torres to voluntarily accompany them to the police station to investigate his connection to the homicide. It assumed the detectives were not going to attempt to arrest Torres, who may have recently committed a murder, and who may have attempted to resist arrest by getting into his car where his gun was available.

Clearly, the detectives stopped and frisked Torres for a reason. They were investigating a possible homicide and the report that Torres was carrying a gun, which could have been the murder weapon. The fact that they did not find the weapon on him did not end the matter, and they would have been remiss to walk away. Whether they arrested him would depend on what information developed. The detectives did not know what would happen next or how accessible the gun was in the shoulder bag. Before making any decisions about their next course of action, as any safety-minded detective would, they checked the shoulder bag for the gun that had been reported by the caller. They checked the bag to ascertain whether the gun that could have had a connection to a homicide was present in the bag.

If a gun had not been found in the bag, then the detectives might have been obligated to conclude that the anonymous caller's information was inaccurate, and, barring other information, they would have had to release Torres.

The court described the gun in the bag as "the supposed gun" when in fact there was a gun. The court, astonishingly, characterized the potential threat to the detectives in this situation as "unrealistic" and "far-fetched." Apparently the judges discounted the high percentage of police fatalities and injuries that result from suspects quickly producing guns, and they discounted the dangerous nature of the area in and around East 116th Street and Third Avenue, which was one of the most violent areas in New York City. In 1985, at the height of the crack epidemic and the related peak homicide rate, this neighborhood was notorious for drug dealing, gang terror, and street violence. The decent, law-abiding people who lived in this area needed and demanded police protection.

Analysis of the 566,523 reported assaults on police officers that occurred between 1995 and 2004 discloses that the rate of assault was far higher in congested urban areas than in less-populated parts of the country. In large urban areas, the rate of assaults was 17.1 per 100 officers per year. In rural areas the rate was 6.2 per 100 officers per year.[7] The detectives in the *Torres* case worked in a congested, high-crime area, knew the level of violence, knew how fast things could happen, and knew they wanted to go home safely to their families. They were also street-wise enough to credit the report that Poppo had a gun in the shoulder bag. Carrying the shoulder bag into the barbershop when he could have left it locked in the car enhanced the credibility of the report.

Police who encounter armed and violent criminals are at a tremendous disadvantage. Many of these criminals have been raised in a violent subculture and have been involved in prior shootings. A study conducted by the Federal Bureau of Investigation focused on incidents in which police officers were shot. The examiners interviewed 42 offenders who were convicted of shooting police officers. Of these offenders, 24 admitted involvement in shootings prior to assaulting the police officer. Twenty-three offenders claimed to be instinctive shooters in that they would simply point and shoot and not use the sights of a gun because there was not enough time. Several admitted to more than five previous shooting incidents. The study found:

> Several of the offenders who were interviewed grew up in an environment where violence was commonplace. They were raised among street sales of narcotics and open-air drug markets. These "street combat veterans" are prepared to use deadly force on a moment's notice. Officers, on the other hand, must consider the legality of their action, use of deadly force policy, various departmental administrative policies, and moral justification before such force can be exercised. It appears that in many cases, the "street combat veteran" may enjoy a distinct advantage over a police officer who is relatively inexperienced

---

7. Unified Crime Reports, U.S. Department of Justice, FBI, Officers Killed or Assaulted, 2004.

ife situations and who must operate

ce courts to abstain from mandating when
irearms. Assuming that our public policy is
t to proactively combat crime by enforcing
the laws, recovering evidence, and confiscating illegal guns and unlawful drugs, we should expect that as part of their mandate officers will stop and search people when it is necessary, appropriate, and reasonable. In the fast-moving events that police encounter, they need to be able to act instinctively. It is unreasonable and unfair for society to direct them to engage in close contact with potentially dangerous criminals while hampering their natural movements and reactions. It is unreasonable for courts to disregard the safety concerns of officers when determining whether a search was reasonable.

Despite the above considerations, in 2006, the New York State Court of Appeals continued on its path of reviewing every movement of police officers during street encounters and added more complexity to its search and seizure jurisprudence. *People v. Moore*, 6 N.Y.3d 496 (2006), is another illustration of the propensity of the judges to substitute their judgment for that of the experienced police officers, and the court's ruling could be interpreted as forbidding the police from approaching suspicious persons with their guns drawn. The effect of *People v. Moore* may be that the discussion in *People v. Torres* is now moot. In *Torres*, the police approached the defendant with their guns drawn, but the court did not address that issue. In *Moore*, the Court ruled that when the police draw their weapons in violation of the constitution, all evidence seized after the violation must be suppressed. Furthermore, *Moore* ratified the legal reasoning in *People v. Hampton*, *supra*, and essentially claimed that it was up to the courts to determine when an officer can take out his gun for self-protection. In *Hampton*, *Torres*, and *Moore*, the New York courts declined to follow the advice of Chief Justice Earl Warren in the landmark decision of *Terry v. Ohio*, 391 U.S. 1 (1968). Warren wrote:

> A rigid and unthinking application of the exclusionary rule, in futile protest against practices which it can never be used effectively to control, may exact a high toll on human injury and frustration of efforts to prevent crime. No judicial opinion can comprehend the protean variety of the street encounter.... [9]

---

8. *In the Line of Fire*, U.S. Department of Justice, FBI, NIJ, October 1997.
9. *Terry v. Ohio*, 392 U.S. 1 (1968).

The facts pertaining to *Moore* occurred on November 12, 1997. Two police officers on routine patrol in their marked police car received a radio call of a dispute involving a male with a gun, described as approximately eighteen years of age, wearing a gray jacket and red hat. The information came from an anonymous phone call. The officers arrived on the scene within a minute of receiving the call. No dispute was taking place, but the officers observed the defendant, Moore, a young man wearing a gray jacket and red hat.

The officers approached Moore, who began to walk away. The officers drew their weapons and yelled, "Police, don't move." Moore walked a short distance before stopping. When the officers told Moore to put up his hands, he made a movement toward his waistband as he raised his arms. One of the officers patted-down Moore and recovered a gun from the defendant's left jacket pocket.

Moore was arrested for possession of the gun, but he moved to suppress the use of the gun as evidence. The motion was denied, but his appeal reached the New York Court of Appeals. That court suppressed the gun, stating:

> Although we agree with the Appellate Division that the anonymous tip authorized only an inquiry, the police here failed to simply exercise their common-law right to inquire. Instead—in ordering him at gunpoint to remain where he was—the police forcibly stopped defendant as soon as they arrived on the scene. Because the officers did not possess reasonable suspicion until after defendant reached for his waistband, however—by which time defendant had already been unlawfully stopped—the gun should have been suppressed. Defendant's later conduct cannot validate an encounter that was not justified at its inception.[10]

The court appears to be mandating that in these "gun run" situations, a police officer must wait for the suspect to draw his weapon before the officer can draw his. It is extremely doubtful that police officers in these situations, fearing for their safety, will follow the court's unrealistic mandate. They will exercise their inherent right to self-defense irrespective of the inadmissibility of the suspect's gun.

The action taken by the police in *Moore* is an example of the kind of police work that occurs every day in New York City. During the 1990s in their efforts to reduce violent crime, taking guns off the street was a priority for the police. The communities that the police serve demanded that they confiscate guns to make their neighborhoods safe, and the state legislature passed stringent anti-

---

10. *People v. Moore*, 6 N.Y.3d 496 (2006).

gun laws based on the obvious connection between guns and violence. The newspapers were rife with stories of innocent people killed for nonsensical reasons only because a gun was available. In 1993, approximately 1500 of the 2456 homicides in New York City were committed with guns, and roughly 5000 people were wounded in shootings. In response, New York City police instituted anti-gun operations, including street crime unit patrols, and from 1994 to 1997 the police made 46,198 arrests for unlawful possession of guns while confiscating 56,081 guns. As a result, by 1997, city homicides committed with guns decreased to approximately 970, and non-fatal shootings decreased to approximately 1400.[11]

Moore, retroactively, has declared many of those gun seizures illegal, and defense attorneys rely on *Moore* as the authority to suppress guns confiscated in street encounters between the police and criminals. This extension of the exclusionary rule undermines law enforcement efforts and works against the best interests of the citizens of the state.

Justice Robert Smith, in his dissent in *Moore*, pointed out that the majority had increased the possibilities for invoking the exclusionary rule by combining two former predicates for the rule. Prior to *Moore*, an anonymous tip alone was an insufficient ground for the police to stop a person, and a person's avoidance of contact with the police was an insufficient ground for a stop, but both of those actions together could have been sufficient for a stop. In *Moore*, the majority held that even the combination of an anonymous tip and the avoidance of contact would be insufficient. Of course, the police officers when they stopped Moore on November 12, 1997, did not know that the court would change the rules on February 21, 2006.

Moore again raises the questions raised by the *Hampton* case. Should the courts control when police officers can draw their weapons? Does the application of the exclusionary rule in cases such as *Moore* and *Hampton* interfere with legislative and executive branch prerogatives regarding public safety? Another question is whether these cases preclude police departments from deployed officers armed with long guns, such as submachine guns, at airports, train stations, and other locations to counteract terrorism threats? These un-holstered weapons are approximately thirty inches in length; they are carried chest-high and are visible and threatening. If an officer with such a weapon approaches a suspect to make a common law inquiry, does *Moore* mandate the suppression of any contraband subsequently found on the suspect?

---

11. "Getting Guns Off the Streets," New York City Police Department, Profile 19, New York (1998).

Police officers carry other weapons besides guns, such as pepper spray, electric dart guns, and traditional nightsticks. Should the courts go further and control the details of when a police officer can take out these weapons? Should the courts control how a police officer can hold these weapons? Is holding a nightstick in hand a threat of force in the same way that holding a gun in hand is a threat? Does it depend on whether the officer holds the nightstick up or down a few inches?

In *Hampton, Torres,* and *Moore,* the courts conceded that the police had lawful authority to approach and question each of the suspects, but only without drawing their weapons. Had the officers not drawn their weapons, the risk of flight or assault would have been increased, and flight and assaults by suspects are costs that must be added to the costs of suppressing evidence.

Furthermore, what are costs paying for? What were the real damages done by the violation of the civil rights of Torres, Moore, and Hampton? None of the defendants were arrested without good reason, and none of them were convicted of crimes they did not commit. They were guilty of their crimes. They suffered the damage of being searched for weapons by police who had legitimately approached them in the course of lawful police duties.

Were Torres, Moore, or Hampton not in possession of guns, they would have suffered the same damages as many people who are stopped, frisked, or searched by police and are not found in possession of unlawful guns. A person stopped but not found with a gun, barring other circumstances, will be released within a few minutes. For such innocent persons, the inconvenience, embarrassment, and humiliation are something to be concerned about. Their remedy is to make a complaint to the police department, to other appropriate government agencies, or to a civilian complaint review board if one exists in the jurisdiction. In cases where additional factors are involved, such as abuse or racial discrimination, the appropriate remedy might be a lawsuit.

Torres, Moore, and Hampton should have been given no greater remedy than the innocent person. They should not have been given the added reward of immunity for their crimes.

Chapter Nine

Freed Criminals and New Victims

On November 27, 2006, Marie Hutchinson, the manager of a Burger King restaurant in Linderhurst, Illinois, was found dead next to the restaurant's open and empty safe. She had been strangled with the bow tie from her uniform. She also suffered several puncture wounds, but strangulation was the cause of death. Mrs. Hutchinson was 45 years old, had a 22-year-old son, and had been a Burger King employee for 14 years.

Five days after the crime, police arrested a former employee, James Ealy, 42 years old, and charged him with the murder and robbery. The State's Attorney said that Ealy made incriminating statements during videotaped questioning, and police recovered from his apartment $2000 that had been taken from the store safe, clothes he allegedly wore during the crime, and a cell phone with which he had placed a call to the restaurant between 4:00 and 4:30 a.m. on the day of the murder. He had tried to conceal the call by first dialing Star-67.

On January 7, 2007, Ealy pleaded not guilty at his arraignment.

If Ealy is responsible for the murder of Mrs. Hutchinson, the exclusionary rule is also responsible. Twenty years ago, Ealy was convicted of the strangulation murders of a pregnant woman, Christine Parker, and her three children—two girls and a boy, Mary Ann, Cora, and Jontae, ages 15, 12, and three, respectively. Jontae, the three-year-old boy, had been found curled up in a corner and had been sodomized anally. However, an Illinois appellate court reversed Ealy's conviction after suppressing his confession and the physical evidence connecting him to the murders. The court ruled that the police had arrested him without probable cause and had conducted an illegal search, and therefore all the evidence obtained after the arrest had to be suppressed. Although the court ordered a new trial, the district attorney, without any admissible evidence, was forced to dismiss the charges.[1]

---

1. Eric Herman, *Chicago Sun-Times*, 12/6/06.

The following is an abridgement of the appellate court decision.

* * *

Illinois v. James Ealy

Appellate Court of Illinois, First District, Fifth Division
146 Ill. App. 3d 557; 497 N.E.2d 101; 1986

OPINION: Following a jury trial, defendant James Ealy was found guilty of four counts of murder and sentenced to natural life imprisonment in the Illinois Department of Corrections, the sentence to be served consecutively with a previously imposed 23-year sentence on a conviction for rape. On appeal, defendant argues that: (1) based on the ground that his arrest was illegal, the trial court erred in denying his motions to suppress his confession and evidence obtained as a result of two searches of his residence.... For the reasons set forth below, we reverse and remand.

The record reveals that at the hearing on defendant's motions to suppress, the following testimony was presented. On August 16, 1982, at approximately 12:55 p.m., Chicago Police Officer Dennis Vavrin discovered the bodies of Christine, Mary Ann, Cora and Jontae Parker in their seventh floor apartment located in the Rockwell Gardens housing project at 2515 West Jackson, in Chicago. Christine, the 33-year-old mother of 15-year-old Mary Ann and 13-year-old Cora, was found in a bedroom of the apartment. Mary Ann and her three-year-old son, Jontae, were discovered in the bathroom. Cora was found in a closet, next to the bathroom. All of the victims bore ligature marks around their necks, with the exception of Mary Ann who was discovered with a green cloth wrapped around her neck. A later examination of the premises by police evidence technicians revealed no fingerprints suitable for comparison. Dr. Robert Stein, the Cook County medical examiner who had been called to the scene, pronounced the victims dead and their bodies were removed from the apartment.

Shortly thereafter the police conducted a canvas of the building residents. Police officers went to defendant's mother's apartment located on the fourth floor and questioned her. Defendant, who was 17 years old, was present at that time but was not questioned. Later that afternoon, the police returned to Mrs. Ealy's apartment and spoke with defendant, who told them that he had dated Mary Ann Parker until earlier that year, he knew the other Parkers and that he did not know anyone who might have killed them. At approximately 11 p.m., several police officers reappeared at the apartment asking to see defendant and, finding he was not at home, told Mrs. Ealy to have him call them if he had any more information regarding the Parker homicides.

The next day, August 17, autopsies were performed on the victims by Dr. Stein. In attendance was Detective Thomas Blomstrand of the Chicago police department. Dr. Stein's examination disclosed that each victim had died as a result of ligature strangulation. His examination of Mary Ann revealed that the green cloth around her neck was a leg portion of a pair of green surgical pants. After removing the cloth from Mary Ann's neck, Dr. Stein also discovered a piece of tan material knotted on the right side and tied tightly around her neck. His examination of Jontae further revealed that he had been raped.

Thereafter, Detective Blomstrand reported to Area 4 police headquarters and communicated Dr. Stein's findings to other detectives present at a 5 p.m. roll call. Detectives Terrence Thedford and Patrick Harrington were among those in attendance. They were assigned to interview two of five individuals, one of whom was defendant, who were known to frequently watch television in the victims' apartment. Thedford and Harrington arrived at defendant's residence, without a warrant, allegedly at 9 p.m. They identified themselves to Mrs. Ealy, stated they were working on the Parker homicides and asked to speak with defendant. Mrs. Ealy invited them in and sent her younger son to get defendant, who was outside on the playground area of the building. When defendant arrived, the detectives asked him if he would come to the police station with them. Both detectives testified that they did not tell defendant that he had to go with them, and defendant never indicated that he did not want to go with them. On direct examination of defendant, defense counsel orally made an offer of proof that defendant would testify that "he felt they [the detectives] would force him to go if he didn't cooperate" and "that one of the officers was standing by the door, blocking the door from his exit."

They then left the apartment — one detective in front of and one in back of defendant. Defendant was not handcuffed and the officers "did not pull their guns on him." He was transported to the police station in a squad car which was equipped with a wire screen between the front and rear seats and which lacked handles to the windows and doors in the rear.

Upon arriving at the Area 4 station at approximately 9:40 p.m., the detectives placed defendant in a second-floor interview room, but did not give him *Miranda* warnings at that time. The room was windowless and contained a table and three chairs. The officers left defendant in the room for 20 minutes, then returned and interrogated him for 30 minutes, asking him to account for his whereabouts during the early morning hours of August 16. Determining that some discrepancies existed between defendant's account of his activities and the one previously given by his mother, the detectives left the room to discuss the inconsistencies. While out of the room, they became aware of the presence of Mrs. Ealy and told her about the inconsistencies between defendant's and her account of defendant's whereabouts on August 16. Contrary to Mrs. Ealy's testimony, they then asked Mrs. Ealy if she would speak to defendant about his story and she agreed. Contrary to defendant's testimony, they further testified that they asked defendant if he would speak with his mother and that he refused to do so.

Shortly thereafter, Thedford and Harrington were informed by another detective that defendant recently had been arrested for a rape which occurred in the same building where defendant and the Parker family lived. After reviewing the case report of that rape, Thedford and Harrington returned to the interview room at approximately 11 p.m. and gave defendant *Miranda* warnings. Defendant said he understood his rights and the officers interrogated him for another 30 minutes. During that time, defendant was asked and agreed to sign a consent to search his bedroom. The detectives did not seek to obtain a search warrant. The officers also testified, contrary to Mrs. Ealy's testimony, that she had agreed to sign a consent to search form.

The next shift of detectives, Ralph Vucko and Victor Switski, were informed by Thedford and Harrington of the status of the investigation. Detective Vucko testified he prepared a consent to search form for Mrs. Ealy's signature. At approximately 1:30 p.m. on August 18, after finding that Mrs. Ealy had left the station, Vucko and Harrington took the form into the interview room. Vucko stated he asked defendant to sign the consent form after reading its contents to him and advising him that he was waiving "his right to the police having to have a search warrant to look in [his] house." Defendant, however, testified that although he signed the form, its contents were not read to him and he did not read it.

At approximately 1:45 a.m., Detectives Vucko and Switski arrived at defendant's residence. They testified they showed Mrs. Ealy the consent to search form signed by defendant, she permitted them to enter the apartment, and she showed them to defendant's bedroom. Mrs. Ealy, however, testified that the detectives asked her to sign a consent form, she asked them if it was a search warrant, they said no, and she said she would not sign it. She stated that they then pushed her aside, entered the apartment and went into defendant's bedroom. The detectives subsequently found a "bundle" underneath defendant's bed. It contained numerous items, including two lengths of khaki-type material, one of which was knotted at each end and the other with one knot in it. Other items found in the bundle were a bone-colored knife handle, a green pair of surgical pants, some bed sheets with red stains, a child's sweater, and a red sock. Vucko took the khaki material and some shoelaces he had found in defendant's dresser.

The detectives then left the apartment and went to Detective Blomstrand's home. They showed him the khaki material taken from the bundle and he told them it looked like the same material he had observed around Mary Ann Parker's neck at the autopsies he attended. Vucko and Switski then returned to the Parkers' apartment. Vucko discovered a khaki-colored trench coat in a closet and noticed that although the coat had belt loops, the belt was missing. He also found a knife blade in the closet which appeared to him to match the handle he had seen in the bundle in defendant's bedroom. Vucko took both items and he and Switski returned to the police station, arriving at approximately 4 a.m. on August 18. At that time, Switski testified that he went to the interview room occupied by defendant and locked the door.

At approximately 5 a.m., Vucko and Switski entered the interview room. Detective Thedford also entered, "took defendant's underwear and gym shoes" away from him and then left. Defendant was again given his *Miranda* rights, he indicated he was willing to further discuss the Parker homicides, and the officers confronted him with the items they had recovered from his bedroom and the Parker crime scene. Thereafter, defendant told the officers that on August 15, at about 11:30 p.m., he was near the Parkers' apartment and saw a large black man running from the apartment carrying a large bundle which he dropped. After picking up the bundle, defendant went into the Parkers' apartment and found the victims' bodies. He said he then left the apartment, taking the bundle with him to his mother's apartment, placed the bundle under his mother's bed and went to sleep. Defendant, however, later denied giving this account to Detectives Vucko and Switski. Defendant also denied that he signed a second consent to search form at the end of this interrogation session, even though he later acknowledged his signature on the form which was admitted into evidence.

At approximately 6 a.m., Detectives Vucko and Switski went to defendant's residence bearing the second consent form. They testified that they showed Mrs. Ealy the consent form and told her that they were there to pick up the rest of the items which were left in the bundle. Contrary to Mrs. Ealy's testimony, Vucko and Switski stated that she permitted them to enter the apartment and to take the items. Mrs. Ealy testified that the detectives shoved her, entered her apartment and went into defendant's bedroom. Finding that the bundle had been removed from its previous location, they told Mrs. Ealy to bring it to them, she did so, and they left.

Vucko and Switski returned to the Area 4 station with the bundle and interviewed defendant again at approximately 9:30 a.m. on August 18. Switski gave defendant *Miranda* warnings, and Detective Vucko then told defendant that his previous story did not make sense. At that point, defendant became excited, started crying and said he "would tell the truth." Vucko and Switski stated that defendant then told them that on August 15 he had been drinking with friends. He later went to the Parkers' apartment at approximately 11:30 p.m. and several members of the Parker family "made fun of his red eyes." Defendant then described to the detectives how he strangled the four victims.

Thereafter, Detective Switski called the State's Attorney's office, and Assistant State's Attorney Christine Campbell arrived at Area 4 at 10:45 a.m. After explaining her position to defendant and giving him *Miranda* warnings, defendant repeated his confession to her and agreed to make a written statement. At 1 p.m., defendant signed a waiver of his constitutional rights, his statement was taken down by a court reporter and at approximately 2:30 p.m. he signed the statement. At 3 p.m., defendant was allowed to see his mother. She had arrived at the station at approximately 10 a.m. and had been told she had to wait before seeing defendant. During that time, Mrs. Ealy called Beverly Bearden, a case worker volunteer for Catholic Charities, who arrived at the station at 2:30 p.m. and was also told she would have to wait to speak to defendant.

Defendant testified that when he spoke with his mother and Bearden, he told them he confessed because he "couldn't take it" any more. He stated that he had not had anything to eat or drink throughout his detention, that the officers would not permit him to sleep and that they would not let him leave. Defendant further stated that he had been repeatedly "punched in the ribs" by an unidentified officer and threatened that he would not be able to sleep or to see his mother until he signed a confession. He also stated that he in fact did not kill the Parkers, that he had been high on wine when he found a bundle by the garbage chute on the seventh floor where the Parker apartment was located, that he had used the bundle as a basketball, tossing it into garbage cans as he made his way down to his mother's apartment on the fourth floor, and that he went home to sleep when he reached his mother's apartment, tossing the bundle on the floor of his bedroom.

At the conclusion of the evidence, the trial court denied the motions to suppress defendant's confession and evidence obtained as a result of the two searches. The court also subsequently denied defendant's motion to exclude the photographs and microanalyst's notes pertaining to the evidence obtained from the searches, but advised defense counsel that he could again raise his objection to this evidence at trial.

At trial, the witnesses' testimony was virtually the same as their testimony at the suppression hearing. Defendant, however, did not testify. In addition, when defense counsel again raised his objection to admission of the photographs and the microanalyst's notes, the motion was denied. Defendant's motion for a mistrial, citing alleged prejudicial and inflammatory statements made by the State in closing rebuttal argument, was also denied, as was his post-trial motion.

On appeal, defendant contends that the trial court erred in denying his motions to suppress his confession and the evidence obtained as a result of the two searches of his bedroom. Specifically, defendant argues that the police, lacking probable cause, arrested him at the time they took him from his residence and, therefore, his confession and other incriminating evidence were the fruits of an illegal arrest, requiring suppression.

Probable cause exists if the facts and circumstances known by the arresting police officers are sufficient to cause a reasonable man to believe that an offense has been committed and that the defendant has committed the offense.... An arrest occurs when the police detain a person in a manner such that a reasonable, innocent person in the same situation would not consider himself free to go.... All evidence directly traceable to an arrest made without probable cause must be suppressed where there are no intervening events to break the connection between a defendant's illegal detention and the evidence obtained as a result therefrom. [Citations omitted].

Here, the State concedes that no probable cause to arrest defendant existed at the time he was taken from his residence, but argues defendant was not "seized" at that time so as to require probable cause. Instead, the State argues that defendant was not considered under arrest until 4 a.m., at which time probable cause existed, and that defendant's consent to the searches and his confession were voluntarily made. In support of its contention that defendant was not seized at the earlier time, the State relies on *People v. Reed* (1982), 104 Ill. App. 3d 331, 432 N.E.2d 979, and *People v. Gale* (1979), 72 Ill. App. 3d 23, 390 N.E.2d 921. We find these cases unpersuasive.

In *Reed*, police officers investigating a murder and robbery did not ask the defendant if he wanted to be questioned at his apartment, but instead asked him to accompany them to the police station. At the station, the defendant was given *Miranda* warnings and, after four hours of interrogation, confessed to the crimes. In *Gale*, the defendant, was asked to accompany an officer to the police station regarding a theft investigation. At the station, the defendant was given *Miranda* warnings, but was not told he was under arrest. After being interviewed for 30 minutes, he confessed to committing the theft. Both the *Reed* and *Gale* courts concluded that the defendants were not illegally arrested because a reasonable, innocent person in the same position as defendants would not have considered himself under arrest.

The circumstances of defendant's detention in the present case greatly differ from those in the *Reed* and *Gale* cases. Here, defendant was continuously interrogated for an 18-hour period during which time he was deprived of the basic necessities of life. For 18 hours defendant had nothing to eat or drink and disputedly was not allowed to sleep. Only once during the entire time was a restroom made available to him. On the other hand, in *Reed* and *Gale*, the defendants were only detained for four hours and 30 minutes, respectively, and were not subjected to the deprivations defendant here endured. We further note that the *Reed* court, in fact, specifically considered the absence of a continuous, lengthy interrogation in concluding that Reed had not been illegally arrested.

We find that the circumstances in the present case are more analogous to those in *People v. Townes* (1982), 91 Ill. 2d 32, 435 N.E.2d 103, *cert. denied* (1982), 459 U.S. 878, 74 L. Ed. 2d 143, 103 S. Ct. 174. There, as here, the defendant was questioned over a lengthy period of time by the police. On the basis of a vague physical description given by a rape victim, the police asked the defendant to accompany them to the police station instead of questioning him at his home. At the station, he was placed in an interview room and interrogated five times during a 12-hour period, during which time he was repeatedly given *Miranda* warnings. The police obtained the defendant's consent to search his home and car, they never told him he was free to leave and they subsequently obtained a confession from him. The *Townes* court, relying on the apposite case of *Dunaway v. New York* (1979), 442 U.S. 200, 60 L. Ed. 2d 824, 99 S. Ct. 2248, held that the defendant's detention resembled a traditional arrest and the circumstances indicated that a reasonable person in the same position as the defendant would not have believed he was free to leave. The court also held that the seizure of the defendant had an improper "quality of purposefulness" in that it appeared that the police were conducting an "expedition for evidence" in the hope of obtaining sufficient information upon which to predicate the probable cause necessary for an arrest.

We believe the circumstances in the instant case present far more compelling reasons than *Townes* for requiring reversal of the trial court's judgment. Here, in addition to the obvious similarities of this case and *Townes*, the police continuously interrogated defendant eight times during an 18-hour period—three interrogation sessions more and six hours longer than the interrogation of the defendant in *Townes*. Throughout his 18-hour detention, as previously noted, defendant also was deprived of the basic necessities of life. He was not offered anything to eat or drink for 18 hours. A restroom was made available to him on only one occasion during his detention. Although it is disputed whether defendant was permitted to sleep during this time, we note that if in fact he did so he would have had to sleep on the floor or sitting up, since there was no bed in the room. In addition, any sleep that defendant may have gotten would have been, at best, minimal due to the interruptions created by the repeated interrogation sessions which usually lasted at least 30 minutes each, *i.e.*, 11 p.m., 1:30 a.m., 5 a.m., 9:30 a.m., 10:45 a.m., 1 p.m. and 2:30 p.m. Finally, we note that defendant was subjected to having his underwear and gym shoes, which he had been wearing, taken away from him prior to giving any confession.

Under the totality of the circumstances, we conclude that defendant's detention, like that of the defendant in *Townes*, resembled a traditional arrest and indicates that a reasonable, innocent person in defendant's position would not have believed he was free to leave. We also find that the unconstitutional misconduct of the police was a purposeful expedition for evidence in the hope of obtaining sufficient information upon which to predicate the probable cause necessary for defendant's arrest. We note that even though the detectives stated they had probable cause to arrest defendant at 4 a.m. as a result of the evidence obtained from their first search of his bedroom, they nonetheless did not call in an assistant State's Attorney at that time, but instead interrogated defendant two more times until obtaining a second consent to search form and a confession from him at 9:30 a.m. Accordingly, since the police lacked probable cause to arrest defendant at the time they took him from his residence, which the State concedes, we hold that defendant was illegally seized in violation of the fourth amendment.

We recognize, although the State does not so argue, that the illegality of an arrest does not *per se* render incriminating evidence inadmissible where there are intervening events to break the connection between a defendant's illegal detention and the evidence obtained as a result therefrom…. Under the facts and circumstances of the instant case, clearly no intervening events occurred. Accordingly, defendant's confession and the evidence obtained as a result of the two searches required suppression since the taint of the illegal arrest was not dissipated….

Finally, we believe that the evidence at trial was sufficient for the trier of fact to conclude that defendant was guilty beyond a reasonable doubt. This does not mean we are making a finding as to defendant's guilt or innocence which would be binding on retrial, but rather our consideration of the sufficiency of the evidence admitted at trial will remove the risk of subjecting defendant to double jeopardy….

For the foregoing reasons, the judgment of the circuit court of Cook County is reversed and the cause remanded for a new trial.

Reversed and remanded.

* * *

Although the court acknowledged that the evidence produced at trial met the high standard of proof beyond a reasonable doubt, they essentially immunized Ealy for the murders he committed, and they released this clearly dangerous individual back into society. The court's action did not lead immediately to a new crime because Ealy had been convicted of rape in an unrelated case and sentenced to 23 years in prison. He was eventually paroled on the rape conviction in 1993, then arrested again in 1996 for the assault of a prostitute, convicted, and sent to prison until he was released on parole in 1999. Had his convictions for the 1982 murders been upheld, he would not have been released to commit the 1996 assault or the 2006 murder of Marie Hutchinson.

Those in favor of the exclusionary rule might argue that it was not the court, but the detectives who were responsible for Ealy's release and, arguably, Mrs. Hutchinson's death because the detectives violated Ealy's Fourth and Fifth Amendment rights. In 1987, Ealy's attorney, Randy Mehrberg, said the justice system had worked: "This is exactly the type of confession the Constitution is intended to protect against. You can't have police going around and picking up people without evidence."[2]

To agree that Mr. Mehrberg was right, one would have to accept that the police could no longer effectively investigate homicides. Mehrberg does not want the police "picking up people without evidence." Does he also want them to disregard and fail to follow leads about potential suspects? A basic police method of investigating crimes is to interview people who may know about the crime or who may, themselves, be suspects. Sometimes reactions of the interviewee immediately indicate that he or she may know about or have been involved in the crime. Should the police ignore that? Should the police stop questioning? Or should they ask the person to come to the police station to explain what he knows? Defense attorneys say the police should stop questioning until the person obtains a lawyer, the result of which would be that the lawyer will advise the person not to talk to the police. In such cases, without additional evidence, the police investigation will be stymied.

Such roadblocks should not be placed in front of investigators. When police investigators contact a person who is a potential witness or suspect, they are gathering information that may lead to evidence. That is their function, and that is the system we use to gather the initial evidence necessary to begin the judicial process.

The detectives investigating the Parker murders learned of Ealy's relationship to the victims, and following long-standing police practices, they asked him to come to the stationhouse to be interviewed, which he did. Pointing to a variety of factors, the court determined that this transport was an arrest, and since probable cause had not been established, the arrest was illegal. An arrest does not have to be formally announced but may occur *de facto* on the basis of conduct and interactions between the police and a suspect. The United States Supreme Court has identified factors that may be considered for determining whether an arrest or seizure has or has not occurred. In *United States v. Mendenhall*, 446 U.S. 544 (1980), the Court stated:

---

2. Associated Press, 12/8/06.

Examples of circumstances that might indicate a seizure, even where the person did not attempt to leave, would be the threatening presence of several officers, the display of a weapon by an officer, some physical touching of the person of the citizen, or the use of language or tone of voice indicating that compliance with the officer's request might be compelled ... In the absence of some such evidence, other inoffensive contact between a member of the public and the police cannot, as a matter of law, amount to a seizure of that person.

The *Ealy* court apparently deemed it significant that Ealy testified that when the police made their request, "One of the officers was standing by the door, blocking the door from his exit." Also, although Ealy was not handcuffed, "He was transported to the police station in a squad car which was equipped with a wire screen between the front and rear seats and which lacked handles to the windows and doors in the rear."

Had the officer not stood by the door, would that have changed anything? Should police in these situations be precluded from standing by the door? Should police investigating quadruple murders be precluded from positioning themselves in a precautionary manner? Should police departments be required to change their squad cars to eliminate the wire screens between the front and back seats, and should they be required to install interior rear door handles, despite the professional judgment that installing wire mesh and removing door handles in police vehicles are necessary safety measures that save lives and prevent injuries?

Addressing none of these questions, the court ruled that because of the *de facto* arrest without probable cause, any evidence obtained—the confession itself, or evidence derived from the confession, or evidence obtained as a result of the consent-to-search form—had to be suppressed. The court cited *Dunaway v. New York*, 442 U.S. 200 (1979), as the precedent for the suppression required in this case. However, in *Dunaway*, which involved a similar station house confession, the detectives were purposefully ordered to arbitrarily "pick up" Dunaway and "bring him in." He "was taken into custody; although he was not told he was under arrest, he would have been physically restrained if he had attempted to leave." It was clear that Dunaway had been purposefully and illegally taken into custody; the question was whether his subsequent confession should have been suppressed.

The detectives who transported Ealy to the station house had not been told to take him into custody. They encountered him during the process of canvassing the building for information and interviewing potential witnesses. At the station house, no one indicated that Ealy would be physically restrained if he attempted to leave, and the detectives did not give Miranda warnings until after information was developed that changed Ealy's status from a witness to a suspect. This is not an uncommon occurrence. During interviews, purported witnesses often implicate themselves to a lesser or greater degree in the crime under investigation. Sometimes they are arrested. Sometimes they become co-operating witnesses and are not arrested.

Through long experience, homicide investigators know that cases are solved while the trail is hot. Once the trail grows cold, the chances of solving the case or obtaining sufficient evidence to convict the murderer are greatly reduced. Evidence is destroyed, the trauma and emotions of the criminal subside, stories are concocted, lawyers are hired, and defense strategies are developed.

As far as the detectives knew, Ealy could have had some knowledge related to the crime. He could have provided information against someone else. As it turned out, he became the prime suspect. When he did, the detectives gave him Miranda warnings.

The ruling in *Ealy* implies that police should not transport witnesses or suspects to a police station for questioning. The ruling implies that even if witnesses or suspects voluntarily agree to go to the station house, the Illinois court will void the agreement because of the inherently coercive circumstances of being transported to a police station. They will void the agreement because the police officer stood by the door or because there was wire mesh in the police car.

How the police could have conducted this investigation according to the parameters of the court is not clear. Several scenarios can be envisioned, depending on what actions were taken by the police or the suspect. Had the police continued questioning Ealy in his apartment, he might have refused to cooperate. Or if he did discuss the matter, in the environment of his apartment, he might not have made any incriminating statements. In such circumstances, the detectives would have had to leave, and when they left, Ealy could have gotten rid of the evidence.

On the other hand, had the detectives continued to question Ealy in the apartment and had they obtained incriminating evidence, they would have been in no better position. This case arose two years after the Supreme Court ruling in *Payton v. New York*, 445 U.S. 573 (1980), that an arrest warrant was required to arrest a suspect in his home. Had Ealy, while in the apartment, made admissions that led to discovery of the physical evidence, the arrest and search would have been challenged under the doctrine of *Payton*, and all the evidence obtained in the apartment would have been suppressed.

The dilemma for the detectives was that arresting Ealy in his apartment without a warrant would have resulted in suppression, and, as it turned out, transporting him to the police station also resulted in suppression. Moreover, an arrest warrant would not have helped. Had the officers attempted to obtain an arrest warrant or a search warrant before taking Ealy to the station house, they would not have had the probable cause necessary for either. Had the judge issued the warrants despite a lack of probable cause, the warrants would have been challenged, and the evidence would have been suppressed. Bound by the dilemma created by the courts, the best course of action for the detectives was to ask Ealy to come to the station house voluntarily so that they could continue the investigation without the specter of *Payton* looming over their heads.

Without the ability to question Ealy, the detectives would have had no basis to ask for the consent forms, and they would not have recovered the incriminating physical evidence. Without the physical evidence and the confession, it is unlikely that the four murders would have been solved.

In addition to the transport of Ealy to the station house, the court focused on the long hours of the interrogation as indicative of an arrest. However, since the court had already determined that taking him to the station house constituted an arrest, the extensive examination of the interrogation period seems redundant and appears to be an indication that the court lacked confidence in its determination that the transport equaled an arrest.

At the police station, the detectives placed Ealy in an interview room that was windowless and contained a table and three chairs. Police stations generally have one interview room. It is used for interviews of complainants, witnesses, suspects, and defendants. Interview rooms are designed for privacy and lack of distractions to make them conducive to obtaining information. The doors are not locked. Unless a person is under arrest, he can leave.

At 9:40 p.m. on August 17, when the detectives placed Ealy in the interview room, they did not have probable cause to arrest him. They questioned him for thirty minutes between 10:00 and 10:30 p.m., and left the room. At 11:00 p.m., after they learned of inconsistencies between his and his mother's accounts of his whereabouts and discovered that he was out on bail in connection with his recent arrest for another rape in the same building, they gave him Miranda warnings, although they did not place him under formal arrest.

The investigation continued, and the detectives found the "bundle" underneath the defendant's bed, which contained the two lengths of khaki-type material with the knots that could be used for choking a person, and the material appeared to match the material found around the neck of one of the victims.[3]

---

3. David Heinzmann and Angela Rozas, "Suspect Freed in '82 Killings," *Chicago Tribune*, 12/6/06.

The detectives discovered a bone-colored knife handle, a green pair of surgical pants, bed sheets with red stains, a child's sweater, and a red sock.

The detectives went to the home of the detective who had witnessed the autopsies of the murder victims and showed him the khaki-type material from the bundle, and he told them it looked like the same material he had observed around Mary Ann Parker's neck at the autopsies he attended. The detectives then returned to the crime scene apartment, discovered a khaki-colored trench coat in a closet, and noticed that although the coat had belt loops, the belt was missing. They found a knife blade in the closet, which appeared to match the handle observed in the bundle in the defendant's bedroom. Based on this evidence, the detectives had probable cause, and at 4:00 a.m., they locked the door to the interview room, six hours and twenty minutes after Ealy's arrival at the police station. At 5:00 a.m., they took Ealy's underwear and gym shoes for examination by the forensics laboratory.

In its focus on the length of the interrogation, the court distinguished *People v. Reed, supra*, where the interrogation in the police station continued for four hours, from *People v. Townes, supra*, where the interrogation lasted for twelve hours. According to those cases, the former did not amount to an arrest, but the latter did amount to an arrest. The court said, "Here, in addition to the obvious similarities of this case and *Townes*, the police continuously interrogated defendant eight times during an 18-hour period—three interrogation sessions more and six hours longer than the interrogation of the defendant in *Townes*."

Putting aside the court's misleading characterization that the police "continuously" interrogated the defendant for eighteen hours, the emphasis on the length of the interrogation was irrelevant to the lawfulness of Ealy's transport to the station house. If the court believed that Ealy's later confessions were involuntary because of the length of interrogation, the court could have suppressed the confessions without suppressing the physical evidence found in his apartment.

The physical evidence from the apartment was recovered well before the full confessions. Ealy had consented to a search of his apartment at approximately 11:00 p.m., and using the court's own correlation to *People v. Reed, supra*, less than four hours of interrogation did not amount to an arrest.

In their written opinion, the court seemed displeased that at 5:00 a.m., the detectives took Ealy's underwear and gym shoes. "Finally, we note that defendant was subjected to having his underwear and gym shoes, which he had been wearing, taken away from him prior to giving any confession." Was the court implying that taking these items was improper or coercive? This occurred after the point at which the detectives arrested Ealy. This is the point at which they conducted the standard search of a defendant, and it is lawful for police to take evidence of the crime from a defendant to secure it and prevent him from destroying the evidence. Considering the murders and the rape of the three-year-old boy, it would have been dereliction of duty for them not to take these items for laboratory analysis.

Furthermore, the fact that the detectives did not conduct the search and did not take these items until 5:00 a.m. is a clear indication that, in their mind, they had not arrested Ealy when they first transported him to the station house.

The expeditious actions of the homicide detectives in this case led to the recovery of the physical evidence connecting Ealy to the crime. Their timely questioning of him about the bundle of evidence caused him to concoct his story that "He was near the Parkers' apartment and saw a large black man running from the apartment carrying a large bundle which he dropped. After picking up the bundle, defendant went into the Parkers' apartment and found the victims' bodies. He said he then left the apartment, taking the bundle with him to his mother's apartment, placed the bundle under his mother's bed and went to sleep."

The recovery of the bundle forced Ealy to give a contradictory and equally incredible story during the suppression hearing, where he testified, "He had been high on wine when he found a bundle by the garbage chute on the seventh floor where the Parker apartment was located, that he had used the bundle as a basketball, tossing it into garbage cans as he made his way down to his mother's apartment on the fourth floor, and that he went home to sleep when he reached his mother's apartment, tossing the bundle on the floor of his bedroom."

Without the work of the detectives over the nights and days after the discovery of the four bodies, the physical and statement evidence would not have been developed. Without their quick work, Ealy might not have been arrested at all. Nonetheless, the court wrote, "We also find that the unconstitutional misconduct of the police was a purposeful expedition for evidence in the hope of obtaining sufficient information upon which to predicate the probable cause necessary for defendant's arrest."

The detectives would agree in part: it was, indeed, a purposeful expedition to obtain evidence for the defendant's arrest. This is what detectives are sworn to do. They tried their best, and it is doubtful they had any intention of engaging in what these judges called "unconstitutional misconduct." They tried their best to remove a dangerous individual from society to protect people like Marie Hutchinson from suffering the same strangulation death as had Christine Parker and her three children. They did not fail; the Illinois court failed; the exclusionary rule failed.

Chapter Ten

Flight and Confusion

Questions of whether a suspect's flight from the police constitutes a sufficient basis for reasonable suspicion or probable cause have confounded courts, and inconsistent rulings on the issue have exposed the flawed logic of applying the exclusionary rule to fast-moving and potentially dangerous police situations. Courts have ruled inconsistently as to whether the initiation of a police chase constitutes a Fourth Amendment seizure and whether property discarded by a fleeing suspect should be considered as abandoned.

As a result of these consistently inconsistent rulings, the practitioners affected by the exclusionary rule place little faith and credibility in the courts. Police and prosecutors who lose suppression motions complain that the courts lack an understanding of the difficulties of police work; defense attorneys who lose suppression motions complain that the courts are pro-law enforcement. Although the adversarial nature of our criminal justice system produces many benefits, including processes to ascertain true and reliable facts, the exclusionary rule, as applied to "street" situations, poisons the adversarial process. It engenders distrust and strong animosity between factions within the criminal justice system. It engenders, not truth and reliability, but falsity and uncertainty.

In 1980, the New York Court of Appeals issued a ruling that exacerbated the differences between those on either side of the flight issue. In *People v. Howard*, 50 N.Y.2d 583 (1980), the Court reversed the conviction of a defendant who had been indicted for criminal possession of a controlled substance in the first degree and criminal possession of a weapon in the third degree. During preliminary proceedings, the defendant had moved to suppress the heroin and a .38 caliber revolver recovered by the police. The court agreed with the defendant's argument and suppressed the evidence. The following is an abridgement of the decision.

* * *

The People of the State of New York, Respondent, v.
Archie William Howard, Appellant

Court of Appeals of New York
50 N.Y.2d 583; 408 N.E.2d 908; 430 N.Y.S.2d 578.
July 3, 1980, Decided

OPINION:

An individual to whom a police officer addresses a question has a constitutional right not to respond. He may remain silent or walk or run away. His refusal to answer is not a crime. Though the police officer may endeavor to complete the interrogation, he may not pursue, absent probable cause to believe that the individual has committed, is committing, or is about to commit a crime, seize or search the individual or his possessions, even though he ran away. Nor when the individual, cornered by his pursuers in the basement of a building and while looking for a way out of the basement, drops or throws a package he was carrying into a pile of junk, has he been shown to have intentionally abandoned the package so as to make a warrantless search and seizure permissible. The order of the Appellate Division should, therefore, be reversed, the motion to suppress should be granted and the indictment should be dismissed.

Indicted for criminal possession of a controlled substance in the first degree and criminal possession of a weapon in the third degree, defendant Howard moved to suppress the gun and drugs which formed the basis for the indictment. They had been taken from him by Officers Charles Hanley and Cornelius Brosnan, who on the day of the seizure were on anticrime patrol in The Bronx in plainclothes and in an unmarked automobile. At about 1 p.m., in broad daylight, on University Avenue in the vicinity of Father Zeiser Place (an area which had a high incidence of burglaries), the officers observed Howard crossing University Avenue diagonally in a southeasterly direction. Their curiosity was aroused by the fact that defendant was carrying what appeared to be a woman's vanity case. As they passed defendant, both officers saw him look over his shoulder in their direction, in a manner described by Officer Hanley as "furtive." Defendant looked in the direction of the car two or three more times until he reached the center of University Avenue. Then as Hanley pulled the car to the right side of the street, defendant reversed direction, walked to the west side of the street and proceeded south on the sidewalk.

The police car made a U-turn and once again the officers saw defendant look in their direction. As the car neared him, defendant's pace quickened. As the car came parallel with defendant, Officer Brosnan displayed his police shield and said "Police Officer. I would like to speak to you." Though looking directly at the officers, defendant ignored them and continued walking south.

The police followed and at the next opening between parked cars, Brosnan re-peated the same words, and began to get out of the car. Defendant, without saying anything, started to run, holding the vanity case to his chest like a foot-ball would be held. The officers pursued and were joined in the chase by Vic-tor Dragaj, a college freshman. Defendant proceeded over an iron fence, through an alleyway and into the basement of a building, at which point, pursued by Dragaj, defendant threw the vanity case into a pile of junk in the corner and sought but was unable to escape through a door which was locked, or a small window on the far side of the room. Dragaj restrained defendant and was joined by Officer Brosnan, who asked defendant why he had tried to get away. About 25 seconds later they were joined by Officer Hanley who identified him-self as a policeman and asked about the vanity case or box. Dragaj pointed to it and Hanley retrieved it from the rubbish pile, which was beyond defendant's reach, and immediately opened it, revealing a .38 caliber revolver and heroin in glassine envelopes. Hanley then placed defendant under formal arrest....

Defendant argues that there was no justification for police action of any kind; that in any event he had a constitutional right to refuse to answer a police in-quiry; that his exercise of that right by walking and then running away did not justify detention of him or seizure of the vanity case; and that as a matter of law there was no abandonment. While we hold that there was a sufficient basis to permit inquiry, we agree that defendant had the right not to answer, that his running did not, absent any indication that any crime had been or was about to be committed, permit detention; that there was no probable cause for de-fendant's arrest; and that the vanity case had not been abandoned.

As we have recently had reason to reiterate in *People v. Belton* (50 N.Y.2d 447), "[the] privacy interest of our citizens is far too cherished a right to be entrusted to the discretion of the officer in the field." That privacy interest is protected by the mandate of the Fourth Amendment to the United States Con-stitution and section 12 of article I of our State Constitution both of which, in identical language, state: "The right of the people to be secure in their per-sons, houses, papers and effects, against unreasonable searches and seizures, shall not be violated."

... The principles that have evolved seek to balance society's interest in the detection and prevention of crime and in the protection of the lives and safety of law enforcement officers with the interest of individuals in living their lives free from governmental interference. Therefore, whether there has been an unreasonable breach of legitimate expectations of privacy involves considera-tion of (1) the nature and scope or severity of the interference with individual liberty, (2) the public interest served, and (3) the objective facts upon which the enforcement officer relied, in light of his knowledge and experience.

We have no difficulty in concluding that the officers' request for information from defendant was justified under those criteria. In an area beset by a high burglary rate defendant was seen carrying a woman's vanity case by the officers, one of whom testified that it was not uncommon for a burglar to carry away loot in his victim's luggage. Considering those facts together with defendant's numerous glances at the officers' car, his change of direction and his quickened pace, we conclude that, though the carrying by a man of a woman's purse does not constitute probable cause … and though defendant could, the car being unmarked and the officers in plainclothes, have acted evasively out of fear for his own safety, the circumstances constituted a sufficient basis for the inquiry made, which of itself constituted no more than a minor inconvenience to defendant.

There was, therefore, basis for questioning defendant, but there was nothing that made permissible any greater level of intrusion. The officers had no information that a crime had occurred or was about to take place, had not seen defendant do anything criminal, and were confronted only by facts susceptible of innocent interpretation. Presence in an area of "frequent burglaries" was an insufficient basis; in this day of unisex haircuts and clothing, the carrying of a woman's vanity case was at best equivocal; and defendant's "furtive" movements (repeated glances, change of direction, quickened pace) were, the car being unmarked and the officers not in uniform as already noted, at best ambiguous. The circumstances justified the inquiry made and would have justified the officers in keeping defendant under observation but were not a predicate for anything more.

But while the police had the right to make the inquiry, defendant had a constitutional right not to respond. This is so both because the Fifth Amendment to the United States Constitution and its State counterpart (New York Const, art I, §6) permitted him to remain silent and because the Fourth Amendment and its State counterpart (art I, §12) protect him from detention amounting to seizure unless there is probable cause. As Mr. Justice Brandeis put it long ago in *Olmstead v. United States* (277 U.S. 438, 478), defendant had "the right to be let alone."

… Nor can the failure to stop or co-operate by identifying oneself or answering questions be the predicate for an arrest absent other circumstances constituting probable cause.…

That does not mean that the police in furtherance of their duties may not continue observation provided that they do so unobtrusively and do not limit defendant's freedom of movement by so doing. Defendant's flight, had there also been indicia of criminal activity, would have been an important factor in determining probable cause, but where, as here, there is nothing to establish that a crime has been or is being committed, flight, like refusal to answer, is an insufficient basis for seizure or for the limited detention that is involved in pursuit ... The circumstances existing at the moment defendant Howard was seized by Officer Brosnan did not constitute probable cause for arrest. The opening of the vanity case cannot be justified as incident to a lawful arrest ... The contents of the vanity case must, therefore, be suppressed unless defendant abandoned it.

Property which has in fact been abandoned is outside the protection of the constitutional provisions. We do not find it necessary to consider whether the facts of this case bring it within the concept of police action short of illegal seizure but sufficiently coercive to nullify an abandonment for Fourth Amendment purposes, for we agree with the hearing Judge that intent to abandon cannot be found on the facts of this case.

... As the hearing Judge noted, the act of defendant in holding on to the case during the entire chase belies intention to abandon. Since Dragaj and the police were in hot pursuit, it cannot be found that defendant's act in dropping or throwing the case in the corner while seeking to open or break down the door and window in the basement was an act "involving a calculated risk" rather than a spontaneous reaction to the necessity of evading his pursuers or that he purposefully divested himself of possession of the vanity case. Under those circumstances he cannot be said to have knowingly waived his constitutional protection against warrantless search of the case.

For the foregoing reasons, the order of the Appellate Division should be reversed, the motion to suppress should be granted and the indictment should be dismissed.

* * *

Obviously, the Court applied a broad perspective and high principles to the issues presented by this typical police case. The "right to be let alone" that they relied on comes from the nicely crafted language of Justice Louis Brandeis in his famous dissent in the 1928 case of *Olmstead v. United States*, 277 U.S. 438. *Olmstead* involved illegal government wiretapping, and the "right to be let alone" was a fit protest against such practices. However, applied to everything else, it brings to mind the legal truism "that small phrases start large wars and simple sentences produce generations of litigation."[1]

The *Howard* court also quoted from its decision *People v. Belton*: "[The] privacy interest of our citizens is far too cherished a right to be entrusted to the

---

1. J. Butler, *People v. Chez Dann*, 161 Cal. App.3d 22 (1984).

discretion of the officer in the field."[2] This curious quote begs the question: Where should the discretion lie? If we cannot entrust our police officers with discretion, why do we employ them? Why do we assign officers to anticrime patrol, which is designed to prevent crime or apprehend criminals in the act or in flight from the act? Clearly, if discretion is to lie only with judges and not with the police, the judges will have very few cases to hear.

Despite the Brandeis quote, the *Howard* court agreed that the officers properly and lawfully attempted to question Howard because of his suspicious actions. The court noted that police officers are not limited to approaching and questioning people only on the basis of reasonable suspicion of criminal activity. They may approach and question a person as a matter of routine inquiry. If while lawfully interacting with the person, they observe evidence of a crime, the inquiry may be expanded to a stop or even an arrest. As long as the police do not first conduct a seizure, it is lawful to approach, question, and observe the person. However, in *Howard,* in the face of the defendant's resistance, the officers could not complete the questioning.

A seizure within the meaning of the Fourth Amendment occurs when a person is deprived of freedom of movement and brought under a police officer's control, either through submission to a show of legal authority or by actual physical restraint.[3] Whether a particular contact between the police and a citizen is deemed a seizure or merely an inquiry often determines the admissibility of evidence obtained as a result of the police contact. A seizure will be lawful when made on the basis of reasonable suspicion or probable cause. Here, the determinative question was whether the suspect's flight was a factor sufficient to established reasonable suspicion or probable cause, which would allow his seizure.

In its explanation for suppressing the evidence, the court diverted its explanation from the actual facts of the case to a fictionalized situation in which a defendant refused to answer questions, although in the actual case the police never had the opportunity to ask Howard questions. The court advised the police that when a suspect refuses to answer questions, "That does not mean that the police in furtherance of their duties may not continue observation provided that they do so unobtrusively and do not limit defendant's freedom of movement by so doing."[4]

Such advice is of little help to police officers in the field. In this case, the defendant ran away. Could the police have "unobtrusively" continued to observe

---

2. 50 N.Y.2d 447 (1980).
3. *California v. Hodari D.*, 499 U.S. 621 (1991).
4. 50 N.Y.2d 583 (1980).

him? Could they have chased him without limiting his freedom of movement? It seems the court believed the police should have just let him run away.

In *Howard,* the court declined to rule that the defendant's flight raised the level of suspicion that would have allowed the police to pursue and seize him for further questioning. Law enforcement advocates argue that while the act of merely running, in and of itself, would not constitute a sufficient basis for a police stop, an unambiguous flight from police is a significant factor that combined with other factors raises the level of suspicion and should allow the police to continue pursuing their investigation. The court, however, held only that the police could have watched the defendant in order to find another opportunity to attempt to question him. In this case, the only way for the police to watch the defendant was to run after him and to follow him into the basement of the building. Nevertheless, the court concluded that the police should not have chased him.

Addressing whether the defendant "abandoned" the vanity case containing the heroin and the gun, the Court stated:

> It cannot be found that defendant's act in dropping or throwing the case in the corner while seeking to open or break down the door and window in the basement was an act "involving a calculated risk" rather than a spontaneous reaction to the necessity of evading his pursuers or that he purposefully divested himself of possession of the vanity.[5]

Equally rational minds can differ regarding the same set of facts. A less obtuse interpretation of the facts was given by J. Jasen, the dissenting justice:

> Here, there can be no doubt but that defendant, by throwing the vanity case on the pile of junk in the corner of the basement, intended to rid himself of the case containing incriminating evidence. He obviously did not harbor an expectation of retrieving the case, nor is there any evidence that he threw the case in the corner after the police arrived. Rather, defendant attempted to divest himself forever of the damning evidence before the law enforcement officers appeared. For this reason, the warrantless search of the vanity case was proper, inasmuch as defendant abandoned the case, thus relinquishing his privacy interest therein.[6]

The dissent would have held that the defendant was responsible for his actions after he ran. The majority, in effect, held that although the police were

---

5. *Id.*
6. *Id.*

authorized to ask the defendant a question, once he ran and the police pursued, the defendant was not responsible for any weapons or contraband on him or that he discarded.

The outcome in *Howard* may have been different had the police arrested the defendant for trespassing and attempting to damage property. Had they done so, they could have asked him whether he still wanted the vanity case. If Howard said that he did, the case would have been searched in accordance with inventory and safety precautions incidental to the arrest. If he did not, that would have indicated abandonment, and the police could have lawfully seized and searched the vanity case. The most likely reason for not arresting him for trespassing and damaging property was that the officers assumed their actions were lawful and they did not anticipate that the gun and narcotics in the vanity case would be suppressed. When they were chasing him in good faith performance of their duty, they could not have anticipated that years later the New York Court of Appeals would overrule other courts and other judges and decide that the officers were wrong to chase the suspect.

California courts also grappled with issues related to a suspect's flight. In *In Re Hodari D.*, 216 Cal.App.3d 745 (1989), as two plainclothes police officers in an unmarked car rounded a corner, "They saw four or five youths huddled around a small red car parked at the curb. When the youths saw the officers' car approaching they apparently panicked, and took flight." One officer chased the defendant. "Looking behind as he ran, [the defendant] did not turn and see [the officer] until the officer was almost upon him, whereupon he tossed away what appeared to be a small rock." After the officer tackled and handcuffed the defendant, the rock was recovered and found to be crack cocaine.

In a pre-trial motion, the defendant moved to suppress the crack cocaine on the grounds that when the officer chased him, the officer had unreasonably seized him without probable cause or reasonable suspicion. The trial court denied the motion, but on appeal, the California Court of Appeals held that the "seizure was unreasonable under the Fourth Amendment, and that the evidence of cocaine had to be suppressed as the fruit of that illegal seizure."[7]

The prosecution appealed to the United States Supreme Court. Although conceding that the officer did not have reasonable suspicion or probable cause to justify stopping the defendant, the prosecution contended that the cocaine had been abandoned and was thus admissible evidence. In *California v. Hodari D.*, 499 U.S. 621 (1991), the Supreme Court agreed, reversed the California of Appeals, and ruled the crack cocaine admissible because it had been aban-

---

7. *In Re Hodari D.*, 216 Cal.App.3d 745 (1989).

doned before any seizure had occurred. By doing so, the Court avoided the issue of whether reasonable suspicion or probable cause existed under the facts of the case. In its decision, the Court reasoned that a Fourth Amendment seizure does not take place without touching or holding by the police or by a suspect's submission to police authority. The Court held the following:

> The narrow question before us is whether, with respect to a show of authority as with respect to application of physical force, a seizure occurs even though the subject does not yield. We hold that it does not.

The Court drew an analogy to naval warfare: "A ship still fleeing, even though under attack, would not be considered to have been seized as a war prize." A police officer chasing a suspect and shouting "Stop, in the name of the law" has not seized the suspect. Since no seizure had occurred, the property discarded by a suspect during a chase was not seized but was abandoned.

Public policy was important in the decision, and the Court stated:

> Street pursuits always place the public at some risk, and compliance with police orders to stop should therefore be encouraged. Only a few of those orders, we must presume, will be without adequate basis, and since the addressee has no ready means of identifying the deficient ones, it almost invariably is the responsible course to comply.[8]

According to the traditions of legal precedent, the ruling should have influenced state courts to decide flight cases in line with *Hodari D.*, and the ruling should have convinced the New York Court of Appeals to overturn *Howard*. Nevertheless, two years later in 1993 when the New York court had the opportunity in *People v. Holmes*, 81 N.Y.2d 1056, it failed to do so. *Holmes* had remarkably similar facts to *Hodari D.*, but the court reached a different result. In *Holmes*:

> Police officers, patrolling in a car ... near a "known narcotics location" in upper Manhattan, observed defendant with several other persons. One officer recognized several of the men as having been previously arrested for drug transactions at the same location. The officers noticed a 'large bulge' in the right pocket of defendant's leather jacket. As the patrol car approached, the defendant began to back off from the group and then turned and walked away. The officers stopped the patrol car, and from inside the vehicle one officer called out to defendant, requesting him to come over. Defendant reacted by turning

---

8. *California v. Hodari D.*, 499 U.S. 621 (1991).

and moving towards the car. As the officer started to get out of the car, defendant turned again and ran in the opposite direction.... The officer on foot, running about 10 feet behind defendant ... saw him throw a plastic bag containing 45 vials of crack cocaine through a chain link fence into a courtyard.

Despite the Supreme Court precedent, which held that discarding property during a chase is the equivalent of abandonment, the New York Court suppressed the crack cocaine evidence, ruling that the police were not justified in pursuing Holmes and causing him to discard the bag of drugs. The Court wrote, "If these circumstances could combine with flight to justify pursuit, then in essence the right to inquire would be tantamount to the right to seize, and there would, in fact, be no right 'to be let alone.' That is not, nor should it be, the law."[9]

To the contrary, Judge Saul Wachtler's dissent in *Holmes* implied there is no right to be let alone when one is committing the crime of selling illegal drugs on a street corner. His dissent said the majority's decision converted the so-called "right to be let alone" into the "right to run away," and complained that "to then leap to the proposition that flight can be given no legal significance whatsoever in an encounter based on an objective and credible reason is a major misdirection in these ever-proliferating cases. While it is supposed to be well established that flight can have some associated legal significance, that is plainly not the way the rules are being applied in fact-finding and reviewing courts.... Judges at every court level are encountering obvious difficulty in deciding, with the benefit of reflection, what is lawful versus unlawful or relevant versus irrelevant or equivocal versus indicative of criminality. It is thus beyond my comprehension how anyone can reasonably expect the recent cascade of precedents from all courts, including this one, to guide the police in their instantaneous on-the-street decisions and actions relating to flight and pursuit."[10]

Although perfectly sensible as it was, Judge Wachtler's dissent in *Holmes* is not the law in New York; the majority opinion is, and lower New York trial courts are mandated to follow the majority's precedent. Moreover, trial courts not only follow bad precedents, but they often exacerbate the problem by going beyond them. A troubling trial court case was *People v. Bain*, decided in Brooklyn Supreme Court in December 1993, wherein an indicted defendant moved to suppress a gun confiscated from him by the police. In *Bain*, two police officers, in a patrol car at 2:50 a.m., heard gunshots. As they drove toward the

---

9. *People v. Holmes*, 81 N.Y.2d 1056 (1993).
10. *Id.*

sound of the shots, they saw a group of males walking. The officers drove alongside the group and asked where they were coming from. At that, the defendant walked away from the group. One officer said to him, "Come over to the car." The defendant began to walk to the police car, but when he was approximately five feet away, he abruptly turned and started to run. One officer got out of the car and began to chase him. The other officer, as he followed in the car, saw the defendant reach into his waistband, remove a black revolver, and throw it into some weeds. The officers apprehended the defendant, and recovered the gun.

Using the *Holmes* ruling that flight alone is not grounds for arrest, the judge in *Bain* suppressed the gun and dismissed the indictment. But there was more than flight alone; there were gunshots! What were the officers supposed to do? They heard gunshots, and they made a simple inquiry. Should they have done nothing? When the defendant broke and ran, should they have ignored him? The judge said they should. According to the judge, by chasing the defendant, they unreasonably seized him and any subsequent search of the defendant or seizure of the gun was unlawful.

To police officers this seems contrary to their job description. It is contrary to the Supreme Court ruling in *Hodari D.* and also seems contrary to other New York precedents. For officers, these conflicts between the cases have created much confusion. The line between encounters that are mere inquiries and those that are seizures is not always easy to discern. Some encounters can change from an inquiry to a seizure within a split second—a slight hand movement or a few steps might be determinative.

People v. DeBour, 40 N.Y.2d 210 (1976), is a case often used to train New York police officers how to divine the differences between inquiries and seizures. In *DeBour*, at 12:15 a.m., on the morning of October 15, 1972, police officer Kenneth Steck was "walking his beat on a street illuminated by ordinary street lamps and devoid of pedestrian traffic … he and his partner noticed someone walking on the same side of the street in their direction. When the solitary figure of the defendant, Louis DeBour, was within 30 or 40 feet of the uniformed officers, he crossed the street. The two policemen followed suit and when DeBour reached them Officer Steck inquired as to what he was doing in the neighborhood."

DeBour, clearly but nervously, answered that he had just parked his car and was going to a friend's house. "The officer then asked DeBour for identification. As he was answering that he had none, Officer Steck noticed a slight waist-high bulge in defendant's jacket. At this point the policeman asked DeBour to unzip his coat. When DeBour complied with this request Officer Steck observed a revolver protruding from his waistband. The loaded weapon was removed from behind his waistband and he was arrested for possession of the gun."

In *DeBour,* the gun was not suppressed, and the conviction was upheld. The Court ruled that because DeBour had "conspicuously crossed the street to avoid walking past the uniformed officers," the officers were authorized to make the brief limited inquiry that they did. When the officer noticed the slight bulge in the defendant's jacket, he was authorized to conduct a further stop and frisk.

To some it might seem that DeBour's crossing the street to avoid the police was less of a reason for the police to stop him than for them to chase Bain when he ran away from them after the gunshots. Yet these are the kinds of results that come from New York's exclusionary rule decisions; the kinds of results that have convinced many officers that such court rulings are impossible to follow.

Setting *DeBour* and *Howard* and *Bain* side by side, the lesson for criminals carrying guns is that they should run when the police approach them. If a defendant has a gun in his waistband and runs, the police will not be able to see it. If the defendant does not run, the police might see it. DeBour did not run, and he was convicted. Howard and Bain ran, and they were not convicted.

In addition to state courts, lower federal courts continue to issue confounding decisions regarding flight. In 1996, Federal District Court Judge Harold Baer, Jr. issued a decision that caused a public outcry and calls for his impeachment. In *United States. v. Carol Bayless,*[11] Judge Baer refused to count flight as an appropriate factor for reasonable suspicion. In *Bayless,* plainclothes police officers in an unmarked car had been patrolling in the Washington Heights area of Upper Manhattan, an area known as a hub for the illegal drug trade. At 5:00 a.m., the officers observed a car with Michigan license plates proceed slowly and double park on the north side of the street. Ms. Bayless was alone in the car. As soon as the car stopped, four males emerged from between parked cars on the south side of the street and crossed the street, walking single file. When Bayless pushed the trunk release button, the first male lifted the trunk open, the second and third males each placed large black duffel bags into the trunk, and the fourth male closed the trunk.

When the officers pulled their vehicle behind the Bayless car, the males noticed them, spoke briefly to each other, and then quickly ran in different directions. The officers stopped and questioned Ms. Bayless. After obtaining her consent to search the trunk, they found 34 kilograms of cocaine and two kilograms of heroin in the duffel bags. The value of the drugs exceeded $500,000.

Judge Baer suppressed the drugs on the grounds that "these facts fail to meet the requisite standard of reasonable, articulable suspicion that any criminal activity was afoot and that is assuming the officer … is to be believed."

---

11. *U.S. v. Bayless,* SDNY, 95 Cr.533, 1/22/96.

That may have been his opinion, but what was startling about this case was the language that gave away the judge's antipolice bias. He wrote, "Even assuming that one or more of the males ran from the corner once they were aware of the officers' presence, it is hard to characterize this as evasive conduct ... residents in this neighborhood tended to regard police officers as corrupt, abusive, and violent ... had the men not run when the cops began to stare at them, it would have been unusual."

Undoubtedly, our Supreme Court would never rule that it was good public policy to encourage citizens to run away when the police approach or stare at them. The law-abiding citizens in such areas as Washington Heights want and demand that the police fight crime. This judge stripped the police, including honest police, of their authority and power to investigate crime.

After the decision, the ensuing public outrage and calls for his impeachment inspired Judge Baer to reconsider his ruling. He held a new hearing and reversed his decision. He even apologized to the residents of Washington Heights and to the "vast majority of honest men and women in blue." Though the reversal was noteworthy, it came about only because the extraordinary amount of drugs in the case attracted public attention. Many other erroneous and injudicious rulings involving lesser amounts of drugs are regularly left uncorrected.

In 2000, perhaps because of *Bayless* and other inconsistent rulings regarding flight, such as in *Howard, Holmes,* and *Bain,* the Supreme Court tried again to address and clarify the flight issue in *Illinois v. Wardlow,* 528 U.S. 119 (2000). In *Wardlow,* Chicago uniformed police officers investigating drug dealing were driving in the last car of a four-car caravan that converged on an area known for heavy narcotics trafficking. An officer observed defendant, Wardlow, "standing next to the building holding an opaque bag ... [he] looked in the direction of the officers and fled." The officers pursued, cornered, and stopped Wardlow. The officer conducted a protective frisk and discovered a .38-caliber handgun with five rounds of live ammunition.

The Illinois courts suppressed the handgun, stating, "Flight may simply be an exercise of this right to 'go on one's way,' and, thus, could not constitute reasonable suspicion justifying a *Terry* stop."[12]

The Supreme Court reversed the decision and allowed the admission of the evidence, stating:

> It was not merely respondent's presence in an area of heavy narcotics trafficking that aroused the officers' suspicion but his unprovoked flight upon noticing the police. Our cases have also recognized that nerv-

---

12. 183 Ill.2d, at 312.

ous, evasive behavior is a pertinent factor in determining reasonable suspicion.… Headlong flight—wherever it occurs—is the consummate act of evasion: It is not necessarily indicative of wrongdoing, but it is certainly suggestive of such … Unprovoked flight is simply not a mere refusal to cooperate. Flight, by its very nature, is not "going about one's business"; it is just the opposite.[13]

The Supreme Court addressed the contention often raised that flight is not necessarily indicative of ongoing criminal activity. Although conduct such as flight may be susceptible of an innocent interpretation, the conduct may also raise a reasonable suspicion of criminal activity. Under such circumstances, the police can detain a person to resolve the ambiguity. *Wardlow* reiterated the police powers enunciated in *Terry v. Ohio*, which allowed the police to stop, question, and, if necessary, frisk a suspect, even when the suspect's conduct could turn out to be innocent.[14]

Questions regarding police street encounters—whether they should pursue a fleeing suspect, take out their guns, conduct a protective frisk, or ask a suspect a question—are a long way from the original purposes of the exclusionary rule. They are a long way from the initial Supreme Court rulings dealing with intrusions into homes without warrants in cases such as *Weeks, Wolf,* and *Mapp.* Police responses to ongoing street-level criminal activity or flight from criminal activity are generally not willful, thought-out decisions to circumvent constitutional protections. They are most often split-second decisions while carrying out the performance of duty. Academic criticisms of the police decisions can be proper subjects of discussion and training, but suppression of evidence obtained as a result of these criticisms is a drastic and inappropriate penalty.

---

13. *Illinois v. Wardlow,* 528 U.S. 119 (2000).
14. *Terry v. Ohio,* 392 U.S. 1 (1968).

Chapter Eleven

Exclusionary Rule Corruption

Most police officers, most of the time, perform their duties honestly and in accordance with the law. However, police corruption has been a widespread and continuing problem throughout police departments and other law enforcement agencies. Governmental committees and academics have attempted to identify the causes of police corruption, but none have focused significantly on one major cause of such corruption—the exclusionary rule.

As a result of the exclusionary rule, large segments of the population believe that police officers are liars, and, unfortunately, there is a basis for this belief. Placed in the untenable position of having the primary responsibility to fight crime while at the same time having to adhere to a wide array of complex, impracticable, and often incomprehensible restrictions, many police officers engage in what has been termed "testilying": tailoring their testimony in a criminal case to avoid the exclusionary rule. They do so because they know that in some circumstances were they to testify truthfully as to their actions during an arrest, search, or interrogation, the evidence would be suppressed and the defendant would be released. Usually, these officers alter their testimony not for personal gain but for what they believe is right.

As William Bratton, who has served as the police commissioner of both New York City and Los Angeles, has said:

> In many cases, "testilying" is not intentional, but is a result of job pressures and an overwhelming sense of frustration brought on by past cases in which defendants were set free on technicalities.... As the cops who "testilie" see it, they don't lie to convict innocent people, but to convict guilty people.[1]

Tailored testimony occurs mostly at evidence suppression hearings, which often determine the outcome of a criminal case. At these hearings, the prose-

---

1. "Bratton Announces Plan to Train Officers to Testify," Clifford Krauss, *New York Times*, November 15, 1995, B3.

cution calls police officers to present a narrative that supports the constitutionality of their actions. Some officers may alter their testimony to avoid the suppression of evidence, but they do not believe they are committing perjury. Their rationale for this belief is that they do not change material facts such as whether the defendant possessed an illegal gun: they change only incidental facts such as whether or not the officer saw a weapon-like bulge in the defendant's pocket before searching the defendant and finding the gun. In their minds, changing or omitting a fact or two in order to avoid the suppression of evidence is necessary and justifiable. Officers who would never testify falsely that a defendant possessed a gun may sometimes testify falsely that they observed the gun in plain view on the floor of a defendant's car, when in fact they actually discovered the gun as they reached under the car seat or looked in the glove compartment.

The first reaction of most people to police officers who engage in this kind of conduct is to arrest and fire them all. However, firing a few officers will not solve the problem, because the new officers hired to replace them will likely succumb to the same exclusionary rule dynamics.

Without a change in the exclusionary rule, testilying will continue, and officers will continue to engage in what has been termed "noble-cause corruption." The officers believe it is up to them to prevent the release of guilty defendants, and within police culture it is acceptable and laudatory to do so. Police view their obligation to protect innocent citizens and the public as a noble cause. Despite legal restrictions and obstacles, they find ways to continue to fight crime. In the street, they circumvent the rules to make arrests and seize evidence, then in court they tailor their testimony to comport their actions with the rules in order to prevent guilty defendants from getting off due to legal technicalities.

A study by Sparrow, Moore, and Kennedy shed light on the building blocks of this aspect of police culture. From the police officer's point of view:

1. The public wants the police to be crime fighters, and the police are the primary crime-fighting organization in government.
2. No one except other police officers can understand the "real" nature of police work and what is necessary to get the job done.
3. Police have to stick together: loyalty to one another is more important than anything else because the public, politicians, and police managers are consistently unfair in their evaluations and criticisms of the police.
4. Police cannot "win the war" on crime without violating legal, organizational, and ethical standards.

5. The public does not support or appreciate the police, and they expect too much of police officers.[2]

Within the culture of them-against-us that exists in most large police departments, it is sometimes a badge of honor to testify in a manner that results in the admissibility of evidence, even when the evidence may have been seized in violation of the Constitution. Officers see their primary responsibility as the enforcement of substantive criminal law, and they see the procedural law made by judges and lawyers as obstacles. They see it similarly to the difference between *mallum in* se and *mallum prohibitum* crimes—some acts are inherently wrong, whereas some acts are wrong only because they are prohibited. For many officers, the crimes of murder, rape, and narcotics trafficking are inherently wrong; violations of search-and-seizure rules and other legalities are wrong only because they are proscribed—tailoring testimony to obtain the conviction of a guilty criminal is necessary to counteract unrealistic prohibitions. To circumvent the rules and avoid the suppression of evidence, officers know what and what not to say. For example, they know that in some instances if they testify that they drew their firearm as they approached a suspect, the court will deem their action to have been a seizure and will suppress any evidence recovered after the seizure. Consequently, officers are tempted to testify that they did not draw their weapon when in fact they did.

Testifying falsely to save a case is not the subject of group disapproval in the closed police culture. As a distinct group under continual scrutiny and criticism, the police have developed a defensive culture that is passed from senior to junior officers.

> Every occupation has a learning process (usually called "socialization") to which its members are subjected. The socialization process functions to make most "rookies" in the occupation adopt the prevailing rules, values, and attitudes of their senior colleagues in the occupation. Very often, some of the existing informal rules and attitudes are at odds with the formal rules and attitudes society as a whole expects members of the occupation to follow.
>
> Police officers may be taught how to commit perjury in court to ensure that their arrests lead to convictions, or how to lie in disciplinary investigations to protect their colleagues.[3]

---

2. M.Sparrow, M. Moore, and D.Kennedy, *Beyond 911: A New Era for Policing.* New York: Basic Books, 1990, p. 51.

3. Sherman, Lawrence, "Learning Police Ethics." In Gaines and Cordner, *Policing Perspectives: An Anthology.* Los Angeles: Roxbury Publishing Company, 1999, pp. 301–310.

Undoubtedly, generalizations about all police officers are not true. Nonetheless, revelations about those who engage in tailored testimony not only damage the officers involved, but also the image of all police officers, even exemplary officers. Such revelations and others like it have produced the exaggerated belief that all police officers perjure themselves, and this perception in turn spreads the equally exaggerated belief that all police are dishonest in all aspects of their job. Such perceptions often unfairly result in accusations and rulings that certain officers purposely tailored their testimony when, in fact, they may have only innocently and inadvertently given inaccurate or mistaken testimony. In any event, the belief that tailored testimony is widespread continues to grow.

Noble-cause perjury not only generates distrust, but also leads to outright corruption, as it starts an officer down that path. Some officers begin with acts of noble-cause perjury to prevent guilty defendants from going free. Others begin by perjury, not to convict a guilty defendant, but to justify their actions and defend themselves during cross-examination. In either case, once an officer commits perjury in a courtroom, it is easier to do it again and easy to graduate to outright corruption for financial gain. Once officers deviate from a complete commitment to uphold the law, they become vulnerable to all forms of corruption; having once committed perjury, the next steps toward corruption are easy. What may begin as a seemingly understandable compromise of principle transforms the officer into a common criminal.

Other participants in the criminal justice system largely ignore the problem of tailored testimony. Many agree that if officers always testified exactly as to how events occurred during an arrest or search, the charges against many defendants would be dismissed and some extremely dangerous criminals would be released. A viewpoint exists that tailored testimony is a necessary evil, and as long as it is not too egregious, it should be given a wink and a nod. However, in recent years, more attention has been paid to the credibility of police testimony. In so-called "dropsy" cases in which a police officer testifies that a defendant dropped illegal drugs to the ground as the officer approached, even district attorneys have raised concerns about the believability of the testimony. In a New York case, *People v. Berrios*, 28 N.Y.2d 361 (1971), the district attorney submitted a report stating:

> For the last ten years participants in the system of justice—judges, prosecutors, defense attorneys and police officials—have privately and publicly expressed the belief that in some substantial but indeterminate percentage of dropsy cases, the testimony is tailored to meet the requirements of search-and-seizure rulings and it is very difficult in many cases to distinguish fact and fiction.

Each dropsy case shown to be false solidifies the view that all dropsy cases are false. Although at most suppression hearings police actions are upheld and the evidence is deemed admissible, it is the rulings against the police, especially those that expose false or incredible testimony, that receive notoriety. Defense attorneys use such cases as propaganda to raise suspicions about all police actions.

Judges, ranging from federal to local criminal court judges, have increasingly joined the chorus of defense attorneys and other critics who have spoken out against falsified police testimony, and many judges have suppressed evidence because of patently unbelievable police statements. In a recent local criminal court case, the judge suppressed marijuana evidence, partly because the actions described in the police testimony seemed to contravene of the laws of physics. Regarding the arresting officer's testimony, the court stated:

> The court finds the balance of his testimony incredible as a matter of law and patently tailored to nullify constitutional objections. To accept [the officer's] testimony, that he ultimately observed the marijuana from the backpack in plain view, would require the court to believe that the closed backpack magically opened, without explanation, either on its flight into the back seat or upon landing on the seat, and that [the officer] could actually see that the backpack had opened when the alleged opening was against the seat and facing away from him.[4]

A survey of suppression rulings in United States District Courts found twenty instances of judges expressing skepticism about the credibility of police officer testimony. The judges used language such as: "patently incredible," "riddled with exaggeration," "unworthy of belief."[5]

Although the above kinds of statements by judges are relatively few, they ratify the viewpoint of defense attorneys and other critical groups that police routinely violate constitutional rights and then lie in court to "legalize" their conduct. This viewpoint has spread to the general public and a consensus has been built, particularly in lower income communities, that the police are corrupt and dishonest.

The problem has been exacerbated by several large-scale police corruption scandals that emerged during the 1990s in Los Angeles, Miami, Detroit, New

---

4. *People v. Lapardo*, NYS, First District Court of Nassau County, J. Engel, Decision and Order, Docket No. 21008NA013502.

5. "Police in Gun Searches Face Disbelief in Court," Benjamin Weiser, *New York Times*, May 12, 2008.

York, and other cities.[6] These scandals involved more than perjury by a few, scattered officers but perjury and other crimes by large concentrated groups of officers who graduated from tailoring testimony to out-and-out corruption. One scandal that emerged at the notorious 30th Precinct in the New York City Police Department began with officers perjuring themselves on the witness stand to justify searches and seizures in drug cases and escalated to the point at which the officers became a criminal gang, specializing in burglaries, robberies, and reselling confiscated narcotics.[7] Eventually, 33 officers were indicted for corruption, and many admitted committing perjury, including a sergeant who admitted lying on the witness stand 75 times. After the indictments of the officers, the district attorney reviewed cases in which the officers had testified, and as a result, the courts had to overturn 125 cases against 98 defendants because their convictions had been based on police perjury. Interestingly, the 98 defendants were interviewed after their cases were dismissed, and 70 of them admitted that they had committed the crimes for which they were arrested—clear proof that the officers' perjury did not pertain to the substance of the underlying crimes but to the procedural aspects of the police tactics and actions.

Although the 30th Precinct case involved a distinct group of officers at a particular time and place, the crimes the officers committed tainted all police officers throughout New York City and beyond. The damage done seems nearly impossible to reverse, and judges and prosecutors wholly agree that it is harder than ever to get jurors to convict defendants where the prosecutor's case rests solely on police testimony.

Besides defendants, criminal defense attorneys obtain the greatest benefit from the exclusionary rule. When they are confronted with overwhelming physical and other evidence against their clients, often their only chance of winning, or, at least, demonstrating that they are doing something, is to challenge the admissibility of the physical evidence, verbal statements, or identifications that the police obtained. In addition to examining the lawfulness of search and seizures, they examine whether the rules related to Miranda warnings and right to counsel were upheld, and they cross-examine the officers and probe the police conduct during investigations, arrests, and subsequent procedures. When they are able to discredit the testimony of an officer defending the police conduct, the evidence will most likely be excluded.

---

6. "Los Angeles Police Scandal May Soil Hundreds of Cases," Todd Purdum, *New York Times*, December 16, 1999.

7. "New York Pays a High Price for Police Lies," David Kocieniewski, *New York Times*, January 5, 1997.

The general perception that police officers lie is of great benefit to criminal defense attorneys and provides them with ample means with which to subvert prosecution cases—exploiting the public's distrust of the police is the bread and butter of many attorneys. They know that jurors will be instructed that if they believe an officer lied about one aspect of a case, they may discredit the officer's entire testimony; so these attorneys will insinuate that the police are lying about some aspect of the case, and they will seize on every contradiction or inconsistency to prove their insinuations. In some instances, they convince jurors to conclude that if police are capable of lying about the facts leading up to the seizure of evidence, they are also capable of "framing" a defendant. Moreover, many criminal defense attorneys will use such tactics despite an absence of proof to support their allegations, and in a fair number of cases, they succeed in undermining the prosecution's case.

Unfortunately, they also succeed in many cases even when the testifying officers are essentially telling the truth. No one's testimony is perfect, including that of police officers, but police officer witnesses are held to a higher standard than civilian witnesses. Inaccurate, mistaken, or confused testimony of civilian witnesses for the prosecution will not necessary result in an acquittal for the defendant, but such testimony by a key police officer witness more than likely will result in an acquittal. Civilian witnesses might be excused for inconsistencies in their testimony, but police inconsistencies—whether within an individual officer's testimony or between different officers—are equated with lies. Although inconsistencies are sometimes evidence of falsity, they can also be evidence of normal mistakes, misperceptions, or faded memories. In any event, police inconsistencies often result in the suppression of evidence or the acquittal of a defendant. For these reasons, defense attorneys make great efforts to attack police witnesses by any opportune means, sometimes establishing that an officer lied, sometimes making it appear as though an officer lied even when the officer told the truth.

Defense attorneys do not have an obligation to ascertain the truth; their obligation is to defend their clients, whether the clients are guilty or innocent:

> If [defense counsel] can confuse a witness, even a truthful one, or make him appear at a disadvantage, unsure or indecisive, that will be his normal course. Our interest in not convicting the innocent permits counsel to put the State to its proof, to put the State's case in the worst possible light, regardless of what he thinks or knows to be the truth. Undoubtedly there are some limits which defense counsel must observe but more often than not, defense counsel will cross-examine a prosecution witness, and impeach him if he can, even if he thinks the wit-

ness is telling the truth, just as he will attempt to destroy a witness he thinks is lying.[8]

The exclusionary rule makes all police officers vulnerable to defense attorney tactics and to an air of distrust and insidious accusations. The false testimony engendered by the exclusionary rule taints all officers, and in a substantial number of cases, honest officers are disbelieved and the evidence they recovered is suppressed. In cases in which the evidence pertaining to the exclusionary rule is not clear-cut, the judge must make a decision on the basis of limited information and the testimony of police officers. Whether the judge believes the police testimony often depends on the judge's own bias, and the same set of facts will result in one judge deciding to suppress the evidence while another judge decides to admit the evidence.

Sometimes decisions are not made on the basis of evidence that is material to the main facts at issue but, instead, on the basis of collateral credibility issues. When a defense attorney can point out inconsistencies in any part of officer's testimony, the main part of the officer's testimony may be discredited. An example is *People v. Lebron*, 184 A.D.2d 784, 585 NYS 2d 498 (1992), wherein the defendant had been convicted of three robberies. Prior to his trial a suppression hearing had been held at which the prosecution had the burden of going forward to show the legality of the police conduct in question. The prosecution had to establish that the officer either saw a weapon visible in the defendant's pocket, in which case it would have been in plain view and the officer could have lawfully seized it, or that the officer had probable cause to arrest the defendant and then search the pocket in which the weapon was found.

The officer testified that he and his partner were driving in their marked patrol car when an unidentified person told them that the defendant had a gun. The officer approached the defendant, and when he was about one foot away, he saw a silvery metallic object in the front pocket of the defendant's coat. He asked the defendant what was in the pocket. When the defendant began to move his hand toward the pocket, the officer reached into the pocket and pulled out a weapon, which was a combination knife and metal knuckles.

The officer arrested the defendant for possession of the unlawful weapon, and during the subsequent investigation the defendant was identified in lineups as the perpetrator of the seven robberies. He also made incriminating statements in connection with the robberies.

After hearing the officer's testimony, the trial court ruled the evidence against the defendant was admissible, and the defendant was subsequently convicted.

---

8. *United States v. Wade*, 388 U.S. 218 (1967), J. White, dissent.

The defendant appealed his convictions, contending that his arrest was without probable cause, and, therefore, under the fruits of the poisonous tree doctrine, the weapon, the subsequent lineup identifications, and the incriminating statements should have been suppressed.

The questions for the New York Appellate Division court pertained to the officer's credibility in establishing the reasonableness of the search of the defendant. Was the officer's account credible that the unidentified witness existed? Was his testimony believable that he observed the silvery metal object in the defendant's pocket before he searched him? Did he tailor his testimony to overcome constitutional challenges?

After reviewing the record, the appellate court reversed the conviction and ruled that the officer's testimony was "so improbable as to be inherently unworthy of belief." The court recounted the discrepancies:

> For instance, at the hearing, the officer stated that the informant had told him and his partner that the defendant had a gun. However, he never recorded that fact in his memo book although he was the "recorder" for that shift, and the stop-and-frisk report he claimed to have prepared was never located. Moreover, although the officer testified that the informant did not tell him that the defendant was wanted for robbery, on the request-for-department-recognition form that he and his lieutenant signed, the officer had written that the informant had indeed said the defendant was wanted for robbery.... In addition, the request-for-department-recognition form did not even mention the informant's statement that the defendant had a gun. Indeed, the officer did not write anything about a gun or a knife on the form. Further, the arresting officer acknowledged that he had written on the form that the officers had "searched the area" after receiving the description and not, as he had testified, merely walking up to the defendant.
>
> Furthermore, even were we to believe the officer's testimony about an unnamed, unknown citizen informer and find that the officer had the common-law right of inquiry based upon the informant's purported description, the officer's claim that, from a distance of a foot, he was able to see into the defendant's six or seven-inch-deep pocket (which was conveniently "standing somewhat open" from the coat) and observe a metal object strains credulity.

The combination knife and metal knuckles, which led to the defendant as a suspect in seven robberies, the lineup identifications of the defendant by robbery victims, and the defendant's statements incriminating himself in the robberies were all suppressed and could not be used against the defendant were he tried again.

Although the court conceded that "it is unclear exactly what happened during the encounter between the officer and the defendant," the court chose to disbelieve the officer's primary testimony because of the non-testimonial statements made by the officer on a request-for-departmental-recognition form. Which account of the incident was closer to the truth did not matter: the discrepancies mattered, as well as the generally accepted belief that police lie to avoid the exclusionary rule.

The inconsistencies that the court relied on to discredit the officer could not be termed direct and significant contradictions to his sworn testimony. It is not unusual for arresting officers to fail to make a memo book entry about the details of an arrest. They have to fill out numerous arrest-related reports on which they recount the details of the arrest. They usually make a cryptic memo book entry about the time and place of an arrest without including the specifics.

The failure to prepare a stop-and-frisk report is also not unusual. Stop-and-frisk reports are primarily designed to record situations in which the police stop and question a suspect then let the suspect go. When an officer makes an arrest and fills out arrest reports, the stop-and-frisk report seems superfluous, and they often neglect to prepare them.

Regarding the inaccurately prepared request-for-department-recognition form, these requests are notoriously exaggerated and inaccurate. Their purpose is to get a medal, and certain formulas will work, others will not. Apparently this form was prepared in a way to meet the standards required for the medal. The foolishness of submitting an inaccurate form led to the impeachment of the officer's credibility, but it did not directly disprove his sworn testimony.

In the typical my-word-against-yours case, courts are often required to choose between the testimonies of adversarial witnesses. They make judgments about each witness' credibility. However, in suppression hearings, the officer generally testifies, but the defendant does not. The officer's credibility can be attacked, but the defendant's cannot. Clearly, this is an advantage for the defendant. Nevertheless, at the actual *Lebron* suppression hearing, the trial court judge observed the officer's live testimony, examined the physical evidence, and was not dissuaded by the inaccuracies on the extraneous request-for-department-recognition form. That judge admitted the evidence.

The appellate court had only a written record to review. It neither observed the officer's live testimony, nor examined the weapon and the coat pocket. The appellate court did not directly observe the demeanor of the officer as he testified, yet they suppressed the evidence without direct and conclusive proof that he had lied. Consequently, the defendant avoided conviction for possession of the weapon and the robberies.

Most, if not all, suppression hearings address the credibility of the testifying officer. Even in apparently straightforward arrest-and-search cases, such as when drivers are stopped and discovered to be driving with suspended licenses or for driving while intoxicated, the officers will be questioned about their reasons for stopping the vehicles in the first place. If the officer did not observe a traffic violation or did not have reasonable suspicion or probable cause regarding a crime, the stop of the vehicle would be unlawful and any evidence derived from the stop including evidence of the driver's intoxication would have to be suppressed.[9] The officers' testimony about their observation of a vehicle going through a red light or committing some other traffic violation can determine the admissibility of evidence subsequently discovered and the outcome of cases emanating from the traffic stop. Defense attorneys will challenge the police testimony and use any means available to impeach their credibility.

The court rulings in suppression hearings made on the basis of an officer's credibility fall into four general categories:

1. Testimony is false: judge rules it is false.
2. Testimony is false: judge rules it is true.
3. Testimony is true: judge rules it is false.
4. Testimony is true: judge rules it is true.

Rulings in the first category (false-false) occur infrequently. Nonetheless, such rulings have widespread and damaging ramifications, causing great loss of confidence in the police.

Rulings in the second category (false-true) occur more frequently than the first, and they also cause severe damage to the public's image of the police. Assuming that it is generally surmised that the testimony is false, the public loses confidence not only in the police, but in the criminal justice system for its incorrect outcomes. Moreover, criminals, in and out of the system, seize on the injustice of such rulings as an excuse to avoid accepting responsibility for their own actions and to shift blame to the unfair system.

Rulings in the third category (true-false) occur with undetermined frequency, but they are more damaging than the rulings in the first and second categories. To the public and to criminals, they are additional reasons to believe that the police lie. To the police, they are slaps in the face, slanderous betrayals by the very system to which the police swear allegiance. The damage to

---

9. *Delaware v. Prouse*, 440 U.S. 648 (1979).

police morale caused by such rulings is incalculable and leads in many directions, ranging from negligence to cynicism to outright corruption.

Rulings in the fourth category (true-true), although correctly decided, do not produce benefits to any degree that can compensate for the damages done in the other categories.

Adding the above kinds of intangible costs to the very tangible costs of releasing guilty defendants, it is clear that the costs of the exclusionary rule far outweigh any benefits—especially when the rule is not effectively achieving its purpose to deter police violations. The exclusionary rule engenders cynicism, defensiveness, and hostility among police officers. Honest and conscientious officers are frustrated, and many eventually adopt the "don't get involved if you can help it" mentality. Cynical and discouraged officers are not the best candidates for the difficult job of police work.

Officers must make split-second decisions in dangerous situations and with limited information. They resent second-guessing by judges, particularly by judges who demonstrate an anti-police bias or a lack of understanding of the nature of police work in the field. Officers sense that the skepticism that has developed about police testimony in suppression hearings has spread to trials, and sometimes guilty defendants are acquitted, not because they are innocent but because the judges and juries distrust the police testimony.

When a decision that officers consider "bad" comes down, especially one that denigrates good police officers, the word spreads through the police ranks and adds to the levels of hostility and demoralization. An example of a "bad" decision that caused extreme resentment among members of the New York City Police Department Narcotics Division was issued by United States District Court Judge John S. Martin, Jr., in *United States v. Carluin Sanchez*, 969 F.2d 1409 (1992). The defendant, Sanchez, was arrested by officers of the New York Drug Enforcement Task Force, a joint city-state-federal task force responsible for investigating large-scale narcotics distribution gangs. On the basis of a search warrant for the defendant's apartment, the officers recovered 480 glassine envelopes of heroin, a 9 millimeter semi-automatic handgun, and $46,000 in cash. Sanchez was convicted by a jury of the federal crimes of conspiracy to distribute heroin, 21 U.S.C. 846, and possession of heroin with intent to distribute, 21 U.S.C. 812, 841.

After the jury's guilty verdict, the judge vacated the verdict because, as he wrote:

> Frankly, on the record before the Court, the Court could not find, certainly beyond a reasonable doubt, that anything the police officers testified occurred in that apartment did in fact occur. Their whole scenario is undermined when it becomes clear that perjured testimony was offered with respect to how the officers gained entrance to the apartment.

In a subsequent decision on the same case, the judge explained his opinion further:

Based on my observations of the witnesses who testified before me, I find as a fact that police officers committed perjury at this trial concerning the way they obtained entry to the apartment and their observations of Carluin Sanchez running towards the bathroom. This conclusion which exists to a moral certainty is based on their demeanor as well as the inconsistencies and contradictions in their testimony.

The judge went on to castigate a sergeant who testified, saying:

[It] is clear to me that he was a person with no respect for the truth. A cold record cannot capture the impression made by [the sergeant], particularly on cross-examination where it became evident that the truth was not as important to him as giving an answer damaging to the defendant.[10]

It is unusual for a judge to vacate the verdict of a jury, as it is generally the jury's province to assess the credibility of witnesses. Several officers had testified about the events leading to the arrest of Sanchez. They testified about their execution of a search warrant in which they used a battering ram to knock open the defendant's door. Differences arose between the accounts of the officers as to whether the door was partially open or closed when the battering ram was used. This was pertinent because the sergeant testified that while the door was partially open, he saw the defendant run into the bathroom and he heard the toilet flush. Later, glassine envelopes of heroin were found floating in the toilet and in the toilet trap. The jury obviously accepted much of the officers' testimony, as they convicted the defendant; the judge, however, substituted his opinion for the jury's. The judge's claim that the officers "committed perjury" was highly unusual since the officers were never charged with perjury, much less convicted by a jury of perjury.

The sergeant whom the judge castigated was a highly regarded officer who had spent many years in the Narcotics Division and was selected for the Task Force because of his outstanding work. He is an African-American officer, known as a person who has dedicated his life to ridding his community of drug dealers. The castigation of this fine officer had a severe demoralizing effect throughout police ranks.

---

10. *United States v. Sanchez*, 813 F.Supp. 241 (1993)

Some recompense was gained when the United States Court of Appeals for the Second Circuit reversed Judge Martin and reinstated the conviction of Sanchez. That court severely criticized Martin's decision, stating:

> We think that it was an abuse of discretion for the district judge to grant a new trial in this case. In the first place, it appears to us that the district judge erred in discounting the testimony of [the sergeant and the detectives] as perjured. While it is true that the testimony of each officer was somewhat different as regards the point in time at which the door to the Sanchez apartment was first opened, whether the battering ram was used on the apartment door and the manner in which the ram was used (if it was applied at all), the testimony was consistent in a number of other respects. All agreed that there was a struggle, with Tito Sanchez pushing on one side of the door and [the sergeant] pushing on the other. All agreed that at some point when the door was partly opened, someone crossed the room inside the apartment. All agreed that the only other person found in the apartment besides Tito was appellant Carluin. And all agreed on what contraband was found and how and where it was found in the apartment.
> Differences in recollection alone do not add up to perjury.[11]

The Court of Appeals' reversal of Judge Martin was less publicized than his original ruling. The police generally only hear of the "bad" decisions, and rarely are these decisions appealed by the prosecution. They are left standing, and for many officers, they are like festering wounds that can diminish their commitment to the profession.

Fortunately, despite police disaffection, despite increasing perjury prosecutions of police officers, despite all the talk about tailored testimony, a substantial number of officers continue to put themselves on the line to fight crime and convict criminals. Unfortunately, the exclusionary rule continues to motivate some officers to bend the rules and tailor testimony.

In December 2007, a New York City detective with nineteen years of service was indicted on twelve counts of perjury in connection with his testimony at the trial of a defendant for attempted murder, possession of a gun, and other crimes for allegedly shooting a man. The detective testified while the defendant was at the station house, his mother came to see him and he spontaneously said to her: "They want to know why I shot this guy." The defendant's statement was used against him as evidence of a spontaneous confession.

---

11. *United States v. Sanchez*, 969 F.2d 1409 (1992).

Under cross-examination, the detective denied that he had been questioning the defendant before the mother arrived. However, unbeknownst to the detective, the defendant had hidden an MP3 player in his pocket and pressed the record button. He recorded an interview between the detective and himself that lasted more than an hour. During the interview, the defendant admitted the shooting but claimed self-defense. The detective repeatedly tried to persuade the defendant to say how he had disposed of the gun and to write a statement confessing to the crime, and he also repeatedly tried to dissuade the defendant from consulting a lawyer.

The MP3 recording came into the possession of the defense because as the mother was leaving the station house, the detective allowed the defendant to give her his personal possessions, including the MP3 player.

At the trial, during his cross-examination, the detective denied interviewing the defendant. Then, the defense attorney confronted the detective with the recording. As a result, the district attorney had to dismiss the attempted murder charge against the defendant, and subsequently he indicted the detective for perjury.[12]

The detective allegedly committed this perjury, not for personal gain, but to convict a criminal. Apparently he thought that if he admitted that he had questioned the defendant, the incriminating statement the defendant made to his mother would have been excluded from evidence.

For officers who tailor testimony for what they perceive as noble reasons, advice to them that they should just tell the truth, no matter that it results in the release of guilty defendants, has not worked—if people were better than they are, it might, but it has not. However, telling the truth when it will not result in the release of guilty defendants will work. Most police officers committed to convicting guilty defendants would tell the truth about their own actions even when they might have violated administrative or constitutional rules. Police officers with a propensity to take the risks associated with noble-cause corruption may well take the risks associated with telling the truth.

On the other hand, some officers are devoid of nobility and are corrupt from the start. These officers come to recognize the rule as an opportunity to obtain an easy payoff. They hold the keys to a case in their hands and can change the outcome simply by altering their testimony in ways to convict or acquit. As far back as 1928, Benjamin Cardozo, while he was a leading judge on the New York Court of Appeals and prior to his appointment to the United

---

12. "Recorded on a Suspect's Hidden MP3 Player, a Bronx Detective Faces 12 Perjury Charges," Timothy Williams, *New York Times*, December 7, 2007.

States Supreme Court, recognized what the exclusionary rule would let loose. In his inimitable style, he wrote:

> We are confirmed in this conclusion when we reflect how far-reaching in its effect upon society the new consequences would be. The pettiest peace officer would have it in his power through overzeal or indiscretion to confer immunity upon an offender for crimes the most flagitious.[13]

Judge Cardozo's prediction has proven correct. While the exclusionary rule pushed more officers to tailor their testimony to avoid the suppression of evidence, some officers, knowing the technicalities of the rule, and in exchange for a bribe or other benefit, have tailored their testimony to cause a suppression of the evidence and a dismissal of charges against a defendant. Without the exclusionary rule, it would be more difficult for the unscrupulous officer to commit perjury for the purpose of acquitting a surely guilty defendant.

As it stands, the exclusionary rule has not proved to be an effective remedy for police misconduct, and it has generated new problems that have had greater detrimental effects than the problems it was supposed to solve. No compelling need exists to continue employing the rule. Other more effective and pragmatic remedies are available to discipline the police and deter them from committing constitutional violations. It is self-defeating for the criminal justice system to maintain a rule that even subtly encourages police to give false testimony and overtly encourages self-interested attorneys to cast a cloud of suspicion over all police testimony. Eliminating the rule would change the climate of mendacity that permeates the criminal justice system. It would take away a motivation for police to tailor testimony, and it would help to restore the public's confidence in law enforcement.

---

13. *People v. Defore*, 242 N.Y. 13 (1926).

Chapter Twelve

Far More Crime

From the end of World War II to 1960, crime rates remained relatively low and stable. Then, in 1961, the Supreme Court imposed the exclusionary rule against the states in *Mapp v. Ohio* and began the defendant's rights revolution and the expansion of legal technicalities. In the 32 years following *Mapp*, from 1961 to 1993, the overall crime rate grew at three times the rate of the population. The most dramatic increase was in violent crime, which grew at more than twenty times the rate of population growth. Violent crimes include murder, manslaughter, rape, aggravated assault, and robbery. According to the Federal Bureau of Investigation (FBI), the number of reported violent crimes increased 565 percent from 289,390 in 1961 to 1,926,020 in 1993, while the population grew by 27 percent.[1] Homicides per hundred thousand of population increased from 4.7 to 9.8.[2]

The period of the crime explosion, 1961 to 1993, coincided with that of the exclusionary rule's greatest expansion, first by the Supreme Court then by state court extensions and broader interpretations. By 1993, intolerable crime levels caused a public outcry, and the pendulum began to swing toward stronger law enforcement. Law enforcement agencies were given increased funding, legislatures passed stricter sentencing laws, and courts imposed longer prison sentences. Following these measures, crime stabilized and then began decreasing.

Remarkably, yet somehow accepted, the crime rate in the United States has settled at a level five times greater than that of the other industrialized democracies, a murder rate eight times greater than the other industrialized democracies, and a growing prison population that constitutes the highest per capita rate in the world.[3] As of June 30, 2007, the United States had 2,221,944 persons incarcerated in federal, state, or local prisons or jails.[4] The number of

---

1. U.S. Department of Justice, Uniform Crime Reports.
2. *Ibid.*
3. E. Fairchild and H. Dammer, *Comparative Criminal Justice Systems*, 2nd Ed. (Belmont, Ca.: Thomson, 2001).
4. U.S. Department of Justice, Bureau of Justice Statistics.

sentenced inmates incarcerated per 100,000 of population has increased from 139 in 1980 to 506 in 2007—an increase of 264 percent. Some believe that these numbers show that we are effectively dealing with our crime problems, that we should incarcerate more criminals, and also lengthen their prison sentences; others argue that the more people we imprison, the more criminality we generate. The latter maintain that prisons are only schools for crime, and the recidivism rate of 67 percent supports their position. Both viewpoints have merit, but neither provides a solution to the level of American criminality. What all should agree upon is that in the most prosperous country in the world, it is a failure, not a success, that so many of our citizens are incarcerated.

The criminality in our society is reflected not only by the common crimes reported in the Index Crimes of the FBI's Uniform Crime Reports, but also by those which pervade all levels of society, from petty pilfering to white-collar crime and the corruption of public officials. The Uniform Crime Reports do not capture the full range of criminal activity. Unlawful drug dealing and usage is rampant, but it is mostly unreported. Moreover, with the advent of the Internet, computer frauds, identity theft, new forms of crime have proliferated, and the amount of such crime is unknown. Discovering the exact causes of this pervasive criminality in our society has proved to be a difficult task, but the negative attitudes, morality, and values so prevalent in our criminal justice system are surely important factors. A criminal justice system that denies swift and certain justice in favor of legal gamesmanship, expends much of its energy on technicalities, shifts blame and responsibility from the criminal to others, and precludes the use of reliable and truthful evidence is undoubtedly a system not functioning effectively to deter criminality or rehabilitate criminals.

To allow criminals to go free because of technicalities encourages many of them to repeat their criminal behavior, inflicting additional pain, injury, and death on the same or new crime victims. Since 1971, more than 700,000 persons have been the victims of murder or manslaughter in the United States.[5] This kind of homicide statistic portrays a nation at war with itself and a nation that has paid too high a price for the putative benefits of the continuation of certain legalisms. Put bluntly, our criminal justice system has failed to prevent an epidemic of murders. Compensating for the system's failure to establish voluntary compliance with the law by incarceration of more and more citizens, year after year, is a short-term solution that will eventually produce disastrous long-term consequences.

During most periods, an inverse relationship exists between number of people incarcerated and the number of crimes reported. Although there is a time

---

5. U.S. Department of Justice, Bureau of Justice Statistics.

lag, as the rate of incarceration increases, the crime rate tends to decrease, and as the rate of incarceration decreases, the crime rate tends to increase. Variations in incarceration rates may explain the variations in the crime rate, but they do not explain why there are so many individuals willing to commit serious crimes. Explanations and solutions to our intolerably high criminality level must be found outside the debate on the pros and cons of building more prisons.

Leading criminologists have offered varying and sometimes contradictory explanations for the levels of crime in the United States. Their theories have focused on such factors as incarceration rates, economic conditions, unemployment, demographics, biology, psychopathology, social context, lack of homogeneity, the availability of guns, drug and alcohol abuse, divorce rates, and out-of-wedlock births. Many criminologists have contributed outstanding scientific and statistical studies, but understanding the causes of crime is as difficult as predicting the future. The criminology community has not found a definitive answer or formed a consensus regarding the causes of crime or why crime rates trend upward or downward.[6]

Criminologists, while analyzing the complexities of crime causation and crime trends, have generally overlooked or discounted the proposition that legal technicalities negatively affect prosecutions, and, in turn, crime rates. Legal technicalities constrain police efforts to solve crimes and apprehend perpetrators. They constrain the ability of prosecutors to construct legally sufficient cases against defendants and to present evidence to juries. At each stage of the criminal process, the ability to obtain or present necessary evidence is hampered. These constraints are manifested by the increasing number of unsolved crimes and failed prosecutions.

In the 1980s, there were frequent calls for the elimination of the exclusionary rule. In 1982, the National Institute of Justice (NIJ), during the Reagan administration, conducted a study of felony arrests in California for the period 1976 to 1979. The study found that "the exclusionary rule exerted a major impact on … state prosecutions."[7] In 1983, Justice Byron White, in his concurring opinion in *Illinois v. Gates*, cited the study as proof that the costs of the rule outweighed the benefits.[8]

In response to the NIJ study, to calls to eliminate the rule, and to Justice White's opinion, the American Bar Association (ABA) commissioned studies of the issue.

---

6. James Q. Wilson and Richard J. Herrnstein, *Crime and Human Nature*, (New York: Simon and Schuster, 1985).

7. National Institute of Justice, "The Effects of the Exclusionary Rule, A Study in California 2" (1982).

8. 462 U.S. 213 (1983).

An ABA-sponsored study of nine counties in three states conducted by Professor Peter Nardulli produced less certain results than the NIJ study. Nardulli's study of legal motions to suppress evidence found that such motions were filed in eleven percent of cases—five percent to suppress physical evidence, two percent to suppress identifications, and four percent to suppress confessions. Since only a portion of these motions were successful, the study concluded that the effects of the rule were marginal.[9] As has been noted by others, the study did not account for appeals of the lost motions, and the study did not account for plea-bargained cases by district attorneys in expectation of motions to suppress. Moreover, the study did not include the largest or most crime-ridden cities.

Another ABA-sponsored study conducted by Thomas Y. Davies examined and challenged the validity of the NIJ and other studies. Davies found that "even if one looks at the cumulative effect of the rule through all stages of the felony process in California, only about 2.35 percent of felony arrests are lost because of illegal searches." (His conclusion was that the available data were insufficient to prove a case one way or the other.)[10] An honest look at the conclusions of these and other studies conducted during this period revealed a strong correlation between the interests of the sponsors and the results. Predilections often influence intellectual conclusions. Those against the rule clearly found its detrimental effects; those in favor of the rule concluded that its effects are equivocal and argued against any change. The resistance of lawyers and bar associations to curtailing the exclusionary rule is reminiscent of the efforts during the nineteenth century to curtail the formalities of the legal pleadings required at common law. For decades, David Dudley Field (1805–1894), a prominent attorney, spearheaded a drive to simplify and codify legal procedure. He argued that the common law pleading requirements were arcane and unintelligible to the public and that meritorious cases were lost because of inadvertent failures to comply with innumerable and complex technical details. Coincidentally, during the period that Field was active, the novelist Charles Dickens was shedding light on the absurdities and injustices of the English legal system in his novel *Bleak House*, pointing out that the only persons who benefited from the system were the lawyers.

The studies in the 1980s by Nardulli and Davies not only failed to account for the exclusionary rule's effect in the area of plea-bargaining, but they failed

---

9. Peter F. Nardulli, "The Societal Cost of the Exclusionary Rule: An Empirical Assessment," *American Bar Foundation Research Journal* (1983): 585.

10. Thomas Y. Davies, "A Hard Look at What We Know (and Still Need to Learn) About the 'Costs' of the Exclusionary Rule: The NIJ Study and Other Studies of 'Lost'' Arrests." *American Bar Foundation Research Journal* (1983): 611.

to account for the rule's impact on police investigations and evidence gathering prior to arrest and prosecution. The deterrent effect of the exclusionary rule is usually framed as deterring illegal police conduct, but it also deters legal and proper police conduct. The uncertainties of the rule often discourage police from taking action when they should. When police officers are not sure that they have sufficient grounds for probable cause to make an arrest or conduct a search, they often refrain from doing so: consequently, arrests are not made, evidence is not recovered, and admissions and confessions from defendants are not obtained. Of the cases that were not solved or not brought to justice because of the lack of police action, a percentage would have passed constitutional standards. Convictions would have followed, some of the criminals would have been incarcerated, and others might have been deterred from further crime.

Measuring the rule's impact requires more than studies of the late stages of prosecutions. The rule influences undocumented police activity that cannot be easily measured, and, perhaps more importantly, sends a message to criminals that they can get away with crime. The effect of these influences and messages is difficult to quantify, and isolating their effects from other causes of crime would be extremely difficult.

During the decade after the NIJ and ABA studies, police chiefs, prosecutors, and political leaders continued to complain about the rule, and several Supreme Court cases kindled hope for overturning the rule. The Court did not overturn the rule, but established several exceptions. Although the exceptions did little to curtail the rising crime rate, each exception initiated further debate and study of the rule's impact.

In 1998, Cassell and Fowles attempted to establish a connection between the imposition of the exclusionary rule and diminished police effectiveness. Their study, published in *The Stanford Law Review*, focused on the Supreme Court's 1966 decision in *Miranda v. Arizona*, which mandated that the police give warnings to suspects before conducting custodial interrogations. FBI statistics showed that crime clearance rates, or police success at solving crimes, "fell precipitously immediately after *Miranda* and have remained at lower levels ever since."[11]

Law enforcement agencies clear or solve a crime when at least one person is charged and turned over to the court for prosecution. Cases may also be cleared by exceptional means, such as when an identified offender is killed

---

11. Paul G. Cassell and Richard Fowles, "Handcuffing the Cops?: A Thirty-Year Perspective on *Miranda's* Harmful Effects on Law Enforcement," *Stanford Law Review* 50 (1998): 1055–1145, at 1059.

during apprehension, commits suicide, or flees the jurisdiction. A cleared case does not mean that it was resolved by a conviction for the crime charged. The defendant could plead guilty to a lesser charge, the case could be dismissed because evidence was suppressed, or the defendant could be acquitted.

Clearance rates are moving averages and not exact measurements, because the classification of cases can change and some cases are cleared years after the event. Nonetheless, even though clearance rates are inexact measurements, substantial changes in the rates indicate significant changes in police performance. A substantial reduction in police clearance rates is a telling measurement of diminished police effectiveness.

After *Miranda*, police effectiveness declined sharply. Clearance rates for total crime fell from between 55 and 60 percent pre-*Miranda* to between 33 and 40 percent post-*Miranda*. The question posed by the Cassell and Fowles study was whether the reduction in clearance rates was partly or substantially the result of *Miranda*. Using multiple regression analysis, they attempted to account for other factors that could affect clearance rates and to isolate the *Miranda* effect. The authors concluded:

> Our regression equations and accompanying causal analysis suggest that, without *Miranda*, the number of crimes cleared would be substantially higher—by as much as 6.6 to 29.7% for robbery, 6.2 to 28.9% for burglary, 0.4 to 11.9% for larceny, and 12.8 to 45.4% for vehicle theft. Moreover, applied to the vast numbers of cases passing through the criminal justice system, these percentages would produce large numbers of cleared crimes. As many as 36,000 robberies, 82,000 burglaries, 163,000 larcenies, and 78,000 vehicle thefts remain uncleared each year as a result of *Miranda*.[12]

Although the correlation between increased robberies, burglaries, larcenies, and motor vehicle thefts and *Miranda* was statistically significant, the authors were unable to establish whether any part of the diminished clearance rates for homicide, rape, or aggravated assault was solely due to *Miranda*. They explained that this result was due to the fact that confessions to homicides, rapes, and assaults most often involve a single crime committed by persons known to the victims. For example, the assault or murder of a woman by an ex-boyfriend is usually a one-time crime of passion. On the other hand, confessions to robbery, burglary, larceny, and vehicle theft generally involve suspects

---

12. *Ibid.*

who have committed many crimes to support themselves or their drug habits. When the police apprehend robbers or burglars, they attempt to obtain confessions to all of their crimes in order to clear their caseload. For these crimes, the numbers of crimes solved as a result of confessions were large enough to generate statistically significant results.

In 2003, a study by Atkins and Rubin published in *The Journal of Law and Economics*, found a promising and reliable way to measure the exclusionary rule's effect on crime rates. Using the 1961 case of *Mapp v. Ohio* as a beginning point, rather than the 1966 case of *Miranda v. Arizona*, the authors compared the change in crime rates in the 24 states that had not employed the exclusionary rule before *Mapp* to the 24 states that had (Alaska and Hawaii were not included in the study). The states that had employed the rule served, in effect, as a control group.

Both groups of states were representative of the nation in that both were randomly distributed across the nation and were not concentrated in a particular region. A presumption of the study was that national economic, social, and demographic variables would have affected both groups of states equally, leaving *Mapp* as the distinct variable.

The goal of the research was to determine whether a change in criminal procedure could cause a change in crime rates. The study found that between 1961 and 1969 crime had increased throughout the nation. However, it increased at a greater rate in those states that had not employed the exclusionary rule before *Mapp* and were forced to implement it afterwards. The study "found a positive and significant effect of the Supreme Court's alteration of criminal procedure on the crime rates of those states affected." In those states, the aggregate data showed that, over and above the rate of increase in the control-group states, larcenies increased by an extra 3.9 percent, auto theft by an extra 4.4 percent, burglary by an extra 6.3 percent, robbery by an extra 7.7 percent, and assault by an extra 18 percent. Their conclusion was that the exclusionary rule clearly increased crime.[13]

Both the Cassell-Fowles and the Atkins-Rubin studies established strong statistical arguments that the exclusionary rule has great social costs. Both studies were scientific, conservative, focused, and should be given great weight. However, an assessment of the exclusionary rule should not be confined only to what can be definitively proved by a conservative analysis of statistical correlations. Common sense dictates that freeing guilty criminals will have detri-

---

13. Raymond A. Atkins and Paul H. Rubin, "Effects of Criminal Procedure on Crime Rates: Mapping Out the Consequences of the Exclusionary Rule." *The Journal of Law and Economics*, vol. 46 (April 2003).

mental social costs. The big picture is that crime increased astronomically after *Mapp* but not only because of *Mapp.* As other exclusionary rule cases, such as *Wong Sun v. United States* in 1963, *Massiah v. United States* in 1964, *Escobedo v. Illinois* in 1964, *Miranda v. Arizona* in 1966, *Katz v. United States* in 1967, *United States v. Wade* in 1967, *Chimel v. California* in 1969, *Brewer v. Williams* in 1977, *Dunaway v. New York* in 1979, and *Payton v. New York* in 1980, further expanded the rule, crime increased at greater rates than it would have without those cases.[14] Those Supreme Court decisions applied the rule to criminal procedure in new and novel ways, and provided the impetus and authority for other federal, state, and local courts to further apply the rule in even more novel ways. Thousands of such applications of the rule cause police and prosecutors to shift their focus from obtaining and presenting evidence for the purpose of convicting criminals to defending and justifying their own actions.

The clearest evidence of the rule's negative impact and social costs is its effect on homicide clearance rates and prosecutions.

Homicide clearance rates are the primary measure of police performance. Homicides are the most accurate crime statistic we have to measure crime trends and consequences, not only because criminal homicide is the ultimate crime against individuals and society, but also because the reporting of homicides is more reliable than reporting of other crimes. Dead bodies must be accounted for, and although some homicides may be erroneously classified as natural deaths, accidents or suicides, most are correctly identified. Police-compiled homicide statistics have been shown to be roughly consistent with reports of homicides by doctors, coroners, and medical examiners to the National Center for Health Statistics.[15]

An analysis using data from 1962, the first full year after *Mapp v. Ohio,* as the beginning point of a study shows a substantial correlation between the drop in homicide clearances and the imposition of the exclusionary rule. In 1962, there were 8,404 murders or non-negligent manslaughters reported. The reported clearance rate for these crimes was 93.1 percent, and law enforcement was confident in its ability to solve these crimes. Thirty-one years later in 1993, well into the defendants' rights revolution, 24,530 murders or manslaughters were

---

14. *Wong Sun v. U.S.,* 371 U.S. 471; *Massiah v. U.S.,* 377 U.S. 201; *Escobedo v. Illinois,* 378 U.S. 478; *Miranda v. Arizona,* 384 U.S. 436; *Katz v. U.S.,* 389 U.S. 347; *U.S. v. Wade,* 388 U.S. 218; *Chimel v. California,* 395 U.S. 752; *Brewer v. Williams,* 430 U.S. 387; *Dunaway v. New York,* 442 U.S. 200; *Payton v. New York,* 445 U.S. 573.

15. P.C. Holinger and E.H. Klemen, "Violent Deaths in the United States, 1900–1975: Relationships between Suicide, Homicide, and Accidental Deaths." *Social Science and Medicine* 16 (1982):1919–1938.

reported, and the reported clearance rate fell to 65.6 percent and since remained at about that level or below.[16]

Table 12.1 estimates the number of murder and non-negligent manslaughter cases cleared and not cleared between 1962 and 2007.

As the table demonstrates, the estimated number of un-cleared murders and negligent manslaughters per year increased 11-fold from 580 in 1962 to 6568 in 2007, and had been much higher at 8437 in 1993. This dramatic increase in un-cleared cases is discerned best by comparing decades. For instance, in the decade from 1962 to 1971, 16,059 homicides were not cleared. From 1985 to 1994, 71,447 homicides were not cleared.

Using a rough and conservative calculation, an estimated 229,205 criminals who committed murder or manslaughter between 1962 and 2007 have not been brought to appropriate justice (this estimate does not include a calculation for the many homicides that are committed by more than one person, which increases the number of perpetrators not brought to justice). The majority of the un-cleared cases remained so not because the police were without a viable suspect but because they were stymied in their efforts to gather sufficient evidence to file charges. As a result of the failure to prosecute such suspects, the goal of swift and certain justice has been drastically undermined, and these unresolved cases are a discredit to our criminal justice system.

In addition to the disturbing number of un-cleared cases, the troubling fact persists that a majority of persons arrested for serious crimes are not convicted for those crimes. The historical conviction rate of offenders charged with homicide is 44.7 percent.

Perhaps many of the individuals who were not convicted did not in fact commit the crime with which they were charged. Perhaps they were rightfully acquitted, and their acquittals could be viewed as a positive outcome. On the other hand, most of them may have been guilty and escaped justice only because of our high standards of proof or because of legal technicalities.

The Cassell-Fowles and the Atkins-Rubin correlation studies proved some level of connection between the exclusionary rule and clearance and crime rates. However, the connection may be far stronger than that which can be proved by direct correlation. As is often said, correlation is not necessarily causation. Here, the Cassell-Fowles and the Atkins-Rubin correlations may be just the tip of the iceberg of the exclusionary rule's contribution to American criminality.

A comprehensive understanding of crime causation cannot be achieved by studying only concrete data, such as clearance, conviction, and incarceration

---

16. U.S. Department of Justice, Uniform Crime Reports.

Table 12.1 Estimated Murder and Non-Negligent Manslaughter Cases Cleared and Not Cleared

Year	Murder or Non-Negligent Manslaughter	Percent Cleared	Estimated Cases Cleared	Estimated Cases Not Cleared
1962	8404	93.1	7824	580
1963	8504	91.2	7756	748
1964	9249	90.2	8343	906
1965	9850	89.9	8855	995
1966	10918	89.2	9738	1180
1967	12093	88.3	10678	1415
1968	13648	85.9	11734	1914
1969	14587	86.1	12559	2028
1970	18515	82.2	15219	3296
1971	17627	83.0	14630	2997
1972	15812	86.5	13677	2135
1973	19640	78.7	15456	4185
1974	20710	79.9	16547	4253
1975	20510	78.3	16059	4451
1976	18780	79.0	14836	3944
1977	19120	75.5	14435	4685
1978	19560	76.2	14904	4656
1979	21460	73.4	15751	5709
1980	23040	72.3	16658	6382
1981	22520	71.6	16124	6396
1982	21010	73.5	15442	5568
1983	19308	75.9	14655	4653
1984	18692	74.1	13850	4842
1985	18976	72.0	13662	5314
1986	20613	70.2	14470	6143
1987	20096	70.0	14067	6029
1988	20675	70.0	14472	6203
1989	21500	68.3	14685	6815
1990	23438	67.2	15750	7688
1991	23760	64.6	15349	8411
1993	24526	65.6	16089	8437
1994	23326	64.4	15022	8304
1995	21606	64.8	14000	7606
1996	19645	66.9	13142	6503
1997	18208	66.1	12035	6173
1998	16974	68.7	11661	5313
1999	15522	69.1	10726	4796
2000	15586	63.1	9835	5751
2001	16037	62.4	10007	6030
2002	16204	64.0	10370	5834
2003	16528	62.4	10313	6215
2004	16137	62.6	10102	6035
2005	16692	62.1	10366	6326
2006	17030	60.7	10340	6690
2007	16929	61.2	10361	6568

Source—U.S. Department of Justice, Federal Bureau of Investigation: Crime in the United States: Uniform Crime Reports (1961–2006).

rates. Intangibles, such as mores, values, attitudes, and respect or disrespect for the law and authority, are fundamental factors influencing crime causation. The exclusionary rule causes both concrete and intangible results. It exacts a high price on society, not only due to the release of guilty criminals, but also by creating disrespect for the law and by undermining public confidence in the system. In 1976, Justice Lewis Powell, in *Stone v. Powell*, 428 U.S. 490, recognized the problem:

> (Although) the rule is thought to deter unlawful police activity … if applied indiscriminately, it may well have the opposite effect of generating disrespect for the law and the administration of justice. The disparity in particular cases between the error committed by the police officer and the windfall afforded a guilty defendant by application of the rule is contrary to the idea of proportionality that is essential to the concept of justice.

On the streets and in the prisons, many of the murderers and dangerous criminals who have avoided arrest or conviction because of the exclusionary rule are role models for others to follow. They brag about how they stonewalled the cops, how they beat the rap. Jailhouse lawyers know the cases, and these inmates school other inmates about the ins and outs of search and seizure law, how to testify that they were in custody when questioned by the police so that they should have received Miranda warnings, or how they should swear they asked for a lawyer even when they had not.

Large segments of our population have adopted a worldview of moral relativism and accepted a moral equivalency between law-enforcement efforts and certain types of criminal conduct. The exclusionary rule ratifies that view. A surprisingly large number of people respond to police activity with such comments as "they can't do that," or "they had no right to look under the seat for the gun," or "the confession is no good because they didn't tell him his Miranda rights." Many of these people place a greater negative value on police actions than on some kinds of criminal activity, and when a case is dismissed because of the suppression of evidence, they view the dismissal as proof that the criminal was innocent, right, and justified.

Whether or not evidence is suppressed often depends on small details — whether the officer took out his gun, whether he pointed his flashlight into a car, whether as he frisked a suspect he could immediately tell that the object he felt was a bullet or a crack vial.[17] The unpredictability and conse-

---

17. *Minnesota v. Dickerson*, 508 U.S. 366 (1993).

quences of suppression hearings do not foster the rule of law or the public perception that a rule of law exists in criminal matters. Patently guilty people, professional criminals, and those who can afford high-priced lawyers are often freed while others, especially poor people, who may have been caught up in a one-time incident or in circumstances they could not control, who may have made a foolish mistake or reacted emotionally to a stressful situation, are convicted and severely punished. The public's perception of a fair criminal justice system is essential to the inculcation of personal morality, conscience, and a sense of social responsibility, but unfairness is too often what they perceive. Such negative circumstances do not provide the positive and moral underpinnings necessary for a beneficial value system. Voluntary compliance to law—the ultimate means of crime prevention—has been undermined by the widespread belief that the criminal justice system is broken and unfair.

Noncompliance with the law is readily apparent in the level of unlawful drug use in our society. The connection of drug use to crime has been well established, and every state legislature has passed stringent laws against the use of certain drugs. The United States Congress has examined the consequences of drug usage, and recognizing the significant danger to the welfare of society, has passed comprehensive legislation to combat its spread.[18] At the same time, counteracting our national efforts and our national interest, the exclusionary rule is in force, providing substantial protection for the drug-trafficking industry. That industry is a major cause of crime, directly and indirectly, and many drug traffickers conduct a risk-versus-rewards analysis while engaging in their illegal activities. They weigh the chances of apprehension and conviction against the large profits they can make. The exclusionary rule gives them a greater than 50–50 chance of avoiding conviction through the efforts of attorneys who specialize in challenging the admissibility of evidence. Since drug dealers caught in physical possession of unlawful drugs find it difficult to deny their guilt, the exclusionary rule and other technicalities are their primary means of escaping punishment. Lawyers, who indirectly share in the profits of the illegal drug industry, have exploited and developed the rule. As they have expanded the theories and applications of the rule, the risk-versus-rewards calculation for the drug dealers has improved. Drug dealers and their lawyers use the rule, which was originally designed to protect individual privacy and possession of legal materials, i.e.,

---

18. Omnibus Crime Control and Safe Streets Act, 18 U.S.C. 2510–20 (1968); Comprehensive Drug Abuse Prevention and Control Act, 21 U.S.C. 801–971 (1970).

private papers, to shield illegal enterprises and the possession of unlawful narcotics.[19]

Our society has declared a war on drugs, has committed substantial resources to the fight, imposed severe punishments for possession or sale of large amounts of illegal drugs, and instituted major programs to rehabilitate addicts and to help the families and children of addicts. These enormous commitments should not be undermined by the counterproductive adherence to legal technicalities that favor drug traffickers. We should not fight a war on drugs while giving the enemy a weapon to use against us.

As Justice Sandra Day O'Connor observed while discussing the exclusionary rule:

> Exclusion in such a situation teaches not respect for the law, but casts the criminal system as a game and sends the message that society is so unmoved by the violation of its own laws that it is willing to frustrate their enforcement for the smallest of returns.[20]

When criminal laws, especially unpopular laws, are enforced unevenly or dishonestly, disrespect for the law follows, and as the exclusionary rule leads to uneven and dishonest enforcement of the law, it becomes another cause of crime.

Drugs, poverty, racial discrimination, and other recognized causes of crime have proven difficult to combat. The exclusionary rule is one cause of crime that can easily be eliminated. Without the rule, prosecutions of drug traffickers, violent criminals, and other criminals could unequivocally focus on the guilt or innocence of the defendant, not on the tactical or inadvertent actions of the police. Eliminating the rule would send a clearer message of society's disapproval of criminal conduct.

---

19. *Weeks v. U.S.*, 232 U.S. 383 (1914); *Silverthorne Lumber Co. v. U.S.*, 251 U.S. 385 (1920).

20. *Duckworth v. Eagan*, 492 U.S. 195, at 212 (1989).

Chapter Thirteen

Irreconcilable Differences

Although the courts have attempted to develop a logical and cohesive set of rules for police to follow as they conduct interviews and interrogations, what their rulings have rendered has been illogical and confusing. Because of the deep divisions between those that favor and those that oppose strict adherence to *Miranda* and other exclusionary rule doctrines, the law remains in flux. Reasoned attempts to find a middle ground have failed, because no matter how reasoned the arguments put forth by those on either side, their differences are not based on intellect alone but spring from emotional and visceral proclivities. Generally, those in favor of preventing and excluding confessions have a strong empathy for the accused, especially those that are downtrodden. They have a strong distrust of a potentially oppressive government, and they believe the benefits of deterring inappropriate police conduct outweigh the costs of leaving criminals unpunished. Those opposed to strict adherence to *Miranda* and the exclusionary rule feel that punishment of guilty criminals is a societal necessity. They believe that law enforcement officers can be trusted not to abuse their authority, and they view the costs of excluding confessions and derivative evidence as too great for any purported benefit to society.

In view of the strength of the disagreement, it is understandable that those active on either side of the debate do not acquiesce to decisions that favor the other side, and both sides have continually argued for reforms or modifications in accordance with their positions.

The Congressional Attempt to Overrule *Miranda*

Two years after *Miranda v. Arizona* mandated the warnings, the United States Congress attempted to overrule *Miranda* as it applied in federal courts by passing Section 3501 of the Omnibus Crime Control Act of 1968.[1] The purpose of the statute was to maintain and reinforce the traditional, common law rule

---

1. Title 18, U.S.C., Section 3501.

that voluntary confessions should be admissible. The statute was not designed to allow law enforcement agents leeway to obtain involuntary confessions; such confessions traditionally have been inadmissible under the common law and the due process clause because of their inherent unreliability. The statute was designed to establish the criteria to determine whether a confession was voluntary or involuntary. Rejecting the *Miranda* rationale that a confession without the warnings was presumptively involuntary and the result of coercion, Congress said that whether a defendant received the warnings or their equivalent should be only one factor in the totality of the circumstances used to determine the voluntary or involuntary nature of a confession. The statute stated:

(a) In any criminal prosecution brought by the United States or by the District of Columbia, a confession, as defined in subsection (e) herewith of, shall be admissible in evidence if it is voluntarily given. Before such confession is received in evidence, the trial judge shall, out of the presence of the jury, determine any issue as to voluntariness. If the trial judge determines that the confession was voluntarily made, it shall be admitted in evidence and the trial judge shall permit the jury to hear relevant evidence on the issue of voluntariness and shall instruct the jury to give such weight to the confession as the jury feels it deserves under all the circumstances.

(b) The trial judge in determining the issue of voluntariness shall take into consideration all of the circumstances surrounding the giving of the confession, including

1. the time elapsing between arrest and arraignment of the defendant making the confession, if it was made after arrest and before arraignment,

2. whether such defendant knew the nature of the offense with which he was charged or of which he was suspected at the time of making the confession,

3. whether or not such defendant was advised or knew that he was not required to make any statement and that any such statement could be used against him,

4. whether or not such defendant was advised prior to questioning of his right to the assistance of counsel, and

5. whether or not such defendant was without the assistance of counsel when questioned and when giving such confession,

The presence or absence of any of the above-mentioned factors to be taken into consideration by the judge need not be conclusive on the issue of voluntariness of the confession.

For three decades, the Justice Department declined to utilize 3501, mostly because some officials claimed it was unconstitutional. During the same period, advocates for 3501 and other critics of *Miranda*, including professor of law Paul G. Cassell,[2] tried to convince the Justice Department to employ the statute. Among other points, they argued that *Miranda* tended to block federal agents from interrogating the more educated, affluent, or savvy individuals who had the knowledge and experience to ask for a lawyer while it tended to allow the successful questioning of those with less education, resources, and experience. In a way, *Miranda* fostered inequality in the criminal justice process.

Eventually the Justice Department attempted to utilize the statute, and the issue of its constitutionality reached the Supreme Court in 2000 in *Dickerson v. United States*, 530 U.S. 28. Before the Court's ruling was issued, many observers thought that the Court would overturn or severely modify *Miranda*, because in the years prior to *Dickerson*, the Court had raised expectations that it was ready to do so. In several cases, it had declined to suppress confessions on the basis of *Miranda* violations, and it had established several exceptions to the exclusionary rule, including the good faith, inevitable discovery, and independent source doctrines.[3]

In addition, in *New York v. Quarles*, 467 U.S. 649 (1984), the Court established the public-safety exception to the Miranda warnings requirement. In *Quarles*, police officers arrested the defendant for committing a rape while armed with a gun. When the police apprehended him inside a supermarket, he did not have the gun in his possession. They asked him where he hid the gun, and he told them where it was hidden in the supermarket. New York courts suppressed the defendant's statement because the police had not given him Miranda warnings before asking him where he hid the gun. Under the poisonous-tree doctrine, the court also suppressed the gun as a fruit of the illegally obtained statement. However, when the case reached the Supreme Court, that Court reversed the New York court, stating, "The need for answers to questions in a situation posing a threat to the public safety outweighs the need for the prophylactic rule protecting the Fifth Amendment's privilege against self-incrimination."[4]

In 1985, in *Oregon v. Elstad*, 470 U.S. 298, the Court decided another case involving a defendant's confession. In *Elstad*, the Oregon Court of Appeals

---

2. Paul G. Cassell, "The Statute That Time Forgot: 18 U.S.C., Section 3501 and the Overhauling of Miranda," *85 Iowa L. Rev. 175* (1999).

3. *United States v. Leon*, 468 U.S. 897 (1984); *Nix v. Williams*, 467 U.S. 431 (1984); *Segura v. United States*, 468 U.S. 796 (1984).

4. *New York v. Quarles*, 467 U.S. 649 (1984).

had excluded a signed, voluntary confession to a burglary. The police, armed with an arrest warrant, had entered Elstad's home, and during the arrest, a detective, without giving Miranda warnings, asked him whether he knew about a burglary. Elstad answered, "Yes. I was there."

At the police station, Elstad was given Miranda warnings and voluntarily signed a written confession. The Oregon court excluded the confession because the defendant's admission at his house "let the cat out of the bag" and "tainted" the voluntary nature of the written confession. The Supreme Court disagreed with the Oregon state court, reversed their judgment, and held that "a suspect who has once responded to unwarned yet uncoercive questioning is not thereby disabled from waiving his rights and confessing after he has been given the requisite Miranda warnings."[5]

In 1986, the Supreme Court, in *Moran v. Burbine*, 475 U.S. 412, reversed a lower court's suppression of a confession. In *Burbine*, police in Cranston, Rhode Island arrested the defendant, Brian Burbine, for a local burglary. An attorney called the detective division and was informed that Burbine would not be questioned regarding the burglary. While the defendant was in custody, he was implicated in an unrelated murder that had occurred several months earlier in Providence, Rhode Island. The murder victim was Mary Jo Hickey who "was found unconscious in a factory parking lot in Providence, Rhode Island. Suffering from injuries to her skull apparently inflicted by a metal pipe found at the scene, she was rushed to a nearby hospital. Three weeks later she died from her wounds."

During the evening in which the defendant was in custody, detectives from Providence arrived and gave the defendant the Miranda rights. They did not tell him that an attorney had called to represent him regarding the Cranston burglary, and they proceeded to question him about the Providence murder. The defendant, in writing, waived his rights to remain silent and to have counsel present and gave three full written confessions to the murder.

The defendant was convicted in Rhode Island of murder in the first degree. He filed a *writ of habeas corpus* in federal court, where the United States First Circuit Court of Appeals reversed the conviction and suppressed the confession, ruling that "the deliberate or reckless failure to inform a suspect in custody that his counsel, or counsel retained for him, is seeking to see him, vitiates any waiver of his Fifth Amendment right to counsel and privilege against self-incrimination."[6]

---

5. *Oregon v. Elstad*, 470 U.S. 298 (1985).
6. *Burbine v. Moran*, 753 F.2d 178 (1st Circ. 1985).

The Supreme Court disagreed, reversed the First Circuit, reinstated the conviction, and allowed the confession to stand, finding that the First Circuit's conclusion was "untenable as a matter of both logic and precedent." The Court stated:

Events occurring outside the presence of the suspect and entirely unknown to him surely can have no bearing on the capacity to comprehend and knowingly relinquish a constitutional right. Under the analysis of the Court of Appeals, the same defendant, armed with the same information and confronted with precisely the same police conduct, would have knowingly waived his *Miranda* rights had a lawyer not telephoned the police station.... We have never read the Constitution to require that the police supply a suspect with a flow of information to help him calibrate his self-interest in deciding whether to speak or stand by his rights....

Granting that the deliberate or reckless withholding of information is objectionable as a matter of ethics, such conduct is only relevant to the constitutional validity of a waiver if it deprives a defendant of knowledge essential to his ability to understand the nature of his rights and the consequences of abandoning them. Because respondent's voluntary decision to speak was made with full awareness and comprehension of all the information *Miranda* requires the police to convey, the waivers were valid.[7]

Rulings such as *Quarles, Elstad,* and *Burbine* signaled the possible demise of *Miranda.* However, in *Dickerson v. United States, supra,* the Court surprised and disappointed the critics of *Miranda.*

In *Dickerson,* the Justice Department argued that 3501 supported the admissibility of an un-Mirandized, voluntary confession. In addition, Professor Cassell filed an *amicus curiae* (friend of the court) brief in which he argued that 3501 required the overruling of *Miranda.* In the case, the defendant was indicted for three bank robberies, using a firearm in the course of committing a crime of violence, and conspiracy. The defendant moved to suppress a confession he gave to agents of the Federal Bureau of Investigation, claiming that he had not received Miranda warnings. The U.S. Fourth Circuit Court of Appeals ruled that although evidence was contradictory as to when the warnings were given to the defendant, the confession itself was voluntary, Section 3501 was applicable, and, therefore, the confession was admissible.[8] This decision

---

7. *Moran v. Burbine,* 475 U.S. 412 (1986).
8. 166 F.3d 667.

was a direct challenge to the absolute requirements of the *Miranda* rule and indirectly to the authority of the Supreme Court.

In a seven-to-two decision, the Supreme Court reversed the Fourth Circuit and suppressed the confession and the evidence derived from the confession. The holding comprised two parts: First, "In sum, we conclude that *Miranda* announced a constitutional rule that Congress may not supersede legislatively." Second, "Following the rule of *stare decisis*, we decline to overrule *Miranda* ourselves."

The first part of the holding addressed important questions regarding the separation of powers and the supremacy of powers between the judicial and the legislative branches of government. The Court rejected the proposition that Congress, by passing Section 3501, could overrule a Supreme Court decision on constitutional issues. This was rather ironic in light of the fact that in *Miranda* the Court encouraged Congress to devise equally effective schemes as alternatives to the mandatory warning and waiver requirements.[9]

In the second part of the holding, the Court gave the following reasons for adhering to *stare decisis* even though the majority of this Court, had it been deciding *Miranda* in 1966, would have ruled differently than the Warren Court:

> Whether or not we would agree with *Miranda's* reasoning and its resulting rule, were we addressing the issue in the first instance, the principles of *stare decisis* weigh heavily against overruling it now.... *Miranda* has become embedded in routine police practice to the point where the warnings have become part of our national culture.

The seven-to-two majority vote was unexpected, since most exclusionary rule cases had been decided five-to-four. Clearly, the Court's decision not to defer to Congress was influenced by the Court's territorial imperative to defend its constitutional authority. Proponents who favored the continuation of *Miranda* and exclusionary rules were understandably jubilant over the ruling. However, their jubilation did not last long because four years later the Court returned to its course of limiting *Miranda*.

Miranda Is Not a Right

Despite the Court's pronouncement in *Dickerson* that "*Miranda* is a constitutional decision," three years later, in *Chavez v. Martinez*, 538 U.S. 760 (2003),

---

9. 384 U.S. 436 (1966), at 467.

the Court backtracked on that proposition. In that case, the plaintiff, Martinez, sued the police for interrogating him without giving him Miranda warnings while he was being treated in the emergency room of a hospital. Two police officers, Salinas and Pena, who were investigating narcotics dealing, had stopped Martinez. Officer Salinas frisked him and discovered a knife in his waistband. A scuffle followed, and the officers claimed that Martinez grabbed Officer Salinas' gun and pointed it at them. Officer Pena shot Martinez five times.

Within minutes, Sergeant Chavez arrived on the scene with paramedics. "Chavez accompanied Martinez to the hospital and then questioned Martinez there while he was receiving treatment from medical personnel. The interview lasted a total of about 10 minutes, over a 45-minute period, with Chavez leaving the emergency room for periods of time to permit medical personnel to attend to Martinez."

During the interview, Martinez admitted that he took the gun from the officer's holster and pointed it at the police. He also admitted that he used heroin regularly.

Martinez was never charged with a crime and his answers were never used against him in any criminal prosecution. However, the shooting left him blind and paralyzed, and he filed a civil rights lawsuit. One of the claims in the suit was that Sergeant Chavez' actions violated his Fifth Amendment rights by coercive conduct and interrogating him without Miranda warnings.

The Supreme Court, in a six-to-three decision, which included six separate opinions, rejected the application of the Fifth Amendment to these circumstances. Justices Thomas' opinion carried the most support. He stated:

> We fail to see how, based on the text of the Fifth Amendment, Martinez can allege a violation of this right, since Martinez was never prosecuted for a crime, let alone compelled to be a witness against himself in a criminal case.... We conclude that Martinez's allegations fail to state a violation of his constitutional rights.... Accordingly, Chavez's failure to read Miranda rights to Martinez did not violate Martinez' constitutional rights.

Chavez v. Martinez brought near apoplexy to the anti-police bar. Alan Dershowitz, the renowned criminal lawyer, Harvard professor, and author, felt compelled to write a book to protest the case.[10] His most vociferous complaint was that *Martinez* would allow the government to use any means to obtain in-

---

10. Alan Dershowitz, *Is There a Right to Remain Silent?* Oxford University Press, New York, 2008.

formation from a person as long as the information was not used against the person in a criminal trial. However, the Court did not say any such thing; all it did was establish that suspects could not sue for a police failure to read them Miranda warnings. The Court did not preclude lawsuits on the basis of other egregious police conduct while interrogating a suspect, such as physical torture, assault, false arrest, unlawful imprisonment, or intentional infliction of emotional distress.

The contradiction between the propositions: "*Miranda* is a constitutional decision," in *Dickerson*, and "Chavez's failure to read Miranda rights to Martinez did not violate Martinez' constitutional rights," in *Martinez*, demonstrates the instability of the foundations on which so much of the exclusionary rule has been built. If *Miranda* is not an enforceable constitutional right, then what is the justification for suppressing evidence derived from a failure to give the Miranda warnings? The exclusionary rules created in *Weeks* and *Mapp*, at least, were designed to enforce the actual Fourth Amendment constitutional right to be free from "unreasonable searches and seizures." Miranda rights are not in the Constitution and do not carry the same legal mandates as actual rights spelled out in the Amendments.

Severing a Branch of the Poisonous Tree

The following year, the Court again cut away at *Miranda*. In *United States v. Patane*, 542 U.S. 630 (2004), it severed the fruits of the poisonous tree connection between a Miranda violation and the exclusion of derivative physical evidence. A Colorado Springs police officer and an Alcohol, Firearms, and Tobacco (ATF) federal agent arrested Patane for violating a court-imposed restraining order. The officers had information that Patane owned a Glock automatic pistol, and the ATF agent questioned him about it. As the agent began to give the defendant Miranda warnings, Patane interrupted and asserted that he knew his rights. The agent did not attempt to complete the warnings and began to question him. Patane then divulged that the gun was in his bedroom and gave the agent permission to retrieve the gun.

The U.S. Circuit Court of Appeals suppressed the gun, ruling that it was derived from the questioning that followed the incomplete Miranda warnings. However, the Supreme Court reversed the decision and ruled that although Patane's statements had to be excluded from use at the trial because the warnings were not properly and completely administered, it was unnecessary to exclude the physical evidence derived from the confession. The Court referred back to *Chavas v. Martinez*, *supra*, pointing out, "Our cases also make clear the related point that a mere failure to give Miranda warnings does not, by itself, violate a suspect's constitutional rights."

While the Court reiterated that physical evidence derived from a coerced, involuntary confession still requires suppression because a coerced confession violates a suspect's actual Fifth Amendment right against self-incrimination, it emphasized that physical evidence derived from a voluntary un-Mirandized confession like Patane's does not require suppression of derivative physical evidence because, in the latter circumstances, no deterrent benefit pertaining to self-incrimination at trial would be obtained.

The Court's reasoning appears to abrogate the doctrine that un-Mirandized questioning creates a presumption of coercion that renders a confession involuntary. It now seems there are at least two categories of involuntary confessions: the first category results from undue physical or psychological coercion; the second from a technical *Miranda* omission. The former requires suppression of physical evidence derived from the confession; the latter does not.

Patane might be viewed as the other side of *New York v. Harris*, 495 U.S. 14 (1990). In *Harris*, with a majority opinion written by Justice Byron White, the Court declined to suppress a confession that had been taken at a police station after the police, acting without a warrant, arrested the defendant in his home in violation of *Payton v. New York*, 445 U.S. 573 (1980).[11] In doing so, the Court applied the attenuation exception to the exclusionary rule, breaking the poisonous-tree connection between a Fourth Amendment search and seizure violation and the purported mandate to exclude a derivative confession. The distance of time and place between the search and seizure violation and a later confession vitiated any benefit that would have been obtained by suppressing the confession. *Harris* broke the connection between a search and seizure violation and a subsequent confession; *Patane* broke the connection between a confession taken in violation of *Miranda* and a subsequent search and seizure.

The majority opinion in *Patane*, written by Justice Clarence Thomas, was perhaps the Court's most far-reaching limitation of *Miranda*; it was not merely an exception, such as the inevitable discovery, independent source, attenuation, or public safety doctrines—it was a direct curtailment of the exclusionary rule. Substantial amounts of evidence will now be admissible in federal courts that otherwise would not have been. However, the vehement dissent of Justices Souter, Stevens, and Ginsburg forecasts that the issue is not yet settled. The dissenters viewed the majority ruling as an attack on *Miranda*, and their argument

---

11. See Chapter Seven.

reiterates the position that *Miranda* is more important than the admission of a voluntary confession to a crime. The dissent stated:

> *Miranda* rested on insight into the inherently coercive character of custodial interrogation and the inherently difficult exercise of assessing the voluntariness of any confession resulting from it. Unless the police give the prescribed warnings meant to counter the coercive atmosphere, a custodial confession is inadmissible, there being no need for the previous time-consuming and difficult enquiry into voluntariness.

The absolute attachment of the dissenters to *Miranda* and the exclusionary rule prevented them from following the traditional practice of common law, to wit: review the facts of a case, follow precedents when the facts are the same, but distinguish cases when the facts are different. In *Miranda*, the Court dealt with the inherently coercive atmosphere of a long interrogation in the backroom of a police station; *Patane* involved short-lived on-the-scene questions for the purpose of retrieving the defendant's gun. The facts of these cases were very different. Rather than a submission to coercion, the defendant's decision to tell the police where the gun was hidden and to give them permission to retrieve it was a rational choice made after the police said that they would get a search warrant. *Patane's* consent to search precluded the police from obtaining the warrant and searching the defendant's entire house.

Moreover, the dissenters' argument that the gun should have been suppressed to avoid "the previous time-consuming and difficult enquiry into voluntariness" is rather weak, especially considering all the time consumed by courts while hair-splitting over the gamut of issues created by *Miranda*.

The majority chose to restrict the reach of *Miranda*; however, the ruling will have only limited effect. Each time the Supreme Court has placed limitations on the exclusionary rule, some state courts have rebelled and turned to state Constitutionalism to decide similar cases differently. Since most criminal cases are under state jurisdiction, state courts are suppressing thousands of voluntary confessions and evidence derived from them. Furthermore, in both the federal and state systems, *Miranda* and absolute right to counsel rules are still deterring many guilty suspects from giving statements or confessions and preventing law enforcement from solving serious crimes.

Chapter Fourteen

Equal Protection of the Laws

When a crime is committed, but the exclusionary rule frees the criminal from responsibility, the victim of the crime is doubly wronged. In addition to suffering the injury caused by the crime, the victim vicariously pays for the violation of the criminal's rights. The criminal is rewarded; the victim is penalized.

Although it has not yet been held that crime victims are protected by the Fourteenth Amendment's equal protection clause, it may be argued that the suppression of evidence results in the unequal treatment of crime victims. The Fourteenth Amendment mandates:

No State shall make or enforce any law which shall abridge the privileges and immunities of citizens of the United States ... nor deny to any person within its jurisdiction the equal protection of the laws.

The Amendment was primarily designed to prohibit unequal treatment of persons because of their race, ethnicity, or religion, but it has also been applied to persons in other categories.

After the passage of the Fourteenth Amendment, the privileges and immunities of citizens were enunciated in the Civil Rights Act of 1866, which provided in part:

That there shall be no discrimination in civil rights or immunities ... on account of race ... but the inhabitants of **every race** ... shall have the same right to make and enforce contracts, to sue, be parties, and **give evidence ... and to full and equal benefit of all laws and proceedings for the security of person and property** ... [emphasis added].

The equal protection clause has been summarized to mean that the government must treat all persons who are similarly situated alike.[1] Two victims of similar crimes with similar evidence should be treated alike, and they should have the "full and equal benefit of all laws and proceedings for the security of

---

1. *Brown v. Board of Education*, 347 U.S. 483 (1954).

person and property." They should not be treated differently and lose their right to security because the police officer in one case "blundered" and the police officer in the other case did not.

Since the nineteenth century the general authority to commence criminal prosecutions has been vested with district attorneys rather than with private citizens, but the common law right of private citizens to file criminal complaints has not been abrogated. The position of district attorney was instituted to bring professionalism, objectivity, and judiciousness to the process, and they have been given broad discretion regarding which crimes to pursue and what strategies to employ. Although they may decline to prosecute some potential defendants while vigorously prosecuting others, the foundation of their authority is to represent crime victims. While it is true that they represent the *People*, they must attain justice for crime victims so that crime victims or their families do not resort to private vengeance.

The concept that district attorneys, in addition to representing the interests of the *People*, also represent the interests of the crime victim has gained recognition and support. The National Organization for Victim Assistance and many local organizations have been instrumental in the passage of legislation to aid crime victims, such as the Crime Victims' Rights Act of 2004, which gives victims and their families the right to be heard.[2] As Professor William Pizzi has noted:

> Criminal cases are often multi-sided, and, in a game that is no longer zero-sum, a macho exclusionary rule that demands that reliable evidence be suppressed without any consideration of the seriousness of the crime becomes very difficult to defend.
>
> In short, our conceptualization of criminal cases has shifted considerably since *Mapp* was decided. In 1961, there was no National Organization for Victim Assistance. . . One can be certain today that there would be strong opposition from victims' rights organizations to *Mapp's* deterrence-based exclusionary rule that has no room in its calculus for factors such as the degree of the violation, the good faith of the officer, or the seriousness of the crime.[3]

Without a functioning system of criminal justice in which victims receive some level of satisfaction, society will revert to a state of constant vendetta. In fact, in many areas of the country, in certain stratums of society, gangs and street

---

2. Title I of the Justice for All Act of 2004, Publ. L. No. 108-405, 118 Stat. 2260.

3. William Pizzi, "The Need to Overrule Mapp v. Ohio." *U. of Colorado Law Legal Studies Research*, (July 2011).

violence thrive because individuals do not believe the criminal justice system will protect them or effectively enforce the laws on their behalf. The growing "don't snitch" phenomenon stems from the system's failure.[4]

When courts suppress otherwise truthful and relevant evidence, district attorneys are frustrated and crime victims are deprived of their right to obtain justice. Despite the purported benefit of the rule, crime victims generally do not understand or appreciate the claim that it is necessary to abrogate their right to justice in order to deter police from committing constitutional violations in the future.

Ultimately, those most victimized by the exclusionary rule are the people attacked, raped, or murdered by criminals who previously avoided imprisonment because of the suppression of evidence. Violent crimes committed by first-time offenders are the exception, not the norm, and persons arrested for serious violent crimes usually have long criminal histories. Recidivism prospers, not only because of the propensity of the offenders, but also because technicalities send many offenders back to the streets without any meaningful intervention, with shortened sentences or acquittals.

The proponents of the rule offer a benefit versus cost analysis in the abstract for its justification: they posit that for some inchoate deterrence against future police misconduct, it is worth immunizing criminals today and disregarding the rights of their victims. But justice cannot be abstract; it cannot be dehumanized. The effects on individual crime victims and their families must be calculated into the equation.

The Murder of Jessica Lunsford

An example of the human costs of the exclusionary rule occurred in the Florida trial of 47-year-old John Evander Couey, who was convicted of the murder of nine-year-old Jessica Lunsford, the girl for whom "Jessica's Law" was named. Although Couey was eventually convicted by a jury, obstacles created by the rule almost prevented the conviction.

On February 24, 2005, in Tampa, Florida, Jessica went to bed in her family home, where she lived with her parents and grandparents. The next morning, the family woke and found her missing from her bed. A full-scale search was undertaken to find the missing girl with newspapers and television used to publicize her photograph. A check of known sex offenders living in the area

---

4. Andrew Karman, *New York Murder Mystery* (New York: New York University Press, 2000).

disclosed that Couey, a registered sex offender, was not living at his registered address, but instead was living in a trailer home across the street from Jessica's house. Couey had a long arrest record, including a previous conviction for a sex crime against a child for which he served five years in prison.

The police located Couey in Savannah, Georgia, and took him into custody for violating the terms of his sex offender registration by leaving Florida without notifying authorities.

On March 18, 2005, police began a two-hour video-recorded interrogation of Couey. Detectives advised him of his Miranda rights. He waived his right to remain silent and agreed to speak with them. At first, he said he knew nothing about Jessica's disappearance. When he was asked to take a lie-detector test, he said he wanted a lawyer. The detectives, however, ignored his request, attributing it to his concern about the lie-detector test, and continued the interrogation. As the police explained later, they believed a chance existed that Jessica was still alive and that Couey knew where she was located. They felt Couey was on the verge of opening up and if they stopped the questioning for Couey to get a lawyer, they would lose the chance to learn of Jessica's whereabouts.

Under further questioning, Couey admitted that he kidnapped and raped Jessica, kept her locked in a closet for three days, then buried her alive. He said, "I dug a hole and put her in it, buried her. I pushed . . . I put her in plastic baggies. She was alive. I buried her alive." He explained that about 3:00 a.m. on the morning of the kidnapping, he simply entered Jessica's house and took her. He said, "I got high on drugs. I went over there and took her out of her house. I walked back into her room . . . I just told her to come with me and be quiet . . . I sexually assaulted her . . . I went out there one night and dug a hole and put her in it and buried her . . . She was still alive. I buried her alive, she suffered. I don't know why I did it."

After midnight on March 19, 2005, based on Couey's information, the police found Jessica's body buried in a shallow grave in Couey's backyard. They found her body in a kneeling position. She was clutching a stuffed animal, her hands tied with speaker wire, and her fingers poking through the garbage bags in which she was buried alive. She had been raped before she died of suffocation.

All of the physical evidence in the case indicated that Couey's confession was reliable and truthful. The details he provided before the body was found matched the evidence found in the grave. The body was found buried in his backyard as he said, and a mattress in his trailer home had blood stains that matched Jessica's DNA.

Couey was charged with first-degree murder, sexual battery on a child, kidnapping, and burglary. Before the trial, his attorney moved to suppress the confession because of the violation of Couey's right to counsel. The defense also moved to suppress Jessica's body and the other physical evidence because he claimed that such evidence was the fruit of the poisonous tree of the unlawfully obtained confession.

The district attorney argued that the confession should be admissible under the public safety exception that the Supreme Court had adopted in *New York v. Quarles*, 467 U.S. 649 (1984), but the trial judge, the Honorable Rick Howard, disagreed and suppressed the confession because Couey had asked for an attorney.

Fortunately, the judge declined to suppress the body or the other physical evidence as the fruits of the poisonous tree of the unlawful interrogation. Notwithstanding his exclusion of the confession, he invoked the inevitable discovery exception under *Nix v. Williams*, 467 U.S. 431 (1984), and ruled that the body and the other evidence would have been found even without the confession. If he had not invoked the inevitable discovery exception, a conviction most likely would have been impossible to obtain.

Judge Howard also allowed into evidence a subsequent incriminating statement that Couey allegedly made to a jail guard. The guard said that Couey told him: "I didn't mean to kill her. I never saw myself as someone who could do something like this."

In relative terms, the unrecorded statement to the jail guard had much less indicia of reliability than the videotaped March 18, 2005 confession to the detectives, but it provided corroboration for the physical evidence. Nevertheless, relying on the jail guard's testimony was problematic: the jury had to make a life-and-death decision based on that testimony, without the videotaped confession that contained the clearly pertinent connections to the physical evidence found with Jessica's body.

Couey's conviction alleviated some of the concern over the suppression of his videotaped confession. However, it was only because of the obvious circumstances and the overwhelming evidence that a judicial disaster was avoided. Had the jury been skeptical of the jail guard's testimony and had the physical and circumstantial evidence not been as strong, the suppression of the confession might have led to Couey's acquittal. Had Couey buried the body somewhere else, such as in Georgia where he was apprehended, and had he gotten rid of the mattress, the inevitable discovery exception would have been inapplicable and the case against him would have been lost. Three other people lived in the trailer with Couey. Had the only evidence been the body that was found in the backyard and the mattress, Couey's guilt would be no more probable in a court of law than that of the other three persons.

Suppressing such an essential element of proof as a direct confession should not be taken lightly, and Judge Howard treated the issue with the gravity it deserved. Surely, he was not pleased to suppress the confession. When handing down his decision to suppress the confession, the judge commented: "Such police misconduct is not a mere technicality. A technicality is signing an order in the wrong color ink. This is a material and a profound violation of one of the most bedrock principles of criminal law."[5]

Clearly, Judge Howard accepted the dogma that the right to counsel is always inviolate and applied that dogma to the circumstances presented in the Couey case. His ruling indicates that asking for an attorney trumps all other considerations, no matter what the circumstances. He said that the Sixth Amendment is "one of the most bedrock principles of criminal law." However, while the Sixth Amendment prescribes a defendant's right to assistance of counsel during a criminal trial, it does not, as written, preclude the questioning of suspects during police attempts to rescue hostages or kidnapping victims. The right to counsel explicitly pertains to a trial, not to police investigations and efforts to prevent imminent death or harm.

The Sixth Amendment mandates:

> In all criminal prosecutions, the accused shall enjoy the right to a speedy and public trial . . . to be informed of the nature and cause of the accusation; to be confronted with the witnesses against him; to have compulsory process for obtaining witnesses in his favor; and to have the Assistance of Counsel for his defense.

The framers of the Bill of Rights were not sloppy writers or poor logicians; they were masters. They would not have crafted the Sixth Amendment in a manner that one of its clauses could be applied to the subject matter of another amendment without specific language authorizing such an application. The right to have assistance of counsel did not mean that an attorney had the authority to stop a criminal investigation, especially an investigation into an ongoing situation in which a life might be at risk. Attorneys can advise and aid their clients, but they should not have the power to stop a critical investigation. They should not have the power to grant immunity to their clients. Moreover, a suspect's utterance of the word "lawyer" or some other talismanic word should not automatically nullify evidence or immunize the suspect from his voluntary statements being used against him.

Judge Howard applied a strict standard regarding the request for a lawyer and decided that Couey's videotaped confession had to be suppressed. Other courts have been more flexible in their determinations regarding equivocal re-

---

5. *St. Petersburg Times*, 7/2/2006.

quests for an attorney. Courts have held that the following statements did not require the police to cease questioning:

"Maybe I should talk to a lawyer."[6]

"Do I get to talk to my attorneys?"[7]

"Should I be telling you or should I talk to an attorney?"[8]

"I don't know if I need a lawyer, maybe I should have one, but I don't know if it would do me any good at this point."[9]

"Didn't you tell me I had a right to an attorney?"[10]

"I can't afford a lawyer, but is there any way I can get one?"[11]

It is nonsensical and inexpedient to base important decisions about the admissibility of confessions on the parsing of words and phrases that may or may not have been remembered correctly. The disparity in justice that results from such word games should be unacceptable in our criminal justice system.

The test for the admissibility of a confession should be whether it was given voluntarily. A magic word or phrase here or there may have no relationship whatsoever to the overall voluntary or involuntary nature of an interview or a confession. By far, the best evidence for a judge or jury to determine the voluntariness of a confession would be a videotape of the interview and confession. In the *Couey* case there was a video, and the video should have obviated the need to adhere to artificial rules.

On August 24, 2007, Judge Howard sentenced Couey to death; however, Couey appealed on a list of issues, including the admission of his incriminatory statements to the jail guard and the application of the inevitable discovery doctrine that allowed the admission of evidence from Jessica's body and other physical evidence.

In September 2009, Couey died in prison, which avoided the need to adjudicate his appeals, the possible reversal of his conviction, and a new trial. Notably, in February 2008, Jessica's family filed a lawsuit against the Sheriffs' Department for negligence and failure to expeditiously search for Jessica. The family contends she was alive for several days in Couey's closet after the kidnapping and could have been rescued before he buried her. As occurs in so many cases, the police are criticized after the fact. In this case, they have been criticized by some for continuing to question Couey after he mentioned the

---

6. *Davis v. United States*, 512 U.S. 452 (1994).

7. *Commonwealth v. Malvo*, 63 Va. Cir 22 (2003).

8. *Clark v. Murphy*, 317 F.3d 1038 (9th Cir. 2003).

9. *United States v. Mendoza-Cecelia*, 963 F.2d 1467 (11th Cir. 1992).

10. *Poyner v. Murray*, 964 F.2d 1404 (4th Cir. 1992).

11. *Lord v. Duckworth*, 29 F.3d 1216 (7th Cir. 1994).

word "lawyer" and by others for not conducting the investigation faster and more aggressively.

Whether the lawsuit against the Sheriffs' Department has any merit remains to been seen. Nonetheless, it raises questions about the effect of the exclusionary rule on police investigative procedures. In critical life-and-death situations, the emergency exception to the rule sometimes applies, but it has limitations, and the police cannot be sure that courts will subsequently agree that an emergency existed. Such uncertainty influences police decision making, and sometimes prevents them from acting expeditiously. In the Jessica Lunsford case, the best decision would have been to immediately search all the houses in the proximity of Jessica's house and question individuals in the area. If the police had done so, they might have saved Jessica's life. However, ever-present exclusionary rule considerations most probably restrained them.

Eliminating the exclusionary rule for such life-and-death situations would increase police options and lift unreasonable restraints on their actions. Every day children are reported missing. When the missing child is under ten years old, the standard police procedure in most jurisdictions is to conduct an immediate and extensive investigation and search in the area of the child's residence or where the child was last seen, including private premises within the designated search area. This is an accepted and necessary police function, and part of the process is questioning witnesses and suspects. Missing children who might be the victims of criminal conduct deserve equal protection to children who might simply be lost or accident victims. Both sets of children should have the benefit of the full police efforts to find them, and the police should not be unnaturally restrained because a crime might have been committed.

Chapter Fifteen

Arguments For and Against

Those who support the exclusionary rule focus on four arguments. They contend that (1) admitting unlawfully obtained evidence violates due process of law, (2) admitting unlawfully obtained evidence taints the court's integrity, (3) police have adequately adjusted to the rule and law enforcement's effectiveness has not been hampered, and (4) suppressing unlawfully obtained evidence in a current case deters police from violating the rights of other citizens in the future.[1]

1. Due Process

Defenders of the exclusionary rule, including Professors Peter Arenella and Yale Kamisar,[2] believe that it is necessary to suppress tainted evidence, such as an un-Mirandized confession, to comply with the requirements of due process. They argue that it is illegal to convict a factually guilty defendant on the basis of evidence the government obtained unlawfully. However, the use of so-called tainted evidence and due process of law are not mutually exclusive. Due process of law applies to every legal process in which a person's life, liberty, or property is at stake, yet the exclusionary rule only applies in criminal trials. Evidence that otherwise would be excludable from a criminal trial is utilized in civil lawsuits (even those brought by the government), forfeiture proceedings, tax suits, immigration hearings, administrative hearings, family courts, child welfare proceedings, and probation and parole hearings,[3] and the use of such evidence

---

1. Yale Kamisar, "In Defense of the Search and Seizure Exclusionary Rule," *Harvard Journal of Law & Public Policy*, vol. 26, issue 1, Winter 2003; Stephen J. Schulhofer, "Bashing Miranda Is Unjustified—and Harmful," *Harvard Journal of Law & Public Policy*, vol. 20, issue 2, Winter 1997.

2. Peter Arenella, *Rethinking the Functions of Criminal Procedure*, 72 Geo. L.J. 185 (1983); Kamisar, *supra*, note one.

3. *United States. v. Calandra*, 414 U.S. 338 (1974); *INS v. Lopez-Mendoza*, 468 U.S. 1032 (1984); *Pennsylvania Board of Probation and Parole v. Scott*, 524 U.S. 357 (1998); *U.S. v. Janis*, 429 U.S. 874 (1976).

does not violate the due process clause as it pertains to these important adjudication venues. To argue that due process of law is different in a criminal case because criminal case are more serious than civil cases defies the facts. Surely, deportation from the United States, removal of a child from a parent's custody, or an adverse monetary judgment that wipes out a person's assets and life savings are sanctions as serious as or more so than a fine, probation, or a year in jail, which constitute the majority of criminal sanctions. Due process of law encompasses more than criminal matters. For the professors who defend the rule to be consistent, they would have to argue that the rule should be applied to all legal proceedings, but consistency is not the hallmark of their arguments. Reading between the lines of their opinions, it is clear that their arguments are imbued with a social agenda. They view the criminal justice system as more than a vehicle for ascertaining guilt or innocence; they believe it should be used for their social policy purposes, e.g., protecting the poor from government action, or penalizing oppressive police officers. Professor Kamisar wrote, "to the extent that the Constitution and statutory law entitles the wealthy and educated to 'beat the rap,' if that's what you want to call it, why shouldn't all defendants be given a like opportunity."[4] To the contrary, why should the wealthy and educated have an opportunity to beat the rap? Due process does not require an escape hatch or a fair chance for a defendant to outmaneuver the government as though a criminal case were a sporting event.

Professor Arenella has written, "Our criminal justice system has deliberately created a discrepancy between perceived factual guilt and legal guilt to promote policies other than conviction of the factually guilty. Thus, our system should not tolerate the conviction of a defendant who is either factually or legally innocent."[5] To put it another way, the professor might have written, our system should tolerate the acquittal of factually guilty defendants because of police errors. The due process clause does not require whole-scale acquittals on the basis of police errors that inevitably occur and cannot be eliminated without stripping the police of their investigative functions.

While the *Mapp* and *Miranda* exclusionary rules are generally considered part of the due process revolution, they do not contribute to the goals of due process. Assuming the purpose of a trial is to fairly ascertain the facts and the truth of a matter in issue, the exclusionary rule is diametrically opposed to that purpose. The rule puts jurors in a difficult quandary, as they are asked to make decisions without all the facts. They are asked to determine the truth,

---

4. Yale Kamisar, *Has the Court Left the Attorney General Behind?* 54 Ky. L.J. 464 (1966).

5. Peter Arenella, *Reforming the Federal Grand Jury and the State Preliminary Hearing to Prevent Conviction without Adjudication*, 78 Mich. L. Rev. 463 (1980).

but are denied access to facts known by others in the courtroom, including the judge, the prosecutor, police, defense attorneys, and the defendants. They are asked to solve a puzzle without all the pieces.

Such a regime is not required by the Constitution, which provides other means of enforcing the requirements of due process of law. The Fifth Amendment proclaimed the rights of persons accused of and prosecuted for crimes. It included the rights against compulsory self-incrimination, double jeopardy, and the cornerstone right not to be deprived of life, liberty, or property without due process of law:

> No person shall be held to answer for a capital, or otherwise infamous crime, unless on presentment or indictment of a Grand Jury, except in cases arising in the land or naval forces, or in the Militia, when in actual service in time of War or public danger; nor shall any person be subject for the same offence to be twice put in jeopardy of life or limb; nor shall be compelled in any criminal case to be a witness against himself, nor be deprived of life, liberty, or property, without due process of law; nor shall private property be taken for public use, without just compensation.

The due process clause encompasses the rights enumerated in other Amendments, particularly, the Sixth Amendment rights to a speedy and public trial, to assistance of counsel, to confront accusers, to call witnesses, and to other common law rights.

In 1868, the Fourteenth Amendment applied the due process clause to the States:

> Section 1. All persons born or naturalized in the United States and subject to the jurisdiction thereof, are citizens of the United States and of the State wherein they reside. No State shall make or enforce any law which shall abridge the privileges and immunities of citizens of the United States; nor shall any State deprive any person of life, liberty, or property, without due process of law; nor deny to any person within its jurisdiction the equal protection of the laws.

In addition to the Fifth and Fourteenth Amendments, all state constitutions have due process of law provisions. Due process procedural rights refer to safeguards that are deemed "implicit in the concept of ordered liberty" and "are so rooted in the traditions and conscience of our people as to be ranked as fundamental."[6] These rights encompass not only rights enunciated in constitu-

---

6. *Palko v. Connecticut*, 302 U.S. 319 (1937).

tions, but also traditional rights dating from before the constitution, such as the presumption of innocence and the proof beyond a reasonable doubt standard for a criminal conviction.[7] Also, defendants should have notice of the charges and should be safe from *ex post facto* laws. They should not be convicted on unsupported allegations. Evidence should be reliable, and judgments should not result from fraud or deception.

The right to counsel is essential to implement all of the above rights. This was recognized at the beginning of the defendants' rights revolution in *Powell v. Alabama*, 287 U.S. 45 (1932), the infamous Scottsboro Boys case, in which nine African-American teenage defendants, facing the death penalty, were convicted of rape within days of their arrests. During their pseudo trials, they were not assigned competent counsel to represent them. The Supreme Court reversed the convictions, ruling that competent counsel was required in death penalty cases:

> The right to be heard would be, in many cases, of little avail if it did not comprehend the right to be heard by counsel. Even the intelligent and educated layman has small and sometimes no skill in the science of law. If charged with crimes, he is incapable, generally of determining for himself whether the indictment is good or bad. He is unfamiliar with the rules of evidence. Left without the aid of counsel he may be put on trial without a proper charge, and convicted upon incompetent evidence, or evidence irrelevant to the issue or otherwise inadmissible. He lacks both the skill and knowledge adequately to prepare his defense.

Thirty years later, in *Gideon v. Wainwright*, 372 U.S. 335 (1963), the Court extended the right to counsel for indigent defendants to non-capital cases. In *Gideon*, the defendant was tried in Florida for breaking and entering to commit a crime. The trial judge rejected his request for an assigned attorney, and the defendant was convicted and sentenced to five years in prison. Reversing the conviction, the Supreme Court stated, "Lawyers in criminal courts are necessities, not luxuries."

Clearly, most defendants require attorneys to competently protect their constitutional rights. When necessary, an attorney can press the court for a speedy trial, challenge a court's jurisdiction, scrutinize indictments and other charging documents for validity and sufficiency, question and cross-examine adversarial witness, and prepare and present favorable witnesses and evidence. When

---

7. *In Re Winship*, 397 U.S. 358 (1970); *Commonwealth v. Webster*, 59 Mass. 295 (1850).

necessary, an attorney can appeal an improper court ruling or jury verdict. Attorneys are essential for the application of proper evidence law. In many cases, attorneys have exposed false confessions and faulty identifications, and by doing so, they have helped protect defendants' rights to a fair trial and due process of law, and they have helped the search for truth. Without an attorney, nearly all defendants would be unable to accomplish the above tasks.

False confessions and incorrect eyewitness identifications are two of the leading causes of wrongful convictions. To guard against these, involuntary confessions are inadmissible under the theory that an involuntary or coerced confession has a substantial probability of being false,[8] and to error on the side of caution, involuntary confessions are kept out of evidence even though they might be truthful. To reduce the likelihood of an identification of the wrong person, overly suggestive police practices during lineups or photograph displays will preclude the admission of a resulting identification.[9] When judges exclude such faulty evidence, they are not invoking the procedural exclusionary rules of *Mapp* or *Miranda*, they are invoking substantive evidentiary rules to protect due process of law in accordance with their duties as gatekeepers—keeping out false, unreliable, and incompetent evidence. However, when judges—because of technical, procedural violations—keep out reliable physical evidence or truthful voluntary confessions, they are not applying substantive evidence law, but are undermining the proper operation of law.

Our process for unearthing truth is sometimes an onerous process and can create difficulties for witnesses. We accept the difficulties in exchange for the truth-finding value of the process, but to exclude reliable evidence is inconsistent with the search for truth. Let the evidence in, and then challenge its accuracy and truthfulness.

Peter Neufeld is a prominent defense attorney (well known for his part in obtaining O.J. Simpson's acquittal) and co-founder of the Cardozo Innocence Project. While speaking of the use of DNA to free innocent prisoners, he noted, "What's happening with the expansion of the innocence project is the emergence of a new civil rights movement ... primarily concerned with making the criminal justice system more about its truth-seeking function, more scientific, and ultimately, more just."[10]

No one should argue with his premise that the criminal justice system should protect and fortify its truth-seeking function. DNA has been admitted into ev-

---

8. *Brown v. Mississippi*, 297 U.S. 278 (1936).

9. *United States v. Wade*, 388 U.S. 218 (1967).

10. Tresa Baldas, *Front Page*, Vol. 26, No. 53, pg.1.

idence to counteract eyewitness identifications and confessions. It has overturned convictions and freed convicts from death row. If, in some odd circumstance, a search conducted in violation of the constitutional uncovered evidence containing DNA evidence that would prove a defendant's innocence, no one would argue that such a violation should keep out the DNA evidence. The converse is not true; defense attorneys would argue that unconstitutionally obtained DNA that incriminates their client must be suppressed.

When DNA evidence is admitted, defense attorneys will attack its reliability by showing that it was improperly collected, processed, preserved, or interpreted. This is a legitimate and proper function of the adversary system; to the contrary, keeping out reliable evidence that may provide a truthful answer to an important question is not. Depriving the victim and the authorities of the use of incriminating evidence makes no more sense than depriving a defendant of DNA that proves innocence.

2. Integrity of the System

The argument that admitting unlawfully obtained evidence taints the court's integrity ignores the incontrovertible fact that such evidence enters the system all the time. Evidence, otherwise excludable, is used in criminal trials when it was obtained in violation of a third party's rights, but not in violation of the defendant's rights.[11] Physical evidence obtained in violation of the Fourth Amendment may be used to impeach the credibility of a defendant who testifies and denies possession of the evidence.[12] Moreover, a defendant's confession, otherwise inadmissible because of a *Miranda* or right to counsel violation, may be admitted to impeach his credibility when he takes the witness stand and tells an inconsistent story.[13]

Cases where the defendant is illegally arrested, unlawfully extradited, or even kidnapped and brought to an American court, nevertheless, proceed.[14] As the Court recounted in *Frisbee v. Collins*, 342 U.S. 519 (1952):

> This Court has never departed from the rule … that the power of a court
> to try a person for a crime is not impaired by the fact that he had been

---

11. *Rakas v. Illinois*, 439 U.S. 128 (1978).

12. *United States. v. Havens*, 446 U.S. 620 (1980).

13. *Harris v. New York*, 401 U.S. 222 (1971); *Oregon v. Hass*, 420 U.S. 714 (1975); *Kansas v. Ventris*, 129 S.Ct. 1841 (2009).

14. *Ker v. Illinois*, 119. U.S. 436 (1886); *Frisbee v. Collins*, 342 U.S. 519 (1952); *United States v. Verdugo-Urquidez*, 494 U.S. 259 (1990); *United States v. Alvarez-Machain*, 504 U.S. 655 (1992).

brought within the court's jurisdiction by reason of forcible compulsion.... There is nothing in the Constitution that requires a court to permit a guilty person rightfully convicted to escape justice because he was brought to trial against his will.

Cases wherein government agents kidnap a defendant to bring him before the court do not result in the dismissal of charges against the defendant. In other words, the body of the defendant is not excluded from the jurisdiction of the court. To be consistent, if the body of the defendant apprehended as the result of an illegal procedure is not excluded, the body of the defendant's victim that was found illegally should not be excluded.

Those advocating the integrity of the system argument often quote Justice Clark in *Mapp v. Ohio, supra,* in which he answered Cardozo's complaint:

The criminal goes free, if he must, but it is the law that sets him free. Nothing can destroy a government more quickly than its failure to observe its own laws, or worse, its disregard of the charter of its own existence.[15]

However, failures to observe the law by government agents constantly occur, and to address Justice Clark's contention, the preclusion of government action would need to be vastly expanded beyond suppression of evidence at criminal trials. Illegal arrest cases would need to be dismissed outright, even though other evidence against the defendant existed. In cases in which a government agent acted illegally, grand juries could not issue indictments, immigration authorities could not deport illegal aliens, and probation and parole boards could not revoke probation or parole. Such remedies have not been seriously contemplated.

The proper government response to illegal actions by its agents is to prosecute or discipline the offender and to compensate the victim. Suppressing evidence neither furthers the prosecution of errant government agents nor provides a just remedy to the person whose rights were violated. Ignoring real evidence, subverting the truth-finding process, and precluding the proper and fitting imposition of justice are what disregard "the charter of our government's existence."

It is not the admission of unlawfully obtained evidence, but the suppression of reliable evidence that taints the system and its participants. In addition to the police officers who testify, district attorneys and defense counsels are also affected, and sometimes infected, by the rule.

---

15. 367 U.S. 643 (1961).

District Attorneys

District attorneys have the difficult and crucial responsibility of presenting truthful and reliable evidence in court to prove the crime charged, and they must strategize how to do so with evidence that may run afoul of the exclusionary rule. Never sure that their evidence will be admissible, they are too often forced to make unpalatable deals with accomplices to obtain their testimony. In exchange for the accomplice testimony, they grant these criminals reduced sentences or dismiss the charges. A notorious instance of such deal making occurred when the United States Attorney for the Southern District of New York granted Sammy "The Bull" Gravano immunity for 19 murders he committed. This immunity was granted in exchange for testimony against John Gotti, the Mafia figure. Had the U.S. Attorney been sure that all the evidence he possessed would have been admissible, he very well may have declined to make the deal with Gravano. However, a district attorney does not know beforehand whether the evidence will be admissible, and if he does succeed in getting it into evidence, it may be suppressed afterwards on appeal. Prosecutors only get one bite of the apple. If they lose a trial because evidence is suppressed, they do not get another chance. After an acquittal, a district attorney cannot appeal.[16] On the other hand, defendants can appeal their convictions on the grounds of an erroneous evidentiary ruling. If they win, a new trial will be granted unless the error was deemed harmless. Prosecutors know that at the new trials they will have to proceed without the suppressed evidence, and they face all the difficulties of trying a case years after the fact. Such considerations often force district attorneys to reduce or dismiss charges for persons who should be held accountable for their crimes.

During investigations, district attorneys, in conjunction with law enforcement officers, will utilize confidential informants, not to testify about past crimes, but to "participate" in ongoing crimes. Most often, these confidential informants are from the jailhouse or under pending criminal charges themselves, and they cooperate with the authorities in exchange for a waiver of their charges or leniency. Once committed to their bargain, they will do and say whatever is necessary to get the results the prosecution needs. Cases built on the word of such witnesses are built on quicksand. How many unwarranted convictions have resulted from the testimony of bought-and-paid-for informants is unknown, but, undoubtedly, many thousands of injustices have resulted from their use. Unfortunately, district attorneys, always wary of the exclusionary rule, are forced to resort to the use of such informers.

---

16. *Benton v. Maryland*, 395 U.S. 784 (1969).

Another critical problem for district attorneys occurs when they are not quite sure that their police officer witnesses have testified truthfully about search and seizure, interrogation, or other exclusionary rule issues. Without definite proof that an officer committed perjury, district attorneys generally must proceed with the presentation of their case even though they have doubts about its veracity. Whatever the outcome of these cases, the moral underpinnings of the justice system are weakened by such circumstances.

Defense Attorneys

Defense attorneys have an indispensable obligation to challenge the accuracy of the evidence offered against their clients or to find exculpatory evidence. By examining the accuracy and truthfulness of the evidence offered by the prosecution, and by cross-examining witnesses to uncover bias, inaccurate perceptions, mistakes, or outright deceit, defense attorneys contribute to a fair trial, protect the integrity of the system, and sometimes prevent miscarriages of justice. However, many defense attorneys are tainted by their reliance on the rule, which undermines and distorts their rightful purpose of finding the truth. Many neglect their obligations and, instead, rely on the suppression of evidence as their best defense. When they succeed, they distort trials, subvert the integrity of the system, and sometimes cause miscarriages of justice.

Defense attorneys cross a line when they go beyond challenging prosecution evidence or presenting truthful exculpatory evidence on behalf of their client. Many are not averse to manipulating the facts either to achieve a technical win or to counteract incriminating evidence. They say that if the police can lie, they can counteract those lies with other lies. Some hold such a rabid hatred for the police that they believe there is justification for engaging in unscrupulous activities.

Although defense attorneys are not foolish enough to openly and directly advise their clients or witnesses to lie, they have ways of steering the testimony. It is standard practice for attorneys not to directly ask a client if they are guilty, but to discuss the evidence and then advise them as to what type of testimony would help and what type would hurt them. Such conduct was dramatized in the famous 1959 classic motion picture, *Anatomy of a Murder*, staring James Stewart as the defense lawyer and Ben Gazzara as the defendant charged with murder for killing a man who had raped his wife. When Stewart interviewed Gazzara in the jail to learn about the case and to determine whether any defense was possible, he explained to Gazzara what kind of testimony would be needed to establish a defense of temporary insanity. He then told Gazzara that he would come back tomorrow and that Gazzara should think about what happened and what had been going through his mind. The next day, of course, Gazzara narrated the events in a manner that fit the exact requirements that would be needed to establish the temporary insanity defense.

For a more common example, if a search and seizure issue depends on whether the client voluntarily consented to a police search of his car, an attorney might advise his client that it might be better for him to testify that the officer had told him that he would be arrested and kept in jail over the weekend if he did not consent to the search. To protect himself, the attorney would add the caveat that the client should only testify in such manner if it was true. The attorney might also advise the client that it would be extremely helpful if the client's companions corroborated such testimony. Out of the attorney's presence, the client and the companions might agree to provide such testimony even though it is not exactly the truth. For the attorney, the truth would not matter. All that would matter is that the witnesses stick to the story, which would help the attorney obtain suppression of any evidence found in the car. Winning a suppression motion on less than truthful testimony can be habit forming, and once an attorney compromises on the veritable values, the path to additional forms of unscrupulous conduct is opened. Moreover, one attorney's unscrupulous behavior encourages others, and together, they contaminate the justice system.

3. Law Enforcement Effectiveness

Another argument put forth by the defenders of the rule is that the exclusionary rule does not detract from law enforcement effectiveness. Professor Stephen Schulhofer admits that crime clearance rates "collapsed in the 1960s," but he maintains that the cause for the collapse was for reasons other than *Miranda* and the exclusionary rule.[17] He points out that although clearance rates declined, the actual number of cases cleared remained the same. This occurred because police personnel resources did not increase commensurately with the increasing crime, thus the police did not have the capacity to handle the additional crimes and clearance rates suffered. Professor Schulhofer's argument poses a chicken-before-the-egg conundrum: either crime increased because the police became less efficient or the police became less efficient because crime increased. He ascribes to the latter. However, his argument has been refuted

---

17. Stephen J. Schulhofer, "Bashing Miranda Is Unjustified—and Harmful," *Harvard Journal of Law & Public Policy*, vol. 20, issue 2, Winter 1997.

by subsequent events. Police and overall law enforcement resources have been greatly increased from the 1980s into the twenty-first century and police departments are far more responsive to crime problems than they have ever been; nevertheless, clearance rates for serious crimes have remained at about the same levels as those after the collapse in the 1960s.[18]

The argument that the rule does not detract from police effectiveness and efficiency is also refuted by the exceedingly high levels of criminality in our society. Between 1961 and 1993, the imposition of the rule contributed to a reduction in police clearance rates and a corresponding increase in crime. The subsequent decrease in crime between 1994 and 2007 was not the result of the police effectively living with the rule, but the result of overcompensation for the low clearance rates by increasing arrests and imposing longer prison sentences even for less serious crimes. The reductions from the extremely high crime levels began only after society mobilized against crime in the 1980s. Legislatures passed stricter sentencing laws, more prisons were built, and law enforcement budgets were increased. The United States Congress passed the Sentencing Reform Act of 1984, the Anti-Drug Abuse Act of 1986, and the Violent Crime Control and Law Enforcement Act of 1994. States across the nation passed similar statutes, including three-strikes-and-you're-out laws that mandated life imprisonment for persistent, recidivist criminals. As a result of this enormous expenditure of resources by federal, state, and local governments, by 2007, the imprisoned population of the United States increased to the highest rate in the industrialized world.[19] The only adjustment law enforcement has made to the exclusionary rule has been to compensate for it by making millions of additional arrests and quadrupling the number of persons incarcerated.

A true measure of criminality includes a combination of crime rates, incarceration rates, and recidivism rates. The reduction in the crime rate in the late 1990s was inversely proportional to the number of persons incarcerated in American prisons. Although sending more people to prison has reduced the crime rate, it has not reduced the amount of criminality. The number of persons willing to commit crime is still increasing. As we imprison a greater percentage of people in one generation, the next generation produces others to replace them as active criminals.

Other democratic, industrialized societies produce far fewer criminals. In 2004, the United States averaged 8.9 willful homicides, 39.4 rapes, and 237

---

18. See chart in chapter 12.
19. U.S. Department of Justice, Bureau of Justice Statistics.

robberies per 100,000 persons. England averaged 1.4 homicides, 9.8 rapes, and 116 robberies per 100,000 persons. France averaged 2.4 homicides, 11.3 rapes, and 126.9 robberies. Germany averaged 1.7 homicides, 7.5 rapes, and 71 robberies. Japan averaged 1.4 homicides, 1.3 rapes, and 2.15 robberies. None of these nations, except the United States, employs the exclusionary rule.[20]

With more police officers making ever more arrests and the courts incarcerating the greatest number of people in history, some commentators insist that the system is functioning effectively. They are correct that the quantity of arrests and prosecutions has increased, but the result has been a growing alienation of large segments of the population. Not only prisoners, but their families and associates are alienated, and many of them view law enforcement as the enemy.

Imprisonment deals with the symptoms of the disease, not the causes, and greater levels of imprisonment, year after year, are neither victories, nor a cure for a culture of criminality. The warehousing of so many people in our prisons is not a success story, but a failure of American society that could have been avoided had our criminal justice system focused on truth-seeking and personal responsibility instead of embarking on a mistaken path of creating artificial legalisms and disregarding the essential requirements of justice.

4. Deterrence of Future Constitutional Violations

Justification for the exclusionary rule has rested on the premise that suppression of illegally obtained evidence and any information derived from the evidence would deter law enforcement from committing future constitutional violations. However, advocates for the rule have failed to put forth tangible evidence to support that contention. Most of their arguments are in the negative. They claim that because other remedies are ineffective, suppression must be imposed. Professor Kamisar quotes Justice Traynor's observation in *Cahan v. California*, 282 P.2d 905 (1955):

> Without fear of criminal punishment or other discipline, law enforcement officers ... frankly admit their deliberate, flagrant acts.... It is clearly apparent from their testimony that they casually regard such acts as nothing more than the performance of their ordinary duties for which the City employs and pays them.

---

20. E. Fairchild and H. Dammer, *Comparative Criminal Justice Systems*, 2nd Ed. (Belmont, Ca: Thomson, 2001).

Professor Kamisar seems to rely on the observation in 1955 that police officers back then did not fear any consequences for their illegal conduct of breaking into a defendant's home and installing listening devices without obtaining a warrant.[21] Times have changed. In the twenty-first century, eavesdropping without a warrant is a felony, and lawsuits against police for violations of 42 U.S.C. 1983 and other torts are a burgeoning business. It is inconceivable today that police officers would regularly volunteer in court that they blatantly committed felonies or violated established constitutional rights. Nevertheless, advocates for the rule still believe that the high price society pays—the release of countless guilty criminals—is necessary to protect the constitutional rights of the general public. However, experience has shown that the deterrence theory was based on a false premise. No empirical evidence has been discovered to support the claim that the rule actually deters illegal conduct by law enforcement officers. Balancing the benefit of deterrence against the detriment of freeing guilty criminals has no validity when there is no deterrence, and excluding evidence merely tips the scales to the side of the criminal without any corresponding benefit for the public.[22]

The reasons for the failure of the deterrence theory are plain: Individual police officers suffer no concrete, personal consequences from the exclusion of evidence. They suffer no monetary detriment or administrative penalty when evidence is excluded from a criminal trial. Police agencies measure the performance of their officers in part by how many arrests they make or summonses they issue, and the agencies do not hold them accountable for convictions. As a matter of policy, law-enforcement agencies, to avoid the appearance of improper influence on the process, do not interfere with courtroom testimony. These agencies would be severely criticized if they were found to demand a certain conviction quota from their officers; therefore, they generally do not monitor the relationship between an officer's enforcement actions and his courtroom testimony.

For many committed police officers and police administrators, taking guns and knives off the streets is a valuable end in itself even when the cases result in dismissals. Disrupting open street-level drug dealing by making large numbers of arrests is a practical problem-solving strategy even when most of the cases are dismissed or reduced to petty offenses. When implementing such tactics, exclusionary rule considerations are of secondary concern. Police know

---

21. Yale Kamisar, "In Defense of the Search and Seizure Exclusionary Rule," *Harvard Journal of Law & Public Policy*, vol. 26, issue 1, Winter 2003.

22. Oaks, "Studying the Exclusionary Rule in Search and Seizure" *37 U. Chi. L. Rev. 665*, 667 (1970).

they must continue to uphold their oaths to protect life and property, maintain order on the streets, and suppress crime. They continue to respond to calls for help, enter into dangerous situations, take necessary action, and enforce the laws. They simply do not consider the second-guessing and criticisms by defense attorneys and judges as equivalent to substantive law. They view suppression rules as complex, procedural technicalities with which they cannot always comply while performing their duties.

Some rules are clear: Police know they cannot break into a home without a warrant or other lawful justification; they cannot forcibly obtain confessions, or use excessive force, and during recent decades, these types of violations have been greatly reduced. However, these violations have been reduced not by the exclusionary rule but, rather, by the prospect of prosecutions, lawsuits, and termination of employment.

Less clear are the rules regarding what police can or cannot do when responding to uncertain situations such as prowler calls, domestic violence incidents, street drug dealing, shooting or stabbing incidents, child abuse, or other suspicious conduct. Police across the nation respond to such incidents thousands of times per day, and they have to make quick assessments and judgments. Given the pressures inherent in police work, errors in judgment inevitably occur, but the police must continue to perform their required functions as best they can. The goal of police administrators should be to reduce the number of persons who are unnecessarily or unreasonably searched or arrested, and a priority should be to ensure that people are not searched or arrested based on racially discriminatory practices. Police administrators can best accomplish these goals by good management, constant monitoring, and a strong disciplinary system. Oversight of police should focus on officers who repeatedly conduct unreasonable and unsuccessful searches of individuals. The officers who should be scrutinized and disciplined are those who stop and search innocent persons, not officers who properly arrest guilty persons. Appropriate administrative measures focusing on specific officers who perform incompetently are far more effective deterrents than suppressing evidence.

For borderline cases, the suppression doctrine as a means of deterring police misconduct is completely ineffective because it is unclear. To deter people from particular conduct, the conduct must be clearly defined and fair warning must be given. That is the reason that criminal laws are spelled out in detail. The rules that courts have established for police work are anything but clear; they are blurry, vague, and inconsistent. Mere suspicion, reasonable suspicion, probable cause, reasonable searches, warrant requirements, warrant exceptions, and exigent circumstances are concepts difficult to define and more difficult to apply. Judges have difficulty even with adequate time to study the issues and circumstances, and police are rarely sure of what the courts will decide about admitting or suppressing evidence. With such uncertainty, the suppression doctrine does not work.

Although the rule is an ineffective deterrent to police misconduct, the rule, unfortunately, deters a significant amount of proper and necessary police work. In some instances, the rule has facilitated the commission of individual crimes. Either because of legal barriers or because of police negligence, the rule has hindered the capture and prosecution of numerous criminals who have committed the worst kinds of heinous and atrocious crimes. Although most officers perform their duties to the fullest despite the rule, some less-than-totally-committed officers have used the rule as a convenient excuse to avoid performing their sworn duties, with the result that atrocious crimes have been committed that should have been prevented. When citizens complain and demand actions about crime, these officers can respond by saying that the Constitution, meaning the exclusionary rule, prevents them from taking action.

The infamous Jeffrey Dahmer case may have been an example of police inaction resulting in subsequent crimes. Dahmer was the serial killer who lured young boys to his apartment, then abused, murdered, and cannibalized them. On May 17, 1991, one of the boys, Konerak Sinthasomphone, a 14-year-old Laotian boy, escaped from Dahmer's apartment and ran into the street where two African-American teenagers spotted him as he wandered around in a dazed state, naked and bleeding. The teenagers called the police, and when Dahmer arrived on the scene and began to take the boy back to the apartment, the teenagers tried to protect the boy from him. When the police arrived, the officers spoke to Dahmer and accepted his explanation that the boy was his 19-year-old lover who had drunk too much. The officers, despite the protests of the teenagers, assisted Dahmer in taking the boy back to the apartment. Shortly thereafter, the boy was murdered.

The boy's family sued the police, claiming that they had failed to heed the complaints because the teenagers were black and Dahmer was white. The police defended their actions claiming that the officers did not believe they had sufficient probable cause to take further action. The case was settled for $850,000 without a resolution of the true reason for the lack of police action.

This is an extremely troubling example of police inaction that, in part, may have been caused by the exclusionary rule providing an excuse for less than committed officers to avoid meeting their responsibilities.

During the two months after the Konerak's murder, Dahmer killed four more young men. Then, on July 22, 1991, he drugged and attempted to handcuff another man, Tracey Edwards, but Edwards escaped with the handcuffs dangling from his wrist. He was picked up on the street by two police officers.

Edwards led the police to Dahmer's apartment, and the police entered without a warrant, apparently with Dahmer's consent. The officers noticed grizzly evidence of the previous murders, including a severed human head. They arrested Dahmer, who subsequently was convicted of 15 murders.

How many instances have occurred in which a police failure to take action resulted in dangerous criminals avoiding detection? Were it possible to estimate the number of such instances, it would still be impossible to determine how many of those instances were attributable to less than committed officers using the exclusionary rule as an excuse and how many instances were attributable to fully committed officers making a judgment based on rules that precluded them from taking action. Notwithstanding such difficulties, notorious cases involving figures such as Jeffrey Dahmer and other serial killers provide demonstrable evidence of missed opportunities by police and other authorities to prevent atrocious crimes.

Chapter Sixteen

The Roberts Court

On September 29, 2005, John Roberts replaced the deceased William Rehnquist as Chief Justice of the Supreme Court. Shortly thereafter, in January 2006, Justice Samuel Alito replaced the retiring Justice Sandra Day O'Connor. These replacements did not occasion a dramatic shift to the right, as Roberts and Rehnquist held similar conservative views, while the conservative Alito replaced the moderately conservative O'Connor. The five-to-four divide, with Justices Roberts, Kennedy, Scalia, Thomas, and Alito leaning right and Justices Stevens, Ginsburg, Breyer, and Souter leaning left, stood largely undisturbed. For exclusionary rule issues the Court has maintained its program of further limiting the application of the rule.

In its first major exclusionary rule case, *Hudson v. Michigan*, 547 U.S. 586 (2006), the Roberts' Court addressed the question of whether a violation of the knock-and-announce rule required suppression of evidence. In common law, it had long been accepted that officers must knock and announce their presence and authority before entering a private premise to execute a warrant. The purpose of the requirement was to:

1. Reduce the potential for violent confrontations;
2. Protect individual privacy;
3. Give the occupant time to voluntarily admit the officers.

A predicate to the exclusionary rule question was the question of how long the police would have to wait before forcibly entering a premise if no one responded to the knocking and announcing.

In *Hudson*:

> Police obtained a warrant authorizing a search for drugs and firearms at the home of petitioner Booker Hudson. They discovered both. Large quantities of drugs were found, including crack cocaine rocks in Hudson's pocket. A loaded gun was lodged between the cushion and armrest of the chair in which he was sitting.... When the police arrived to execute the warrant, they announced their presence, but waited only a short time—perhaps 'three to five seconds'... before turning the

knob of the unlocked front door and entered Hudson's home. Hudson moved to suppress all the inculpatory evidence, arguing that the police should have waited more than five seconds before entering and the premature entry violated his Fourth Amendment rights.

The Michigan trial court had suppressed the evidence, holding that the police did not wait long enough after knocking to enter the premises and that a violation of search warrant knock-and-announce requirements mandated the suppression of evidence found during the execution of the warrant.

The Supreme Court, in a five-to-four decision, reversed the Michigan court, and held that the exclusionary rule was inapplicable for this kind of police action. The Supreme Court pointed out that the knock-and-announce rule's purpose "is the protection of life and limb, because the unannounced entry may provoke violence in supposed self-defense by the surprised resident." Other purposes are to protect property and individual dignity. The Court stated, "What the knock-and-announce rule has never protected ... is one's interest in preventing the government from seeing or taking evidence described in a warrant. Since the interests that were violated in this case have nothing to do with the seizure of the evidence, the exclusionary rule is inapplicable." The Court observed that the social costs of excluding relevant incriminating evidence outweigh any deterrent effect the exclusionary rule might provide, and that civil rights lawsuits and improved internal police discipline now provide sufficient deterrents. The Court recognized that it was unrealistic to expect that police officers investigating serious crimes will make no errors, and before penalizing the police through the application of the exclusionary rule, it should be determined whether suppressing the evidence serves a valid and useful purpose.

In *Herring v. United States*, 129 S.Ct. 695 (2009), the Roberts Court again emphasized the theme that suppression should be employed only when it would effectively deter police misconduct. In *Herring*, a police officer arrested the defendant on the basis of a purported outstanding warrant recorded in a police database. Incidental to the arrest, the officer searched the defendant and found illegal amphetamines and a gun. Shortly thereafter, it was determined that the warrant had been rescinded and was no longer in effect, but it had not been removed from the database due to a clerical error. As a matter of course, the defendant's arrest for possession of the drugs and the gun went forward. When the defendant was indicted, he moved to suppress the evidence on the grounds that no probable cause to arrest him had existed and the search therefore violated his Fourth Amendment rights.

In its ruling, the Supreme Court indicated that the search may not necessarily have been unreasonable; however, the government in lower court proceedings had conceded that point. Consequently, the only issue preserved for the Court was whether applying the exclusionary rule in these circumstances would have a deterrent effect on future police misconduct. The Court ruled that it would not—the clerical error that prompted the arrest was the result of isolated negligence and, therefore, any benefit obtained by suppressing the evidence would be marginal or nonexistent and would not outweigh its social costs. Following its precedents in *Franks v. Delaware*, 438 U.S. 154 (1978), *Illinois v. Gates*, 462 U.S. 213 (1983), *United States v. Leon*, 468 U.S. 897 (1984), *Massachusetts v. Sheppard*, 468 U.S. 981 (1984), *Arizona v. Evans*, 514 U.S. 1 (1995), and *Hudson v. Michigan*, 547 U.S. 586 (2006), the Court stated:

> To trigger the exclusionary rule, police conduct must be sufficiently deliberate that exclusion can meaningfully deter it, and sufficiently culpable that such deterrence is worth the price paid by the justice system. As laid out in our cases, the exclusionary rule serves to deter deliberate, reckless, or grossly negligent conduct, or in some circumstances recurring or systemic negligence. The error in this case does not rise to that level.

The Roberts Court also overturned several other court rulings that had suppressed evidence. In *Brigham City, Utah v. Stuart*, 547 U.S. 398 (2006), with Chief Justice Roberts writing the majority opinion, the Court applied the emergency exception and upheld the warrantless entry of police into a private home to handle a domestic fight.

In *Moore v. Virginia*, 128 S.Ct. 1598 (2008), the Supreme Court reversed the Virginia high court's suppression of evidence. In *Moore*, a police officer, rather than issuing a citation as required by Virginia law, arrested the defendant Moore for the misdemeanor of driving with a suspended license. A search incidental to the arrest yielded crack cocaine, and Moore was tried and convicted of drug charges.

Virginia statutory law mandated that driving with a suspended license does not warrant a custodial arrest except in the case of those who fail or refuse to discontinue the violation, those reasonably believed likely to disregard a citation, or those likely to harm themselves or others.[1] Virginia's high court ruled that the arrest was unauthorized under Virginia law; therefore, the search and seizure was unreasonable and violated the Fourth Amendment. Consequently, they suppressed the evidence and reversed Moore's conviction.

The Roberts Court, however, reversed the Virginia court, holding that as long as the police had probable cause to arrest the defendant, the Fourth

---

1. Va. Code Ann. Section 19.2-74.

Amendment was not violated and the exclusionary rule need not be invoked. The Supreme Court explained that linking Fourth Amendment protections to state law would cause the protections to vary between places, and incorporating the nuances of state arrest laws into the Constitution would produce a vague and unpredictable regime: "The constitutional standard would be only as easy to apply as the underlying state law, and state law can be complicated indeed."

Adhering to the bright-line probable cause rule, the Court reiterated the holding of *United States v. Robinson*, 414 U.S. 218 (1973): "A custodial arrest of a suspect based on probable cause is a reasonable intrusion under the Fourth Amendment; that intrusion being lawful, a search incident to the arrest requires no additional justification." Moreover, no matter whether the charges are serious or minor, the officers face the same uncertainties and risks that provide "an adequate basis for treating all custodial arrests alike for purposes of search justification."

The Court noted that Virginia is free to employ an exclusionary rule under the authority of its own constitution, but it has not chosen to do so. The remedies that Virginia has adopted for violations of the citation-only instruction are administrative discipline and/or a tort suit against the officer. It would be illogical for the Supreme Court to invoke its exclusionary rule to enforce an unusual state statute that the state does not see fit to enforce by employing its own prerogative to invoke a state-based exclusionary rule.

Although the Roberts Court has repeatedly emphasized that its Fourth Amendment decisions should provide a consistent regimen for the police to follow, the Court will be unable to meet that standard: Trying to draw fine lines between proper and improper police conduct as a means of refining the exclusionary rule only leads to more confusion. This was recently demonstrated by two decisions involving automobile stops: *Arizona v. Lemon Johnson*, 129 S.Ct. 781, decided January 26, 2009, and *Arizona v. Gant*, 129 S.Ct. 1710, decided April 21, 2009. These cases added further complexity and inconsistency to exclusionary rule jurisprudence without adding any effective deterrence value.

In *Arizona v. Lemon Johnson, supra*, police officers serving in the Arizona gang task force, while patrolling near a Tucson neighborhood associated with the Crips gang, stopped an automobile after learning that its registration had been suspended. The car had three occupants. One officer directed the driver to step out of the car; another officer stayed with the front-seat passenger, who remained in the vehicle throughout the stop; and Officer Maria Treviso questioned Johnson, who was seated in the backseat. Treviso had noticed that as the police approached, Johnson looked back and kept his eyes on the officers. Treviso observed that Johnson was wearing clothing and a bandana consistent with Crips membership, and she also noticed a police scanner in Johnson's jacket pocket.

Treviso testified that she wanted to question Johnson away from the front-seat passenger to gain intelligence about gang activity. She asked him to step out of the car, and he complied. Suspecting that he might have a weapon on him, she patted him down for officer safety and found a gun near his waist.

Johnson was convicted of possession of a weapon by a prohibited possessor, and appealed on the grounds that the gun should have been suppressed. Essentially, he claimed that the officer had no right to pat him down because the traffic stop had evolved into a consensual conversation about his gang affiliation, which was unrelated to the traffic stop, and, therefore, the authority for the frisk had ended, unless additional authority stemmed from a reasonable suspicion that Johnson had engaged in, or was about to engage in, criminal activity.

The Supreme Court disagreed and upheld the frisk, stating:

> A lawful roadside stop begins when a vehicle is pulled over for investigation of a traffic violation. The temporary seizure of driver and passengers ordinarily continues, and remains reasonable, for the duration of the stop. Normally, the stop ends when the police have no further need to control the scene, and inform the driver and passengers they are free to leave.... An officer's inquiries into matters unrelated to the justification for the traffic stop, this Court has made plain, do not convert the encounter into something other than a lawful seizure, so long as those inquiries do not measurably extend the duration of the stop.

Lemon Johnson continues the line of cases from *Terry v. Ohio*, 392 U.S. 1 (1968), in which the Court has sided with the interests of officer safety rather than individual privacy. Significantly, the majority decision was written by Justice Ruth Bader Ginsburg, long noted for her support of defendant's rights and privacy protections. Justice Ginsburg's positioning, here in favor of a law-enforcement interest, marks an interesting a shift in the jurisprudence of the Court.

In *Arizona v. Gant, supra*, the Roberts Court broke the string of cases in which it had reversed lower court rulings that had suppressed evidence. *Gant* surprised court watchers as it marked another interesting shift in the Court's jurisprudence in an unexpected direction. Justices Scalia and Thomas, who have usually sided with law enforcement in search and seizure cases, joined with four liberal members of the Court to suppress a gun retrieved from a vehicle, and Justice Breyer who usually sided with defense counsel in search and seizure cases voted with the conservative members in dissent. The result was an unusually structured five-to-four decision to suppress a gun and drugs that police found while searching an automobile.

In *Gant*, acting on an anonymous tip that a residence was being used to sell drugs, Tucson police officers knocked on the front door and asked to speak to the owner. Gant answered the door and, after identifying himself, stated that the owner would return later. The officers left the residence and conducted a records check, which revealed that Gant's driver's license had been suspended and an outstanding warrant for his arrest existed.

When the officers returned to the residence that evening, they found a man at the back of the house and a woman seated in a car in front of the house. They arrested the man for providing a false name, and the woman for possession of drug paraphernalia. After the arrests, they observed Gant driving his car. They saw him park the car at the end of the driveway, get out, and shut the door. The officer's met Gant ten to twelve feet from the car and arrested him on the warrant and for driving with a suspended license. They handcuffed Gant and locked him in the backseat of their patrol vehicle, searched his car, and found a gun and a bag of cocaine in the pocket of a jacket on the backseat.

Gant's motion to suppress the evidence was denied, and he was convicted of drug crimes. The Supreme Court, however, reversed the decision and ruled that the evidence should have been suppressed. In doing so, the Court distinguished the precedent set in *New York v. Belton*, 453 U.S. 454 (1981), which held that when the police have made a lawful arrest of the occupant of an automobile, they categorically may search the passenger compartment of that automobile. However, since Gant had been secured away from the car and the officer-safety rationale for *Belton* was to protect against a defendant reaching into the vehicle to obtain a weapon or destroy evidence, the Court determined that *Belton* did not apply. Although the decision has an internal logic consistent with some exclusionary rule precedents, it creates conflicts with other precedents. *Gant* will not lead to consistent rules for police to follow nor will it deter improper police conduct. As a practical matter, it will create an incentive for police to keep suspect drivers and passengers of stopped vehicles near the vehicle rather than removing them to a secure location. It will be a rare situation in which they are not able to do so, and therefore the unintended consequence of *Gant* will be to endanger officers, suspects, and the public.

In situations in which an officer keeps a suspect near the stopped vehicle, *Gant* raises the question of whether the officer should have removed and secured the suspect. Will courts begin to examine the subjective motivations of officers? Furthermore, with only reasonable suspicion, officers generally may not handcuff a suspect; whereas, with probable cause, they may. Consequently, *Gant* may produce the inverse result that an officer acting on sufficient evidence for an arrest may be precluded from searching a suspect's vehicle, while an officer acting on less than sufficient evidence for an arrest may be allowed to search a suspect's vehicle in accordance with *Michigan v. Long*, 463 U.S. 1032 (1983).

In *Long*, the Supreme Court held that a police officer was justified in searching the passenger compartment of a vehicle as a safety precaution during a lawful investigation. Two officers on night patrol had observed a car being driven erratically before it swerved into a ditch. The driver, who appeared intoxicated, met the officers at the rear of the car, then turned and began to walk toward the open door of the car. The officers saw a hunting knife on the floorboard of the car. They frisked the suspect, and one officer shined his flashlight into the car and saw something under the armrest. Upon lifting the armrest, he saw an open leather pouch that contained marijuana. The Court ruled that a "search of the passenger compartment of an automobile, limited to those areas in which a weapon may be placed or hidden, is permissible if the police officer possesses a reasonable belief based on 'specific and articulable facts which, taken together with the rational inferences from those facts, reasonably warrant' the officer in believing that the suspect is dangerous and the suspect may gain immediate control of weapons."

Gant may create situations in which officers have stronger evidence than in *Long* but will not be authorized to conduct the search that the officers in *Long* conducted. The majority in *Gant* apparently gave no consideration to the legitimate investigative functions of the police or to the substantial evidence that gave them probable cause to search Gant's vehicle. The police had information that the residence was being used to sell drugs. They investigated and found that the occupant of the residence was not the owner and was wanted on a warrant. They found two people hanging around the house. One gave a false identity; the other had drug paraphernalia. Then they observed Gant unlawfully driving a car with a suspended license, which was a misdemeanor. Criminal drug dealing was surely afoot, and it was reasonable to believe that the car contained evidence of this ongoing criminal activity. Furthermore, drug dealers frequently have weapons handy to protect their product and their proceeds, and associates might quickly gain access to such weapons. Considering the intrusions on privacy that the Court has countenanced in the stop-and-frisk of automobile passengers in such cases as *Pennsylvania v. Mimms*, 434 U.S. 106 (1977), *Maryland v. Wilson*, 519 U.S. 408 (1997), and *Arizona v. Lemon Johnson, supra*, and the automobile exception cases, such as *Carroll v. United States*, 267 U.S. 132 (1925), *Husty v. United States*, 282 U.S. 694 (1931), *Chambers v. Maroney*, 399 U.S. 42 (1970), searching Gant's car in connection with his arrest seems a relatively minor intrusion.

A comparison of *Arizona v. Gant, supra,* to *Arizona v. Lemon Johnson, supra,* also highlights the incongruous, uneven results produced by the nuanced doctrines of the exclusionary rule. The police had more justification to stop and investigate Gant than they had to stop and investigate Johnson, yet Gant escaped justice while Johnson did not. Moreover, it seems the Court has granted more protection for a person like Gant, who the police reasonably suspected of selling drugs and who was wanted on a warrant, than it has granted to a person like Johnson, who was merely a passenger in a car stopped for a traffic violation. If the exclusionary rule is designed to protect all citizens from unreasonable intrusions by the police, it seems the level of protection is unequally distributed.

Rather than eliminating the rule, the mistake the Court makes in trying to keep it viable by drawing fine lines between reasonable and unreasonable searches is that lower court judges and the national army of criminal defense attorneys can find ways to smudge the lines. As the Court restricts the exclusionary rule in some areas, lower court judges and lawyers working in synchronization continually find ways to expand the application of the rule. In *Michigan v. Fisher,* 558 U.S. 130 S.Ct. 546 (2009), the Court again had to correct a lower court's expansion of the rule. In *Fisher,* two police officers responded to a complaint of a disturbance. As they approached the area, a couple directed them to a residence where a man was "going crazy." The officers observed a pickup truck in the driveway with its front smashed, damaged fence posts, three broken house windows, and glass on the ground outside. They noticed blood on the hood of the pickup, on clothes inside of it, and on the doors to the house. Through a window, they could see the defendant, Jeremy Fisher, inside the house, screaming and throwing things. One of the officers, Christopher Goolsby, pushed the front door open, and through the window of the open door, he saw Fisher pointing a long gun at him. The officer withdrew.

When backup officers arrived, Fisher was arrested and tried for assault with a dangerous weapon and possession of a firearm. The judge at the trial court suppressed the officer's testimony that he saw Fisher pointing the gun at him. The judge concluded that Officer Goolsby violated the Fourth Amendment when he entered Fisher's house without a warrant. This ruling was appealed to the Michigan Court of Appeals, and that court affirmed the suppression of the officer's testimony.

The Attorney-General of Michigan appealed to the Roberts Court, which reversed the Michigan rulings and pointed out that the Michigan courts had not followed the emergency entry exception established in *Brigham City, Utah v. Stuart,* 547 U.S. 398 (2006). The Court stated, "It does not meet the needs of law enforcement or the demands of public safety to require officers to walk away from a situation like the one they encountered here…. The role of a peace officer includes preventing violence and restoring order, not simply rendering first aid to casualties."

As impractical as the Michigan court ruling was in this matter, far more disturbing was the prospect that an officer would have had to testify, after swearing to tell the whole truth and nothing but the truth, without being allowed to say what he saw. A jury listening to such incomplete evidence might well have been confused.

Right to Counsel

In the 2009 and 2010 terms, the Roberts Court issued five significant rulings pertaining to right to counsel issues that had emanated from the *United States v. Massiah*, 377 U.S. 201 (1964), and *Miranda v. Arizona*, 384 U.S. 436 (1966), line of cases.

In April 2009, in *Kansas v. Ventris*, 129 S.Ct. 1841 (2009), Justice Scalia wrote the seven-to-two majority opinion in which the Court built upon the impeachment exception for statements obtained in violation of *Miranda* warnings and extended the exception to statements obtained in violation of the *Massiah* right to counsel.

In 1971, the impeachment exception to *Miranda* had been firmly established in *Harris v. New York*, 401 U.S. 222. In that case, the defendant had given an un-Mirandized incriminating statement to the police. While that statement could not be used against the defendant during the prosecution's direct case, when the defendant chose to testify and told a contradictory story, the prosecution was allowed to cross-examine him and to impeach his credibility by using the prior un-Mirandized inconsistent and incriminatory statement.

In *Ventris*, Donnie Ray Ventris and Rhonda Theel entered the home of Ernest Hicks. One or both of the pair shot and killed Hicks. They also stole his truck, approximately $300 in cash, and his cell phone. After they were arrested and charged with the murder and robbery, Theel agreed to testify against Ventris. In exchange for reduced charges, she agreed to identify him as the shooter.

While Ventris was in jail awaiting trial, the police planted an informant in his cell. They instructed the informant to "keep his ear open and listen" for incriminating statements. According to the informant, in response to his statement that Ventris appeared to have "something more serious weighing in on his mind," Ventris divulged that he had shot a man, taken his keys, his wallet, about $350 dollars, and a vehicle.

At the trial, Ventris' statement was not introduced during the prosecution's direct case. However, when Ventris took the stand and blamed the robbery and shooting entirely on Theel, the prosecution called the informant to testify to Ventris' prior contradictory statement in which he admitted to the shooting. The purpose of the informant's testimony was to impeach Ventris' credibility.

Although Ventris was not convicted of the murder, he was convicted of burglary and robbery. He appealed those convictions on the grounds that the informant's statement should not have been admissible. The Kansas Supreme Court agreed and reversed the convictions, because "once a criminal prosecution has commenced, the defendant's statements made to an undercover informant surreptitiously acting as an agent for the State are not admissible at trial for any reason, including impeachment of the defendant's testimony."

The Supreme Court reversed the Kansas Supreme Court, unequivocally ruling that such statements may indeed be used for impeachment purposes. The Court reiterated several of its prior pronouncements, quoting that "it is one thing to say that the Government cannot make an affirmative use of evidence unlawfully obtained. It is quite another to say that the defendant can turn the illegal method by which evidence in the Government's possession was obtained to his own advantage, and provide himself with a shield against contradiction of his untruths."[2] Simply, a defendant cannot use the exclusionary rule as a license to commit perjury.

Ventris has apparently simplified the impeachment exception by eliminating the distinctions between statements obtained in violation of *Miranda* and those taken in violation of *Massiah*, and it has reaffirmed the Court's position that the introduction of illegally obtained evidence during a trial is not absolutely barred by the Constitution, particularly when barring the evidence would not provide a substantial deterrent to police misconduct. The Court's seven-to-two adoption of the impeachment exception establishes that the truth-seeking process is more important the exclusionary rule.

In May 2009, the Roberts Court, again with Justice Scalia writing the five-to-four majority opinion, decided *Montejo v. Louisiana*, 129 S.Ct. 2079, which overturned *Jackson v. Michigan*, 475 U.S. 625 (1986), and lifted some restrictions on when defendants can be interrogated without their lawyers present. *Jackson* had held that once a defendant affirmatively invoked his right to counsel at an arraignment or a similar proceeding, the police were forbidden to interrogate the defendant without his lawyer present, even when the defendant voluntarily waived his right to an attorney at the interrogation.

---

2. See, *Walder v. United States*, 347 U.S. 62 (1954); *Harris v. New York*, 401 U.S. 222 (1971); *Oregon v. Hass*, 420 U.S. 714 (1975); *Stone v. Powell*, 428 U.S. 465 (1976); *Michigan v. Harvey*, 494 U.S. 344 (1990).

The problem *Montejo* addressed was that in some states, attorneys are automatically assigned to represent indigent defendants without a request from the defendant, while in other states indigent defendants are required to affirmatively request the appointment of an attorney. Consequently, under *Jackson*, defendants who were automatically assigned counsel would not have the same right to counsel protections as defendants who were required to affirmatively request an attorney and who did so. This was the kind of distinction that commonsense people without legal training quickly identify as legal nonsense.

In *Montejo*, the defendant was arrested for murder and robbery. He was read his Miranda rights, and while being interrogated, he repeatedly changed his story, at first blaming another person, then admitting that he had shot the victim during a botched burglary. At a preliminary hearing, a judge ordered that a public defender be appointed. Then at some point afterwards, without his appointed attorney present, the defendant was given his Miranda rights again and he agreed to accompany detectives to locate the murder weapon, which he had thrown in a lake. During the trip, he wrote a letter of apology to the victim's widow.

At Montejo's trial, the letter of apology was admitted into evidence. He was convicted, and appealed on the grounds that because of a violation of his right to counsel the incriminating letter should have been suppressed. However, the Louisiana Supreme Court upheld the conviction, ruling that the *Jackson* rule did not apply to him because in Louisiana, lawyers are assigned automatically to indigent defendants and Montejo had not specifically requested counsel at the preliminary hearing.

The Supreme Court affirmed the Louisiana ruling on similar reasoning, but went further by overruling *Jackson* entirely, because *Jackson* mandated an unworkable standard that led to arbitrary and anomalous distinctions between defendants in different states and "when the marginal benefits of the *Jackson* rule weighed against its substantial costs to the truth-seeking process and the criminal justice system, we readily conclude that the rule does not pay its way." The Court emphasized that it was not abrogating a defendant's right to the presence of counsel at critical stages of a prosecution as per *Massiah*, but it was only overturning the *Jackson* rule that a represented defendant could not voluntarily waive that right.

Justice Scalia concluded his opinion with the famous quotation that the Supreme Court "is forever adding new stories to the temples of constitutional law, and the temples have a way of collapsing when one story too many is added."[3] By removing the *Jackson* story from the edifice of right to counsel ju-

---

3. *Douglas v. City of Jeannette*, 319 U.S. 157 (1943).

risprudence, the Court has attempted to move toward simplification; however, *Montejo* was a five-to-four decision, and it raised strong objections from the dissenting justices. Justice John Paul Stevens, who wrote the opinion in *Jackson* that the Court here overruled, displayed considerable emotion when he read his dissenting opinion in which he claimed, "Such a decision can only diminish the public's confidence in the reliability and fairness of our system of justice." The four dissenting justices would have gone in the opposite direction and extended the *Jackson* rule to all arraigned defendants, including those who were automatically assigned counsel. To be sure, projected changes on the court may someday revive the issues raised in *Jackson* and *Montejo*.

The Roberts Court shifted further in the direction of law enforcement in *Maryland v. Shatzer*, 130 S.Ct. 1213 (2010). Justice Scalia wrote the nine-to-zero unanimous opinion, holding that the police are not barred from re-questioning a suspect who previously had invoked his right to remain silent until his attorney was present. Perhaps, the egregious nature of the case—a father sexually abusing his three-year-old son—convinced even the usually liberal members of the Court, including Justices Ruth Bader Ginsburg (a former president of the American Civil Liberties Union), John Paul Stevens, and Stephen Breyer, to shift right and join the unanimous opinion.

In the case, a detective attempted to interview the defendant Shatzer regarding the allegation that he sexual abused his son. At the time, the defendant was already incarcerated in a correctional facility serving a sentence for an unrelated child-sexual-abuse offense. The defendant invoked his Miranda rights and declined to speak without his attorney present. Accordingly, the detective ended the interview, and Shatzer returned to the general prison population.

Without enough evidence to prosecute, the police closed the case. However, two years and seven months later, the police received more specific allegations about the sexual abuse incident. A detective interviewed the child, who was now eight years old and able to provide more details about the crime. The detective reopened the case and re-interviewed Shatzer. The detective gave him Miranda warnings and obtained a written waiver, and this time Shatzer agreed to speak without the presence of an attorney. During the questioning, he made incriminating statements and agreed to submit to a polygraph examination. When Shatzer failed the polygraph test, the detective asked follow-up questions, and Shatzer further incriminated himself by saying, "I didn't force him." Shatzer's statements corroborated the occurrence of the crime and he was tried and convicted.

He appealed his conviction on the grounds that his incriminating statements should have been suppressed because they were taken in violation the rule of *Edwards v. Arizona*, 411 U.S. 477 (1981), which held that once a defendant requests an attorney during custodial interrogation, the police cannot initiate any further attempts at interrogation unless the attorney is present. When the Maryland Court of Appeals agreed and reversed the conviction,[4] the Maryland Attorney General appealed to the U.S. Supreme Court.

In February 2010, the Supreme Court held that the two-years-and-seven-months break between the interviews was a substantial break in custody that modified the *Edwards* doctrine and allowed the police to re-approach Shatzer and obtain a voluntary waiver of his right to counsel and the right to remain silent. Consequently, the incriminating statement was admissible and his conviction should have been affirmed.

The Court distinguished the *Edwards* circumstances in which the defendant had been arrested pursuant to a warrant and taken to a police station, where he was interrogated until he requested counsel. The police ended the interrogation and lodged him in the county jail to await arraignment. The next morning, other police officers approached him at the jail and began a new interrogation at which the defendant made incriminating statements. In that case, the Court suppressed the incriminating statements, holding that subsequent requests by the police to interrogate such a defendant pose a significantly greater risk of coercion, which results not only from the police persistence but also from the increasing pressure of prolonged custody.

In *Shatzer*, although the defendant was in prison, he was living among the general prison population. He was not in police custody or in a confined location cut off from other people, and the break in police custody of more than two years relieved the pressure of continued custody. His waiver and statements could not be deemed the result of prolonged coercion, and, therefore, his incriminating statements were admissible.

The Court, in order to provide a guideline for the police to follow, specified fourteen days as the necessary break in custody between attempts to interrogate a suspect. The Court said, "That provides plenty of time for the suspect to get reacclimated to his normal life, to consult with friends and counsel, and to shake off any residual coercive effects of his prior custody."

Also in February 2010, the Court decided *Florida v. Powell*, 130 S.Ct. 1195 (2010), in which Justice Ginsburg wrote the seven-to-two majority opinion upholding the use of a confession that was challenged on *Miranda* grounds. Justices Ginsburg and Sotomayor sided with the right-leaning side of the Court, leaving only Justices Stevens and Breyer adhering to the left-leaning jurisprudence reminiscent of the 1960s opinions of Justices Brennan and Marshall.

---

4. *Shatzer v. Maryland*, 405 Md. 585 (2008).

In *Powell*, police in Tampa, Florida arrested the defendant, Kevin Powell in connection with a robbery investigation. They apprehended him in his girlfriend's apartment as he came out of a bedroom. They then searched the bedroom and found a loaded nine-millimeter handgun under the bed.

At the police station, the officers read Powell their department's version of the Miranda rights from a waiver form, the pertinent part as follows:

> You have the right to talk to a lawyer before answering any of our questions. If you cannot afford to hire a lawyer, one will be appointed for you without cost and before any questioning. You have the right to use any of these rights at any time you want during this interview.

Powell signed the waiver form and admitted that he owned the handgun found in the apartment. Subsequently, he was convicted of unlawful possession of the gun, but appealed on the grounds that the Miranda warnings given to him did not adequately convey his right to the presence of an attorney during the questioning. He contended that the warnings were misleading because they suggested that he could only consult with an attorney before questioning, but they did not convey his entitlement to counsel throughout the interrogation.

The Supreme Court disagreed and ruled that the warnings were sufficient because the police informed Powell that he had the right to talk to a lawyer before answering any of their questions and the right to use any of his rights at any time he wanted during the interview. "In combination, the warnings reasonably conveyed his right to have an attorney present, not only at the outset of interrogation, but at all times."

Powell is significant as it provides another example of the Roberts Court's more flexible application of the exclusionary rule in contrast to the absolutist application of the rule by the Warren Court of the 1960s.

In June 2010, the Supreme Court addressed another *Miranda* issue in *Berghuis, Warden v. Thompkins*, 130 S.Ct. 2250 (2010). In this case, the Court retrenched to a five-to-four decision with Justice Anthony Kennedy writing the majority opinion for the right-leaning side of the Court.

The facts of the case were that the defendant, Thompkins, exchanged "words" with two young men, victim one and victim two, in a parking lot. The two victims got into their car, and Thompkins with several other men got into a van, and pulled alongside the victims' car. Multiple gunshots were fired into the victims' car, wounding victim one and killing victim two.

Detective Helgert investigated the shootings, and he interviewed a friend of Thompkins who told him and later testified that Thompkins had told him "he had to pop them."

A year after the shootings, Thompkins was arrested, and Detective Helgert attempted to interview him about the shootings. Helgert read Thompkins the Miranda rights and asked him to sign a form acknowledging that he understood the rights. Although Thompkins orally confirmed he understood his rights, he declined to sign the form. Nevertheless, the detectives questioned him for about three hours. During the questioning, Thompkins was mostly silent, although he did give a few limited verbal responses, such as "Yeah," "No," or "I don't know." On occasion, he communicated by nodding his head. He also said that he "didn't want a peppermint" and the chair he was "sitting on was hard."

About two hours and 45 minutes into the interrogation, Helgert asked Thompkins, "Do you believe in God?" The defendant answered "Yes." Helgert asked, "Do you pray to God?" The defendant answered "Yes." Helgert asked, "Do you pray to God to forgive you for shooting that boy down?" Thompkins answered "Yes" and looked away.

At Thompkins' trial, his incriminating statement, the testimony of the victim who survived and identified him, the testimony of his "friend," and other pieces of evidence were used against him, and he was convicted of first-degree murder. He appealed on the grounds that he had invoked his privilege to remain silent by not saying anything for such an extended period that the interrogation should have ceased before he made the incriminating statement. The Supreme Court ruled against Thompkins. Relying on their prior ruling in *Davis v. United States*, 512 U.S. 452 (1994), the Court held that an assertion exercising the right to remain silent must be made unambiguously. If an accused makes an ambiguous or equivocal statement or makes no statement, the police are not required to end the interrogation. *Davis* was decided in the context of the right to counsel, but the same principle applies to the right to remain silent.

The Roberts Court has not remained static; it has undergone a degree of directional shift and additional personnel changes. In the fall 2009 term, Justice Sonia Sotomayor replaced the retiring Justice David Souter, and in the fall 2010 term, Justice Elena Kagan replaced the retiring Justice John Paul Stevens. Justices Sotomayor and Kagan are the third and fourth women to be appointed to the Court. It remains to be seen whether their addition to the Court will significantly change exclusionary rule jurisprudence. Most observers assume both justices will lean to the left; however, that may not make much difference as Justices Souter and Stevens had also leaned left, and, just as the appointments of Roberts and Alito did not upset the Court's balance, the additions of Sotomayer and Kagan will not change the ideological balance on the Court.

Of course, predicting how justices will decide cases has often proven to be humbling. Justice Sotomayer may not be so left leaning in criminal justice matters as some would assume. She has been a prosecutor, a tough-minded trial judge for many years, and a former Solicitor-General of the United States in President Clinton's administration. In *Shatzer* and *Powell*, she voted with the right-leaning side of the Court. In 2011, she sided with the government in other criminal justice cases. In *Kentucky v. King*, 131 S.Ct. 1849 (2010), she joined the eight-to-one majority upholding the lawfulness of a police search under the exigent circumstances exception to the warrant requirement, and in *Michigan v. Bryant*, 131 S.Ct. 1143 (2011), she wrote the majority opinion holding that the Sixth Amendment confrontation clause did not prohibit the admission into evidence of statements by a witness made to the police in an emergency situation.

Justice Kagan, by all indications, also has a practical approach to issues and may not be trapped in a fixed Warren Court ideology. In *Kentucky v. King*, *supra*, she joined Justice Sotomayer's opinion upholding the exigent circumstances search.

A wildcard for those predicting the future direction of the Court has been a discernable shift by Justice Ginsburg. In *Florida v. Powell, supra*, she wrote the majority opinion upholding the admission of a confession and the resulting conviction of the defendant; in *Arizona v. Lemon Johnson*, supra, she wrote the majority opinion upholding the search of an automobile passenger and his resulting conviction, and in *Moore v. Virginia, supra*, and *Maryland v. Shatzer*, *supra*, she sided with the right-leaning side of the Court.

What direction the Court takes in the future will depend, as it should, on debate and persuasiveness as much as on the order and timing of the next retirements and replacements. If the Court leans conservative, it may substantially limit the exclusionary rule by creating new exceptions or extending established exceptions; if it leans liberal, it may reignite the rule's growth and expansion. In any case, the police will have to continue functioning while dealing with growing uncertainty. Rather than such uncertainty, the best outcome may be to relegate the exclusionary rule to history while ensuring the maintenance of genuine due process protections that do not undermine the truth-seeking process.

Chapter Seventeen

Privacy and Policy Privileges

With the invention of the telephone, a new realm of personal communication and interaction was created. With it also came the problems of eavesdropping and wiretapping. The Fourth Amendment states:

> The right of the people to be secure in their persons, houses, papers, and effects, against unreasonable searches and seizures, shall not be violated.

Legal questions arose as to whether conversations are included in the terms—persons, houses, papers, and effects, and, if so, whether the Fourth Amendment protected a person's conversation from unreasonable search and seizure. The Supreme Court and society has unequivocally answered in the affirmative, but more difficult questions relate to when, where, and why.

In 1928, the Supreme Court examined the issues in *Olmstead v. United States*, 277 U.S. 438, a case in which the defendant was convicted of conspiracy to violate the National Prohibition Act. Evidence was obtained against him by intercepting his telephone conversations by means of a wiretapping device that federal agents had placed on a telephone pole outside his house. The question for the Court was whether this interception of the defendant's conversations by federal agents violated the Fourth Amendment right against unreasonable search and seizure. The Court's majority ruled that it was not a violation because the agents had not physically trespassed on the house, person, effects, or papers of the defendant. The Court reasoned that the telephone wires and the conversations passing through them were within the public sphere and not protected as private. The majority stated:

> The language of the Amendment can not be extended and expanded to include telephone wires reaching to the whole world from the defendant's house or office. The intervening wires are not part of his house or office any more than are the highways along which they are stretched.

Olmstead has been most remembered, not for its ruling, but for its marvelous dissenting opinions and their famous quotations, one by Justice Oliver

Wendell Holmes, "It is less evil that some criminals should escape than that the government should play an ignoble part." Another by Justice Louis Brandeis included a prophecy of coming government intrusiveness and omnipresence long before George Orwell's novel *1984*, which dramatized totalitarian government as "Big Brother." Brandeis wrote:

> When the Fourth and Fifth Amendments were adopted, "the form that evil had theretofore taken," had been necessarily simple. Force and violence were then the only means known to man by which a Government could directly effect self-incrimination. It could compel the individual to testify—a compulsion effected, if need by, by torture. It could secure possession of his papers and other articles incident to his private life—a seizure effected, if need be, by breaking and entry. Protection against such invasion of "the sanctities of a man's home and the privacies of life" was provided in the Fourth and Fifth Amendments by specific language ... Subtler and more far-reaching means of invading privacy have become available to the Government. Discovery and invention have made it possible for the Government, by means far more effective than stretching upon the rack, to obtain disclosure in court of what is whispered in the closet.

Brandeis believed that the language of the Amendments had to be expanded to encompass protections for private thoughts and expressions.

> The makers of our Constitution undertook to secure conditions favorable to the pursuit of happiness. They recognized the significance of man's spiritual nature, of his feelings and of his intellect. They knew that only a part of the pain, pleasure and satisfactions of life are to be found in material things. They sought to protect Americans in their beliefs, their thoughts, their emotions and their sensations. They conferred, as against the Government, the right to be let alone—the most comprehensive of rights and the right most valued by civilized men. To protect that right, every unjustifiable intrusion by the Government upon the privacy of the individual, whatever the means employed, must be deemed a violation of the Fourth Amendment.

Irrespective of the dissenting opinions of Holmes and Brandeis, the Court's majority upheld the use of the evidence against Olmstead and retained the physical trespass rule. However, the majority suggested:

Congress may of course protect the secrecy of telephone messages by making them, when intercepted, inadmissible in evidence in federal criminal trials.

Partly in response to the suggestion in *Olmstead*, Congress enacted the Federal Communications Act of 1934, which addressed telephonic communications and provided:

> No person not being authorized by the sender shall intercept any communication and divulge or publish the existence, contents, purport, effect or meaning of such intercepted communications to any person.[1]

This statute had a limited effect on law enforcement, because it did not specifically prohibit eavesdropping and wiretapping. The statute was interpreted to mean only that since intercepted telephonic communications could not be divulged, the contents of an intercepted communication could not be used as evidence in a federal court. As it did not definitely prohibit wiretapping, federal agents and local police continued to wiretap for intelligence gathering purposes, but not for use in court. Moreover, eavesdropping by other electronic means, e.g., bugging a room or vehicle, was not addressed by the Federal Communications Act, and the *Olmstead* trespass doctrine remained the primary method of regulating such law-enforcement conduct.

In time, however, further technological advances caused the Court and Congress to reconsider the rule. Police obtained even more sophisticated eavesdropping and surveillance devices that have made it possible to invade a person's privacy without a physical trespass. They utilized electronic tracking devices, telescopic lenses and cameras, heat sensors, metal detectors, and drug-sniffing dogs to obtain evidence without having to trespass physically. Doors and walls could no longer assure a person's privacy.

As technology changes, constitutional jurisprudence has to adapt. In *Katz v. United States*, 389 U.S. 347 (1967), the Court replaced the trespass doctrine with the reasonable expectation of privacy doctrine. In *Katz*, federal agents, investigating the defendant for illegal gambling, placed a listening and recording device on the exterior of a public telephone booth that they knew he used regularly to make gambling calls. Under the trespass rule, the interception of Katz' conversations (not over the phone wires, but in the phone booth) would not have been a violation for two reasons: first, Katz did not own the phone booth, and second, the device was not placed inside the phone booth.

Discarding the trespass rule, the Court abandoned *Olmstead* and declared:

---

1. Former 47 U.S.C. 605

The Fourth Amendment protects people, not places. What a person knowingly exposes to the public, even in his own home or office, is not a subject of Fourth Amendment protection. But what he seeks to preserve as private, even in an area accessible to the public, may be constitutionally protected.

Closing the phone-booth door established Katz' expectation of privacy; therefore, as the Court stated:

> The Government's activities in electronically listening to and recording the petitioner's words violated the privacy upon which he justifiably relied while using the telephone booth and thus constituted a "search and seizure" within the meaning of the Fourth Amendment. The fact that the electronic device employed to achieve that end did not happen to penetrate the wall of the booth can have no constitutional significance.

The agents investigating Katz' activities needed a search warrant to lawfully intrude upon his privacy. Without a warrant, his verbal statements or tangible evidence derived from his statements would be suppressed.

The Omnibus Crime Control and Safe Streets Act of 1968

In response to *Katz*, Congress enacted Title III of the Omnibus Crime Control and Safe Streets Act of 1968,[2] which included authorization for eavesdropping warrants for both wiretapping and listening devices in private locations. Congress spelled out the requirements to obtain such warrants, and most states passed similar laws, many of which provided greater protection for individuals than the federal law.

Eavesdropping in the legal context is knowingly and without lawful authority engaging in the following conduct:

> (a) Entering into a private place with intent to listen surreptitiously to private conversations or to observe the personal conduct of any other person or persons therein; or
>
> (b) Installing or using outside a private place any device for hearing, recording, amplifying, or broadcasting sounds originating in such place, which sounds would not ordinarily be audible or compre-

---

2. 18 U.S.C. 2510–2521.

hensible outside, without the consent of the person or persons entitled to privacy therein; or

(c) Installing or using any device or equipment for the interception of any telephone, telegraph or other wire communication without the consent of the person in possession or control of the facilities for such wire communication. Such activities are regulated by state and federal statutes, and commonly require a court order.[3]

Under the statutes, violations of the eavesdropping and wiretap laws are felonies, whether committed by private persons or government agents. In addition, evidence obtained by law enforcement acting without a court-authorized warrant in violation of the statutes will not be admissible in any court, civil or criminal, and such evidence obtained by private persons will not be admissible.

Not allowing illegal eavesdropping or wiretap evidence into the courtroom is not the same as invoking the judge-made exclusionary rule. The admissibility or inadmissibility of such evidence is controlled by legislative statutory law. Although the Supreme Court initiated the prohibition, the legislature ratified the Court's ruling and promulgated extensive rules and procedures that supersede the Court's mandate.

Legislatures have noted that wiretap and eavesdropping warrants are far more intrusive than the conventional search warrant for physical evidence. Conventional search warrants are normally executed during a designated 10-day period. They are executed once; additional searches require additional warrants. Police officers search through a home, office, or other premise for contraband or evidence of a crime; when they are finished, they leave. On the other hand, wiretap and eavesdropping warrants are not one-time events, but are of a continuing nature, intruding into a person's private conversations and private life for extended periods of time. Such intrusions pose a greater threat to privacy than a one-time physical search. For this reason, extremely strict rules and standards have been established for the issuance and execution of such warrants.

By enacting the eavesdropping and wiretap laws, legislatures have created a confidential communications privilege, and they have prohibited the introduction into evidence of confidential conversations overheard by unlawful means. Such illegally obtained evidence is prohibited for use in any judicial or administrative proceeding, not just in criminal cases.

This public policy is in keeping with other evidentiary privileges established by Congress and state legislatures. Other privileges also protect a person's con-

---

3. *Black's Law Dictionary* (St. Paul, MN: West Publishing, 1979).

fidential communications from use in court. The doctor/patient, attorney/client, clergy/penitent, and husband/wife privileges serve public policy considerations larger than the benefits of courtroom use; these privileges originated in common law but have been ratified by statutory law. They were designed to provide protection to persons seeking professional advice or assistance and to support the institution of marriage. We have determined that it is important that persons seeking professional advice be truthful with their doctors, attorneys, and clergy, and it is important for spouses to confer in complete confidence with one another. If such persons could not be sure that their confidential communications would be protected, they might be discouraged from seeking assistance or they might be less than truthful in these essential communications.

The Fourth and Fifth Amendment exclusionary rules are unquestionably different than the Title III prohibitions. The former apply in criminal cases and do not apply to other proceedings; Title III prohibitions, by virtue of statutory law, apply "in any court, department, officer, agency, regulatory body, or other authority of the United States, a State, or a political subdivision." Title III may be invoked by a party in a bail hearing, a parole proceeding, or a police department disciplinary proceeding.[4]

The ability to have private conversations is an essential element of liberty, and protecting private conversations from unreasonable government intrusion is a crucial and broad public policy confirmed by society and its legislatures. It is not in the same arena as the much narrower application of exclusionary rules to specific items of evidence in criminal cases.

Tracking a Person's Movements

It is clear that an individual's confidential conversations are protected by the Fourth Amendment and by the statutory prohibitions of Title III, but it is questionable as to whether an individual's movements in the public sphere enjoy such privacy protection. Cell phones, EZ pass, Global Positioning Systems (GPS), and ubiquitous security cameras have diminished privacy in American society. The location of a person's cell phone can be tracked by the signals sent between the phone and cellular receiving tower. Electronic beepers and GPS enable law enforcement officers to track the movements of a vehicle. Nevertheless, most courts have held that as long as the law enforcement agent attaches the beeper or GPS device to the outside of a vehicle (usually to the undercarriage) while it is parked in a public place, no search or seizure occurs.

---

4. LaFave and Israel, *Criminal Procedure*, (St. Paul, MN: West Publishing, 1992): 4.6.b.

In *United States v. Knotts*, 406 U.S. 276 (1983), the Supreme Court held that it was not a Fourth Amendment violation when government agents, who were investigating an illegal drug laboratory, placed a beeper in a five-gallon drum of chloroform to track the container's movements. The agents then followed the vehicle that transported the drum by monitoring the received signals from the beeper. The drum was tracked to Knott's cabin. He was arrested, and after being charged, filed a motion for the suppression of the chloroform on the grounds that his privacy rights had been violated.

The Supreme Court held that a person's public movements are not protected by the Fourth Amendment, as "a person traveling in an automobile on public thoroughfares has no reasonable expectation of privacy in his movements from one place to another."

The tracking device could be viewed merely as an enhancement of an officer's ability to observe a vehicle in a public place, similar to the use of binoculars. As the Court stated, "Nothing in the Fourth Amendment prohibited the police from augmenting the sensory faculties bestowed upon them at birth with such enhancement as science and technology afforded them in this case."[5] However, *Knotts*, did not address the issue of whether placing a tracking device for prolonged periods of time would bring about a different result.

Keying on the silence in *Knotts* regarding prolonged periods of tracking, the D.C. Circuit Court of Appeals, in *United States v. Maynard*, 615 F.3d 544 (D.C. Cir. 2010), ruled that 24-hour tracking for 28 days violated the defendant's expectation of privacy and required a warrant. Three state courts, on the basis of their state constitutions, have ruled that warrants are required for GPS vehicle tracking.[6]

The New York Court of Appeals, in *People v. Weaver*, 12 N.Y.3d 433 (2009), held that the government's use of a GPS tracking device violated the right to privacy. The majority four-to-three opinion was written by Chief Judge Jonathan Lippman and was his first major criminal procedure opinion since his appointment as New York's Chief Judge. He outlined the facts of the case as follows:

In the early morning hours of December 21, 2005, a State Police Investigator crept underneath defendant's street-parked van and placed a global positioning system (GPS) tracking device inside the bumper. The device remained in place for 65 days, constantly monitoring the

---

5. *United States v. Knotts*, 460 U.S. 276 (1983), at 282.

6. *People v. Weaver*, 12 N.Y.3d 433 (2009), *Commonwealth v. Connolly*, 454 Mass. 808 (2009), *State v. Jackson*, 150 Wash. 2d 251 (2003).

position of the van. This nonstop surveillance was conducted without a warrant.

The GPS device, known as a "Q-ball," once attached to the van, operated in conjunction with numerous satellites, from which it received tracking data, to fix the van's location. The Q-Ball readings indicated the speed of the van and pinpointed its location within 30 feet. Readings were taken approximately every minute while the vehicle was in motion, but less often when it was stationary.... To download the location information retrieved by the Q-ball, the investigator would simply drive past the van and press a button on a corresponding receiver unit, causing the tracking history to be transmitted to and saved by a computer in the investigator's vehicle.

[The defendant] was eventually charged with and tried in a single proceeding for crimes relating to two separate burglaries—one committed on July 2005 at the Latham Meat Market and the other on Christmas Eve of the same year at the Latham K-Mart.

The prosecution sought to have admitted at trial GPS readings showing that, on the evening of the Latham K-Mart burglary at 7:26, defendant's van traversed the store's parking lot at a speed of six miles per hour.

Over the defendant's objection, the trial court admitted the electronic surveillance evidence. That evidence, combined with testimony of the defendant's accomplice, resulted in his conviction for the burglaries. Weaver appealed, and the New York Court of Appeals reversed the conviction, ruling that the evidence obtained from the GPS should be suppressed.

Justice Lippman distinguished the *Knotts* case from *Weaver*. In *Knotts*, the beeper was used to track a single trip from the place where the chloroform was purchased to the cabin. To the contrary, in *Weaver*:

We are not presented with the use of a mere beeper to facilitate visual surveillance during a single trip. GPS is a vastly different and exponentially more sophisticated and powerful technology that is easily and cheaply deployed and has virtually unlimited and remarkably precise tracking capability. With the addition of new GPS satellites, the technology is rapidly improving so that any person or object, such as a car, may be tracked with uncanny accuracy to virtually any interior or exterior location, at any time and regardless of atmospheric conditions. Constant, relentless tracking of anything is now not merely possible but entirely practicable, indeed much more practicable than the surveillance conducted in *Knotts*. GPS is not a mere enhancement of human sensory capacity, it facilitates a new technological perception of the world in which the situation of any object may be followed and exhaustively recorded, over, in most cases, a practically unlimited period....

One need only consider what the police may learn, practically effortlessly, from planting a single device. The whole of a person's progress through the world, into both public and private spatial spheres, can be charted and recorded over lengthy periods....

Judge Lippman pointed out that the *Knotts* court had reserved for another day the question of whether the Fourth Amendment would be implicated if "twenty-four hour surveillance of any citizen of this country were possible, without judicial knowledge or supervision."[7] He differentiated the voluntary use or submission to GPS technology from the government's secret use of such technology:

It would appear clear to us that the great popularity of GPS technology for its many useful applications may not be taken simply as a massive, undifferentiated concession of personal privacy to agents of the state. Indeed, contemporary technology projects our private activities into public space as never before. Cell technology has moved presumptively private phone conversation from the enclosure of Katz' phone booth to the open sidewalk and the car, and the advent of portable computing devices has re-situated transactions of all kinds to relatively public spaces. It is fair to say, and we think consistent with prevalent social views, that this change in venue has not been accompanied by any dramatic diminution in the socially reasonable expectation that our communications and transactions will remain to a large extent private. Here, particularly, where there was no voluntary utilization of the tracking technology, and the technology was surreptitiously installed, there exists no basis to find an expectation of privacy so diminished as to render constitutional concerns *de minimis*.

According to Judge Lippman, though a citizen has a lesser expectation of privacy while traveling in his vehicle on public highways, a residual expectation of privacy exists. In this case, the prolonged invasion of privacy was inconsistent with even the slightest reasonable expectation of privacy. Furthermore, even if a warrant had been obtained, it would not have been justified under these circumstances.

Judge Lippman explained his divergence from federal law:

---

7. Id. at p. 283.

In reaching this conclusion, we acknowledge that the determinative issue remains open as a matter of federal constitutional law, since the United States Supreme Court has not yet ruled upon whether the use of GPS by the state for the purpose of criminal investigation constitutes a search under the Fourth Amendment ... Thus, we do not presume to decide the question as a matter of federal law. The very same principles are, however, dispositive of this matter under our State Constitution. If, as we have found, defendant had a reasonable expectation of privacy that was infringed by the State's placement and monitoring of the Q-Ball on his van to track his movements over a period of more than two months, there was a search under Article I, Section 12 of the State Constitution. And that search was illegal because it was executed without a warrant and without justification under any exception to the warrant requirement. In light of the unsettled state of federal law on the issue, we premise our ruling on our State Constitution alone.

It is likely that in the near future the U.S. Supreme Court will have to address the issue of prolonged government GPS tracking. To which future case they choose to grant *certiorari* will be interesting. The type of crime and the length of time of the tracking in the case they choose will be an indication of the Court's direction. However, in light of *Knotts*, which held that tracking did not implicate the Fourth Amendment, it would seem arbitrary to pick a specific time limit that if exceeded would transform a non-violation into a violation. In any event, if the Court determines that prolonged tracking without a warrant should be prohibited, the remedy should not be the exclusionary rule. Procedural time limits, by their nature, are not constitutional principles. If necessary, they should be left to the legislature, and sanctions for failure to comply should be in the nature of an administrative remedy.

Chapter Eighteen

More Effective Remedies

The objective of the judicial exclusionary rule was to deter the police from violating specific constitutional rights, and it was part of the broader objective to deter all forms of egregious police misconduct. However, the rule has failed to meet the objective.

Police misconduct takes many forms, and the rule fails to curtail the worst kinds of such misconduct. For example, assume the police arrest a defendant for a serious crime on the basis of eyewitness evidence and substantial physical evidence of the defendant's guilt. Assume, further, that the police attempt to extract a confession from the defendant by beating and inflicting substantial pain on him, but the defendant refuses to confess or admit anything in connection with the crime. At the defendant's trial, he is convicted on the basis of the eyewitness and physical evidence. Has the exclusionary rule protected the defendant's rights? No. The defendant's Fourth and Fifth Amendment rights were violated, but the exclusionary rule had nothing to suppress. The eyewitness and physical evidence were not derived from the police misconduct toward the defendant but were obtained independently before the misconduct and, therefore, that evidence would not be the subject of the poisonous-tree doctrine. The defendant's conviction will stand, and his remedy for the injury he suffered must be elsewhere.

Assume another example. The police, without a warrant, force their way into a residential apartment on an unconfirmed tip that narcotics are being stored therein by a drug-dealing gang. The apartment is occupied by a married couple and their two children, ages seven and 14. At gunpoint, the police handcuff the parents and the 14-year-old, and make the seven-year-old sit on the floor. For more than an hour, they search the apartment but do not find any unlawful drugs, except a half-smoked marijuana cigarette. They arrest the parents for possession of the marijuana cigarette, and because the parents vociferously protest the invasion of their home, they are charged with disorderly conduct and obstructing governmental administration. The children are removed to a Department of Social Services shelter.

A hearing is held at which the judge suppresses the marijuana and dismisses all the charges. Although the application of the exclusionary rule provided some benefit for the parents, it was surely an insufficient remedy for the injuries they and their children suffered. Furthermore, it did not provide a deterrent to such future police misconduct. The police officers would be unconcerned about the suppression of the marijuana cigarette; other sanctions would be required to deter future misconduct.

At the time of *Mapp* and *Miranda*, the imposition of the exclusionary rule on the states was perhaps an understandable measure. During the 1960s, civil rights issues were prominent in the nation's mind. Abuse of underprivileged and minority citizens, particularly by police departments, needed to be rectified. The Supreme Court had addressed individual abuses in such cases as *Powell v. Alabama* (the Scottsboro Boys case), *Brown v. Mississippi* (confession as a result of physical abuse),[1] and *Gideon v. Wainwright* (the right to counsel for indigent defendants).[2] Then in Mapp and *Miranda*, the Court imposed across-the-board structural protections in criminal procedure law that had general application but would be most helpful to the underprivileged in society. The decisions implementing the exclusionary rule were considered in relation to a costs-and-benefits analysis of the effect on the judicial system, the police, and the public. Arguably, at the time they were decided, *Mapp* and *Miranda* may have been warranted, but weighing the costs and benefits should be a continuing process. As circumstances change and balances shift, the analysis should be revisited.

Significant developments in civil rights law and improved accountability within the law-enforcement community have changed the circumstances and conditions that existed in the 1960s. During recent decades, incidents of police invading homes without warrants or extracting confessions from suspects by physical duress or coercion have been greatly reduced. The exclusionary rule cases began the process, but it was the utilization of civil rights lawsuits, criminal charges filed against police officers, and improved internal discipline that succeeded in changing these police practices. If the exclusionary rule were a necessary medicine at a time when no other medicines were effective, that time has passed. More potent medicines are available for use today. Civil rights lawsuits and criminal charges against abusive officers, when appropriate, are the strongest remedies, and they do not have the side effect of allowing dangerous criminals to escape justice.

---

1. *Powell v. Alabama*, 287 U.S. 45 (1932); *Brown v. Mississippi*, 297 U.S. 278 (1936).
2. *Gideon v. Wainwright*, 372 U.S. 335 (1963).

Civil Lawsuits

Mapp's proclamation that lawsuits against the police were ineffective has been invalidated by the Court's subsequent decisions in *Monroe v. Pape, Bivens v. Six Unknown Named Agents of the Federal Bureau of Narcotics, Monell v. Department of Social Services, Owen v. City of Independence, Canton v. Harris*, and the Attorney's Fees Act passed by Congress.[3] These developments have empowered citizens to sue the police, and such lawsuits are extremely effective deterrents, far more so than the suppression of evidence.

In 1961, in *Monroe v. Pape*, 365 U.S. 167, the Supreme Court held that state and local police officers could be personally liable for violations of federal civil-rights law.

Title 42, United States Code, Section 1983 states:

> Every person who, under color of any statute, ordinance, regulation, custom, or usage, of any state or territory, subjects or causes to be subjected any citizen of the United States or person within the jurisdiction thereof to the deprivation of any rights, privileges, or immunities secured by the Constitution and the laws, shall be liable to the party injured in an action at law, suit in equity, or other proper proceeding for redress.

Monroe v. Pape, supra, ignited a revolution against officials acting under color of state law. For police officers, almost any police-related action taken, even while off-duty, falls within the definition of acting under color of state law. Consequently, any police-related action subjects officers to potential lawsuits under Section 1983.

Monroe was clearly a case that called for a remedy. During the investigation of a murder, thirteen police officers kicked in the door and entered the home of Mr. Monroe, while he, his wife, and their children were sleeping. The officers did not have an arrest or search warrant. They ransacked the house and physically threatened Monroe before taking him to the police station, where they interrogated him for ten hours. No evidence was uncovered against him, and he was subsequently released without charges.

As a remedy for these violations, the exclusionary rule was inapplicable. However, a civil lawsuit was filed, the officers were found personally liable for

---

3. *Monroe v. Pape*, 365 U.S. 167 (1961); *Bivens v. Six Unnamed Agents*, 403 U.S. 388 (1971); *Monell v. Department of Social Services*, 436 U.S. 658 (1978); *Owen v. City of Independence*, 445 U.S. 622 (1980); *Canton v. Harris*, 489 U.S. 378 (1989); Attorney's Fees Act, 42 U.S.C. 1988(b).

their actions, and a monetary judgment was rendered against them. For the plaintiff, this remedy was not completely satisfactory because the judgment was against only the individual officers, not their employer. The Court ruled that municipalities were not "persons" under Section 1983 and could not be liable for the judgment; therefore, the employing municipality of the officers did not have to pay the judgment for them. As a new remedy for future cases, *Monroe* was limited, as individual police officers generally do not have the assets to pay large monetary awards. Without good prospects to collect on a judgment against police officers, most attorneys would not bother to take a case against them.

In 1978, in the seminal case *Monell v. Department of Social Services*, 436 U.S. 658, the Court in part reversed *Monroe* and held that municipalities were "persons" and could be held liable for violations of Section 1983. This decision and others that followed provided the "deep pockets" from which persons whose constitutional rights were violated could obtain sufficient compensation. To win such a lawsuit, a plaintiff needs to prove that a police officer, acting under color of state law, violated the plaintiff's constitutional rights and that the municipality contributed to the violation by conduct that indicated "deliberate indifference" or "governmental custom." The municipality could be held liable even though the alleged conduct "had not received formal approval through the body's official decision-making channels."

In 1980, in *Owen v. City of Independence*, 445 U.S. 622, the Court ruled that municipalities could not raise a qualified-immunity defense even when their employees could. The Court reasoned that when a constitutional violation occurred but the individual officials responsible for the violation enjoyed qualified immunity that protected them from liability, the accountability should shift to the municipality so that damages could be paid.

In 1989, in *Canton v. Harris*, 489 U.S. 378, the Court held that a municipality may be liable under Section 1983 for injuries caused by the inadequate training of its officers when the degree of fault amounts to deliberate indifference to the rights of persons with whom the police come in contact.

In addition to the above line of cases, in 1976 Congress passed the Attorney's Fees Act, 42 U.S.C, Section 1988(b), to compensate attorneys who filed civil-rights cases against state actors and to allow attorneys who win their suits to collect their reasonable fees and costs without regard to the amount of the award. As a result, when attorneys settle a case, even for a moderate amount, they can demand a substantial payment from the defendant in addition to the award. For example, a judge could enhance a settlement or jury award of $1,000 dollars rendered against a police officer to compensate the plaintiff for damages by adding an award of $50,000 for reasonable attorney's fees, which would be paid by the municipality directly to the attorney. This, no doubt, encouraged attorneys to file even "small" cases against those acting under color of state law.

In 1990, federal legislation provided that federal district courts exercising original jurisdiction to hear a Section 1983 claim had the supplemental jurisdiction to adjudicate related state tort claims that arose out of the same operative facts of the case.[4] This has encouraged attorneys, using *Monell* and *Canton* municipal liability, to include in their federal actions such tort claims as negligent hiring, supervision, training, retention, direction, discipline, or investigation. As a result of such cases and legislation, non-prisoner Section 1983 civil-rights actions increased from 150 in 1961 to 42,354 in 1998.[5] Additionally, Section 1983 civil-rights claims can be filed in state courts in conjunction with tort claims, such as intentional or negligent police misconduct. Many states have liberalized the ability to sue police in their courts, and, as a consequence, attorneys can combine federal and state claims in state courts.

The above developments have created a favorable environment for lawsuits against police officers and their agencies, and overall lawsuits against the police now number more than 30,000 per year. In response, municipalities have greatly increased their training, supervision, and discipline of police officers regarding their obligation to protect the constitutional rights of citizens.

Proof that civil lawsuits against police are a better deterrent than suppressing evidence is clearly evident in the reduction of police shooting incidents across the nation. A dramatic inverse relationship exists between the increase of lawsuits related to police shootings and the decrease in police shootings. Although accurate national statistics are difficult to verify, New York City statistics are well documented and reliable. From 1971 to 2009, New York City police shooting incidents steadily decreased from 810 to 105, persons killed by police shootings decreased from 93 to 12, and persons injured by police shootings decreased from 221 to 20.[6] These astounding decreases had nothing to do with the exclusionary rule but were brought about in response to the increasing number of lawsuits against the police and large monetary payouts for damages. The lawsuits incentivized the police department to improve its education, training, supervision, and disciplinary standards, and these standards contributed to the reduction in shootings. Other cities across the country have experienced similar decreases for the same reasons.

A civil lawsuit is a broader and fairer remedy than the exclusionary rule. For innocent persons who are unlawfully searched by the police and not found

---

4. 28 USCA, Section 1367(a).

5. Theodore Eisenberg, *Civil Rights Litigation*, 5th Ed. (New York: Matthew Bender, 2004), 170.

6. NYC Police Department Firearms Discharge Report 2009.

with evidence or contraband, the exclusionary rule provides no benefit, because there is no evidence to suppress. A lawsuit by the innocent person may recover monetary compensation, the amount depending on the nature of the unlawful search. If the person was searched briefly on the street and released, the compensation might be minimal; if the person's home was thoroughly searched and the person was held for an extended period before being released, the compensation might be substantial.

Whether the person unlawfully searched was innocent or guilty should make no difference: an unlawful search does not become lawful because contraband or evidence of a crime was uncovered. The violation is the same; the results are irrelevant. Therefore, an innocent person and a guilty person subjected to the same improper police conduct should receive the same remedy. If the remedy for an innocent person as the result of a lawsuit is $10,000 in compensation, a guilty person subjected to the same police misconduct should receive the same amount— no more and no less. The guilty person should not receive the windfall of suppression of evidence, which often results in immunity for the crime. The exclusionary rule bestows an unfair and unequal reward on the guilty while providing nothing for the innocent person whose constitutional rights were violated.

The debate over the most effective way to deter police misconduct was the focus of *Bivens v. Six Unknown Named Agents of the Federal Bureau of Narcotics*, 403 U.S. 388 (1971), a landmark decision that established the right to sue federal agents for violations of constitutional rights. Within the decision, the justices debated the merits of the exclusionary rule, lawsuits, and administrative sanctions as feasible means to deter police misconduct.

In *Bivens*, the plaintiff alleged that federal agents violated his Fourth Amendment rights when, acting without a warrant and without probable cause, they entered his apartment, used unreasonable force to arrest him, searched the apartment, interrogated him, and subjected him to a visual strip search. Lower federal courts dismissed the plaintiff's action because Congress had not passed legislation authorizing such a cause of action against federal officers. Although Congress had enacted Civil Rights Law, 42 U.S.C. 1983, which allowed lawsuits against state officers who had acted under color of state law, Congress had not passed a comparable statute regarding federal officers acting under federal law.

The Supreme Court, with the majority opinion written by Justice William Brennan, reversed the lower courts and held that the Fourth Amendment prohibition against unreasonable searches and seizures was self-executing and a cause of action against federal agents arose directly from the Constitution even though Congress had not passed enabling legislation.

In a concurring opinion, Justice Harlan, agreed that one of the reasons Bivens should have a right to sue for damages was because the exclusionary rule was irrelevant to his case. Justices Black and Blackmun dissented on the grounds that Congress should be the branch of government to create such a cause of action.

Administrative Remedies

Justice Burger also dissented in *Bivens* on the grounds that the question should be left to Congress, but he further explored the issues surrounding the need to find practical remedies for police misconduct, and he proposed a legislative solution to Congress. Justice Burger opined that the exclusionary rule had proved ineffective and that it came at too high a cost. He quoted *Irvine v. California*, 347 U.S. 128 (1954):

> Rejection of the evidence does nothing to punish the wrong-doing official, while it may, and likely will, release the wrong-doing defendant. It deprives society of its remedy against one lawbreaker because he has been pursued by another. It protects one against whom incriminating evidence is discovered, but does nothing to protect innocent persons who are the victims of illegal but fruitless searches.

As for the deterrence rationale for the rule, Justice Burger wrote, "But the hope that this objective could be accomplished by the exclusion of reliable evidence from criminal trials was hardly more than a wistful dream ... Suppressing unchallenged truth has set guilty criminals free but demonstrably has neither deterred deliberate violations of the Fourth Amendment nor decreased those errors in judgment that will inevitably occur given the pressures inherent in police work have to do with serious crimes." Nevertheless, he would not abandon the rule until a meaningful substitute was developed. He proposed a legislative solution as follows:

> Congress should develop an administrative or quasi-judicial remedy against the government itself to afford compensation and restitution for persons whose Fourth Amendment rights have been violated. The venerable doctrine of *respondeat superior* in our tort law provides an entirely appropriate conceptual basis for this remedy. If, for example, a security guard privately employed by a department store commits an assault or other tort on a customer such as an improper search, the victim has a simple and obvious remedy—an action for money damages against the guard's employer, the department store ... Such a statutory scheme would have the added advantage of providing some

remedy to the completely innocent persons who are sometimes the victims of illegal police conduct—something that the suppression doctrine, of course, can never accomplish.

He outlined the skeleton of a statute, as follows:

a.   A waiver of sovereign immunity as to the illegal acts of law enforcement officials committed in the performance of assigned duties;

b.   The creation of a cause of action for damages sustained by any person aggrieved by conduct of governmental agents in violation of the Fourth Amendment or statutes regulating official conduct;

c.   The creation of a tribunal, quasi-judicial in nature or perhaps patterned after the United States Court of Claims, to adjudicate all claims under the statute;

d.   A provision that this statutory remedy is in lieu of the exclusion of evidence secured for use in criminal cases in violation of the Fourth Amendment; and

e.   A provision directing that no evidence, otherwise admissible, shall be excluded from any criminal proceeding because of a violation of the Fourth Amendment.

Three years later in 1974, Congress, apparently taking Burger's recommendations, amended the Federal Tort Claims Act (FTCA), 28 U.S.C. 2680-h, to permit recovery against the federal government "with regard to acts or omissions of investigative or law enforcement officers of the United States Government" for any claim arising out of "assault, battery, false imprisonment, false arrest, abuse of process, or malicious prosecution." This amendment essentially replicated for the federal government the doctrine of *Monell v. Department of Social Services, supra,* which provided that state municipal entities could be responsible for monetary damages caused by their employees.

Although Congress in the FTCA implemented Burger's suggestion regarding the responsibility for damages, it neither implemented a quasi-judicial tribunal to adjudicate complaints, nor substituted a statutory remedy for the exclusionary rule. Nevertheless, these recommendations have been implemented to some extent, though indirectly, by the establishment of various boards, agencies, and offices to oversee police conduct and the allocation of increased resources for administrative oversight of federal and state law enforcement agencies.

Whether police agencies can engage in satisfactory self-policing is still a major cause of debate; though, in recent years, *Mapp's* holding that they cannot has been undercut by the development of professional and responsible law enforcement and by the greatly increased number of disciplinary actions and employee terminations initiated by police agencies.[7] The strengthening of ad-ministrative authority and the implementation of disciplinary sanctions has been spurred by concerns of civil rights litigation. Police agencies and munic-ipalities have been forced to institute controls, training, and discipline to avert their own liability. The exclusionary rule, which does not result in financial costs for the municipalities, did not spur this important change in direction and policy; rather, civil litigation, which has become extremely costly, spurred po-lice agencies to improve the conduct and performance of their officers. Con-sequently, blatant violations, such as unjustified entries into homes without warrants and overly coercive interrogations of suspects, are now uncommon.

Prosecutions

Mapp's contention that district attorneys are not likely to bring criminal charges against police officers with whom they work closely, has been disproved by the substantially increased number of arrests and convictions of police officers. News-papers on a daily basis carry stories of arrests of police officers that belie the con-tention that prosecutors are overly reluctant to prosecute them. Federal and local district attorney offices have specialized branches that focus on allegations against police. Though police officers are most often arrested for excessive force or cor-ruption charges, prosecutions for search and seizure violations have received much notoriety and have been given extensive press coverage.

Violations of civil rights have been prosecuted under the federal criminal statutes, Title 18 U.S.C. Section 241, Conspiracy against Rights, and Title 18 U.S.C. Section 242, Deprivation of Rights under Color of Law. The latter statute provides:

> Whoever, under color of any law, statute, ordinance, regulation, or cus-tom, willfully subjects any inhabitant of any State, Territory, or Dis-trict to the deprivations of any rights, privileges, or immunities secured or protected by the Constitution or laws of the United States shall be fined or imprisoned …

These statutes apply to both state and federal law enforcement officers. De-pending on the nature of the crimes, the authorized sentences under these statutes range from fines and imprisonment up to life imprisonment, and if death results from the act, the defendant may be sentenced to death.

---

7. S. Walker, *Taming the System: The Control of Discretion in Criminal Justice 1950–1990*, (New York: Oxford University Press, 1993): p.51.

In 1991, the United States Attorney in New York indicted Immigration Agent Joseph Occhipinti on 25 counts of criminally violating the civil rights of twelve plaintiffs. The indictment accused Occhipinti of systematically using coercive tactics to obtain consent to search the premises of dozens of supermarkets in the Washington Heights area of New York City. Occhipinti was tried, convicted, and sentenced to three years in prison for conducting the unlawful searches. Supporters of Agent Occhipinti contend that he was the victim of a frame-up orchestrated by groups of drug dealers. Whatever the merits of the case, its effect on police tactics was dramatic: police learned that relying on consensual searches can be fraught with danger. They know that if the searches are challenged in court, the burden of proof will be on them to show that any consent given was done so voluntarily and not as the result of coercion. Moreover, Occhipinti's searches were not the most egregious in police history, and police know that more serious violations are likely to result in more severe prison sentences.

A few civil rights prosecutions of police officers are enough to deter sensible police officers from committing serous violations. The possibility of indictment is a far greater deterrent than the nebulous effect of the exclusionary rule. Indictments involving violations of civil rights laws may also charge standard crimes such as burglary, trespass, robbery, larceny, assault, or unlawful imprisonment.

A New York City case that began in 1990 had a significant deterrent impact on law enforcement across the nation. The New York County District Attorney's Office of Robert Morgenthau filed state criminal charges against four police officers for their conduct while on duty. Stealing or corruption was not involved; the focus of the case was an unlawful search conducted by the officers to retrieve a stolen police radio from alleged drug dealers. During a police incident on an East Harlem street in Manhattan, a police two-way radio was dropped by an officer and was picked up and stolen by someone in the crowd. Four days later, Lieutenant Patricia Feerick, who was the platoon commander, received information that drug dealers in a building on East 122nd Street had the radio. Lieutenant Feerick led a team of three police officers (two male officers and one female officer) into the building, and conducted searches in two apartments to recover the radio. The officers maintained that they had obtained the consent of the apartment occupants for the searches. Nonetheless, several people were allegedly held against their will while the police ransacked the apartments. The radio was not found, and the officers told the occupants they would keep coming back until the radio was returned. Shortly after the raid, an unidentified person dropped off the radio at the police precinct.

Residents of the building filed complaints about the police conduct, and an investigation resulted in the indictment of the officers.

Lieutenant Feerick was known as a dedicated, hard-working, and competent supervisor. She had a nursing degree and a law degree. She had achieved a high score on the captain's test, and was awaiting promotion. At 35 years of age, she was considered a rising star in the department. However, she and the other officers were tried and convicted of charges ranging from criminal trespass to unlawful imprisonment. Lieutenant Feerick was sentenced to two years in prison. One of the male police officers received one to three years in prison, the other male officer a one-year sentence, and the female police officer was given probation.

This was the first time that police officers had been convicted in New York State of criminal charges for conducting an unlawful search. The occupants of the apartments had turned the tables on the officers, or, more accurately, the officers had turned the tables on themselves. Plainly, recovering the radio was not worth the risk of entering the apartments without a search warrant. It was not an emergency situation in which lives were threatened. The police could have conducted an investigation to develop information about the whereabouts of the radio by building cases against the drug dealers on the block. Inevitably, one of them would have made a deal to locate the radio, and then the police could have obtained a search warrant.

The notoriety of the case raised emotions throughout the law-enforcement community. Many in law enforcement, of course, thought the treatment of the officers was overzealous. Police unions and associations complained. Nonetheless, right or wrong, the notoriety and complaints served to disseminate a clear message to all police officers: entering dwellings to conduct searches without a warrant or absent an emergency is fraught with danger.

While the growing trend to bring federal and state prosecutions against police officers for violating constitutional rights is a powerful deterrent, such prosecutions should be limited to the most serious cases. By and large, district attorneys use appropriate discretion, as they know that a few criminal prosecutions are all that are needed.

The cost of prosecuting a few police officers is very high for those individuals, and many people are empathetic to the plight of the officers who are made examples of in order to establish a general deterrent. However, this cost is far less than the cost of the exclusionary rule that allows large numbers of dangerous criminals to escape conviction for their crimes, giving them the opportunity to commit additional crimes.

Stop and Frisks

Since the most serious kinds of police misconduct have been substantially reduced, of greatest concern to the public is not police breaking down doors without a warrant or beating confessions out of prisoners, it is the street encounter in which police violate search and seizure rules. While criminal prosecutions and civil lawsuits arguably have a limited deterrent effect on such street encounters, the exclusionary rule has virtually no deterrent effect. In fact, police have increasingly used the stop-and-frisk laws to aggressively fight crime. This apparently has been an effective tactic, but it has also alienated many citizens who have been subjected to such frisks, especially when the stop-and-frisks were perceived as mistaken or unfair.

In New York City, such police activity is especially common. A study by the New York State Attorney General's Office found that between January 1998 and March 1999, members of the New York City Police Department (NYPD) prepared 174,919 stop-and-frisk reports, which are required whenever a police officer stops and questions a person. Sixty-nine percent of the persons stopped were frisked. Eleven percent of those stopped (19,409 persons) were arrested as a result of the stops.[8]

The study was aimed at concerns over racial profiling in police stop-and-frisk practices; however, the study did not follow up to ascertain conviction, suppression, or dismissal rates, and it did not attempt to ascertain the lawfulness of the stops. Nonetheless, the study demonstrated that the exclusionary rule had not deterred the police from this aspect of investigative activity.

After the Attorney General's study, criticism arose that reports were not submitted for many stop-and-frisks. In response, the NYPD implemented procedures to fully capture the actual number of stop-and-frisk incidents, and in 2006, according to an internal department study, NYPD officers stopped, questioned, or frisked 508,540 persons. This was either a significant increase over prior years or a more accurate accounting. How many of these police actions were violations of the Fourth Amendment was not ascertained; nevertheless, it is clear that the exclusionary rule has not deterred the police from taking such actions, even though courts would surely deem a substantial number of these actions as unconstitutional.[9] In fact, rather than being deterred from this activity, the NYPD has embraced it as a crime-fighting tool. New York City

---

8. Office of New York State Attorney General, *The New York City Police Department's "Stop and Frisk" Practices*, 12/1/1999.

9. Emily Vasquez, *New York Times*, "Numbers Show How Police Work Varies by Precinct," 2/5/07.

Police Commissioner Raymond Kelly has attributed the 76 percent drop in major crime in New York City between 1993 and 2009 to aggressive and innovative police activity, including increased stop-and-frisks. He stated, "This [stop-and-frisk] is a proven law enforcement tactic to fight and deter crime; one that is authorized by the criminal procedure law."[10]

Left unaddressed is the resentment of all the people who were unfairly subjected to stop-and-frisks. Some of these people have been stopped over and over again, and in minority neighborhoods these constant stops are perceived as a form of racism. The effect of these stops is to harden the belief that the exclusionary rule should be maintained or even expanded. Clearly, such a belief is illogical because the rule obviously has not deterred such stop-and-frisks: what is needed is strong administrative oversight of police street conduct.

Although most police departments have improved internal discipline during the past decades, legislatures, in line with Justice Burger's recommendations in *Bivens*, should create appropriate administrative or quasi-judicial boards to collect information and review matters related to possible violations of constitutional rights. Depending on the authority granted, the boards could make recommendations or take appropriate action. A power that might be considered is a remedy against the government itself to afford compensation and restitution for innocent persons whose Fourth Amendment rights have been violated—something that the exclusionary rule does not accomplish. Also, an added benefit of such a regime would be that the board's determinations would become part of an officer's personnel record so that the need for additional training or disciplinary action could be identified or the officer's continued employment evaluated.

Another alternative would be to adopt the English model for deterring police violations here. In England, the distinctly American exclusionary rule is not employed. Nonetheless, the rights of English citizens have been well protected and any dissatisfaction with the police appears relatively mild. Since the inception of the Metropolitan Police Force, discipline of individual police officers for violating police standards and guidelines has been quite strict. The Judges' Rules, which originated in a letter written in 1906 by Lord Alverstone, then Lord Chief Justice, to the Constable of Birmingham, became the centerpiece of the guidelines that police have followed while investigating criminal matters. These guidelines and other rules developed during the century were followed until the passage of the Police and Criminal Evidence Act of 1984,

---

10. Michael Goodwin,"Speech to The Association for a Better New York," *New York Post*, 9/20/09.

which built upon the Judges' Rules. Part IX of the 1984 Act set up the Police Complaints Authority (PCA), which consists of a chairperson appointed by the Queen and eight other members appointed by the Home Secretary. The PCA oversees the administration of police discipline, supervises investigations of complaints against the police, and has the authority to appoint independent investigators.[11]

In the American criminal justice system, states could adopt suitable variations of the English model as a major deterrent to police misconduct, and an enhanced three-tier structure of criminal, civil, and administrative remedies for constitutional violations would allow an appropriately graded response based on the seriousness or willfulness of the violation. This would be a great advantage over the exclusionary rule, which is an all-or-nothing remedy. Under our rule, an honest, inadvertent mistake by a police officer during a spontaneous street encounter is treated the same as a willful, flagrant, and abusive use of force while violating the privacy of someone's home. As written by Justice Warren Burger:

> Freeing either a tiger or a mouse in a schoolroom is an illegal act, but no rational person would suggest that these two acts should be punished in the same way. From time to time judges have occasion to pass on regulations governing police procedures. I wonder what would be the judicial response to a police order authorizing "shoot to kill" with respect to every fugitive. It is easy to predict our collective wrath and outrage. We, in common with all rational minds, would say that the police response must relate to the gravity and need; that a "shoot" order might conceivably be tolerable to prevent the escape of a convicted killer but surely not for a car thief, a pickpocket or a shoplifter.[12]

Since we have better available remedies than the exclusionary rule, it is now justifiable, practical, and sensible to eliminate or severely restrict the application of the rule. The primary remedies now are lawsuits for violations of civil rights under 42 U.S.C. 1983. Such lawsuits can be brought in either federal or state courts along with related claims of intentional or negligent torts. For violations at a criminal level, prosecutions may be instituted. For less serious violations, such as when an officer conducts an improper street-level search, substantial administrative sanctions on the officer are more practical and appropriate than excluding evidence against criminals.

---

11. Charles Wegg-Prosser, *The Police and the Law*, 3rd Ed. (London: Longman Professional, 1986).
12. 403 U.S. 388 (1971), dissent.

Chapter Nineteen

Conclusions

It is revolting to have no better reason for a rule of law than that so it was laid down in the time of Henry IV. It is still more revolting if the grounds upon which it was laid down have vanished long since, and the rule simply persists from blind imitation of the past. Oliver Wendall Holmes, "The Path of the Law," 10 Harv. L. Rev. 457, 469 (1897).

The Supreme Court has reached general agreement that the exclusionary rule should be applied to a particular case only where it would establish an appreciable deterrent to similar acts of police misconduct in the future. In addition, the benefits of the deterrent must outweigh the substantial social costs of guilty defendants going free or receiving reduced sentences. Where the questioned police conduct was not intentional or willful but resulted from negligence or an inadvertent mistake, the Court has repeatedly refused to apply the rule because suppression cannot provide an effective deterrence to those errors in judgment that will inevitably occur as police confront the fast-moving and uncertain challenges of fighting crime. As the Court noted in *Michigan v. Tucker*, 417 U.S. 433 (1983):

> Just as the law does not require that a defendant receive a perfect trial, only a fair one, it cannot realistically require that policemen investigating serious crimes make no errors whatsoever. The pressures of law enforcement and the vagaries of human nature would make such an expectation unrealistic. Before we penalize police error, therefore, we must consider whether the sanction serves a valid and useful purpose.[1]

In cases in which police officers acted in good faith, the Court has found that although a mistake occurred in the instant case, there was nothing that needed to be deterred in the future.[2] Even in cases of willful and flagrant violations of

---

1. *Michigan v. Tucker*, 417 U.S. 433, at 445–446 (1983).
2. *United States v. Leon*, 468 U.S. 897 (1984); *Massachusetts v. Sheppard*, 468 U.S. 981 (1984); *Arizona v. Evans*, 514 U.S. 1 (1995); *Herring v. United States*, 129 S.Ct. 695 (2009).

constitutional rights, the Court has ruled against suppression of the evidence when the questioned evidence would have been uncovered through other sources. In the inevitable discovery and independent source cases, the Court held that although illegally obtained evidence should not enhance the government's case, the government should not be placed in a worse position than it would have been without the violation.[3] In other words, where the government had or was going to get the evidence anyway, it is too much of a cost, too much of a penalty, to suppress the evidence.

The same practical logic used in declining to apply the exclusionary rule to specific cases should also be applied to the exclusionary rule as a whole. While the costs-and-benefits analysis has precluded the use of the rule in specific cases and categories of cases, the same analysis warrants the general elimination of the rule. The rule's detrimental effects, both tangible and intangible, overwhelmingly outweigh any benefits it may produce.

The costs of the rule are not paid for by any benefit, particularly when the police acted in good faith. Moreover, even when officers acted in bad faith and committed willful violations, the rule serves little purpose. Officers, who knowingly and willfully decide to violate constitutional rights in order to make an arrest or obtain evidence, by definition, are not going to be deterred by the rule. Either they do not care that the evidence will be suppressed or they intend to tailor their testimony to avoid suppression. Other sanctions are needed to remedy this kind of bad faith conduct.

Remedies should be commensurate with the severity of the violations. Officers who engage in flagrantly abusive misconduct may be prosecuted or sued in civil court and sanctioned with punitive damages for which they cannot be indemnified by their employer. On the other hand, officers who act in good faith but make an error can be better dealt with administratively. Good management can effectively address overzealousness, inexperience, or incompetence. Higher personnel standards, professionalism, training, discipline, and accountability are the best means of deterring police misconduct or mistakes. As the Court noted in *Hudson v. Michigan*, 547 U.S. 586 (2006), "Modern police forces are staffed with professionals; it is not credible to assert that internal discipline, which can limit successful careers, will not have a deterrent effect."

When a police officer brutalizes or unnecessarily shoots a suspect, suppression is not employed as the remedy. When police apprehend a murderer and out of cruelty or revenge unnecessarily beat him up, the murderer is not

---

3. *Nix v. Williams*, 467 U.S. 431 (1j984); *Segura v. United States*, 468 U.S. 796 (1984).

exonerated, and evidence is not suppressed because the police used excessive force when making an arrest. If the evidence in a defendant's pocket is not excluded because the police beat him up, it hardly seems sensible to exclude the evidence because the same officer reached into the defendant's pocket. The best remedy for such a violation is a lawsuit or prosecution, not the exclusionary rule.

Nevertheless, the exclusionary rule still flourishes, and judges at all levels in the system continue to utilize and expand it. Often they apply it incorrectly, but rarely are their incorrect decisions appealed. Furthermore, as long as the rule is available, defense attorneys will use it as their most effective means of getting off guilty clients. For many defense attorneys, especially those that defend narcotics charges, it is their bread and butter and keeps them employed. They continually seek new and creative applications, and for each new application of the suppression doctrine to a particular set of circumstances, similar cases are affected, and those similar cases breed additional cases.

Although, at its inception, the rule served the useful purposes of framing problematic issues and chastising the police for illegal conduct, the resolution of these issues and the improved discipline of the police have been largely accomplished by other means, including tort and civil rights lawsuits, criminal prosecutions, and administrative penalties. At this time, with the bulk of the work of reducing serious and blatant police abuses already completed, the rule serves no beneficial purpose, yet it continues to encourage disrespect for the law, criminality, and corruption.

The adoption of the rule came about as part of a movement to provide protections for an accused against the overwhelming power of the state. Undoubtedly, there were sound reasons to do so; however, during the last half-century, defendants have gained significant protections that lessen any basis for the continued existence of the rule. The right to counsel for all defendants from the inception of the accusatory process to trial has been effectively implemented.[4] Indigent defendants are provided counsel free of charge.[5] Defense attorneys have the recognized right to challenge the fairness of a lineup and identification procedures.[6] Discovery rules mandate that prosecutors provide exculpatory information to defense counsel, and prior notes, records, and statements of witnesses must be turned over to the defense.[7] Courts increasingly allow into evidence third-party hearsay statements that exonerate a de-

---

4. *Ferguson v. Georgia*, 365 U.S. 570 (1961); *Cuyler v. Sullivan*, 444 U.S. 823 (1980).
5. *Gideon v. Wainwright*, 372 U.S. 335 (1963).
6. *U.S. v. Wade*, 388 U.S. 218 (1967).
7. *Jencks v. U.S.*, 353 U.S. 657 (1957).

fendant.[8] At the same time, the prosecution has lost the use of certain hearsay exceptions that allowed the admission of third-party statements that incriminate a defendant.[9] All of these measures inure to the benefit of the defendant and generally enhance the truth-seeking aspects of the criminal justice process. As a result, the enhanced capability of defense attorneys to challenge the accuracy of the evidence presented against their clients has resulted in the prevention of many wrongful convictions. With these enhanced protections for defendants in place, the use of the exclusionary rule as a means of providing a general sense of protection for defendants against the government has lost an important premise for its purported justification.

When appropriate, defense attorneys can argue against imputing guilt to their clients based on physical evidence recovered by the police. They can argue that their client did not knowingly possess the physical evidence or that a connection from the evidence to their client cannot be established. However, they should not be able to argue that actual physical evidence did not exist and does not exist for use during a truth-seeking trial. The suppression of evidence, contrary to the objectives of the trial process, allows attorneys to act and argue as though the evidence does not exist. It allows them to perpetrate a fraud on juries and the public, and this fraud provides little countervailing benefit to the justice system or the general welfare.

When witnesses take the stand in a trial, they are required to swear or affirm that they will tell, "The truth, the whole truth, and nothing but the truth." Preventing a witness from testifying that concrete, reliable evidence exists and can be produced shatters the basis of his oath or affirmation. Truth telling is the foundation of the trial process. It is far more important than any supposed benefit the exclusionary rule could serve.

Today's notion that we should exclude truthful and reliable evidence for the sake of some vague and uncertain deterrent value is as absurd as the medieval notion that a judge with private knowledge that the accused was innocent had nevertheless to convict if the record developed in court so dictated.[10] As Saint Thomas Aquinas wrote:

> Suppose that a man has been incriminated by false witnesses, but the judge knows that he is innocent. The judge must, like Daniel, exam-

---

8. *Chambers v. Mississippi*, 410 U.S. 284 (1973); *Holmes v. South Carolina*, 547 U.S. 319 (2006).

9. *Lilly v. Virginia*, 527 U.S. 116 (1999); *Crawford v. Washington*, 541 U.S. 36 (2004).

10. James Q. Whitman, *The Origins of Reasonable Doubt*, (New Haven and London, Yale University Press, 2008) 167.

ine the witnesses with great care, so as to find a motive for acquitting the innocent: but if he cannot do this he should remit him for judgment by a higher tribunal. If even this is impossible, the judge does not sin if he pronounces sentence in accordance with the evidence. For in that case, it is not the judge that puts an innocent man to death. Rather, it is those who declared him to be guilty.[11]

Today's absurdity is not that the innocent are being regularly condemned, it is that the guilty are being regularly exonerated.

The old maxim—It is better that ten guilty men go free rather than one innocent man be convicted—has been converted into a new maxim—It is better that a hundred guilty men go free rather than one person be convicted as a result of an unreasonable stop and frisk or an un-Mirandized question by a police officer attempting to prevent crime. Unfortunately, it is not just a hundred guilty criminals going free, it is tens of thousands.

The social fabric of society suffers when the integrity of the truth-seeking process is diminished. A justice system not founded on truth spreads dishonesty throughout society. As Justice George Sutherland wrote:

The fundamental basis upon which all rules of evidence must rest— if they are to rest upon reason—is their adaptation to the successful development of the truth.[12]

To enhance the truth-seeking process, several major components of the exclusionary rule must be eliminated. They can be eliminated in three stages. First, regarding the admissibility of physical objects as evidence, the principle should stand that the judiciary cannot rightfully deny the existence of objects that in fact exist. Therefore, for physical objects, the Court should clearly and unequivocally eliminate any applications of the rule. Creating exceptions to avoid unacceptable and troubling results has only created further complexity. Half measures such as the inevitable discovery or independent source doctrines have provided inconsistent solutions. For truth and simplicity's sake, if an object exists, its existence should not be denied.

Second, regarding confessions and statements, the Court does not have to subordinate its constitutional authority to Congress, but it could readily adopt the principles that Congress promulgated in 18 U.S.C. Section 3501 regarding voluntary or involuntary confessions, with Miranda warnings being only one factor in the totality of circumstances. Also, whether or not a suspect asked

---

11. Saint Thomas Aquinas, *Summa Theologica.*
12. *Funk v. United States*, 290 U.S. 371 (1933).

for or inquired about an attorney would not be absolutely determinative but only another factor in the assessment of voluntariness.

One way Congress could provide the impetus for the Court to return to the voluntariness standard would be to provide funds for video-recording equipment in police vehicles and facilities so that the police can record their interactions and interrogations of suspects and defendants. Video recording would go a long way toward addressing the concerns that the Court voiced in *Miranda* regarding coercive tactics in police stations. Although not absolutely determinative, a video recording or a lack thereof would be an important factor in assessing whether a confession was voluntary or not.

Third, the right to counsel should apply to the formal stages of a criminal prosecution and to the relationship between an accused and his counsel; it should not apply to a defendant's voluntary statements to persons other than counsel or outside the formal process of investigation or prosecution. When defendants, even represented defendants, freely interact with persons whom they believe are their friends or associates and recount the details of their past, present, or future crimes, they deserve no special immunity and the attorney-client privilege should not apply. Defendants are advised at arraignment that they have a right to remain silent and that anything they say can be used against them; however, they can speak freely if they wish. In fact, defendants, while in court with their attorneys by their sides, often ignore their counsel's advice and respond to statements made by witnesses and others by blurting out voluntary admissions, and those admissions can be used against them.

Similarly, defendants have a right to remain silent outside of court, and, just as in court, anything they say outside of court should also be useable against them. The ubiquitous right to counsel and deliberate elicitation doctrines pronounced in *Massiah v. United States*, 377 U.S. 201 (1964) and *Brewer v. Williams*, 430 U.S. 387 (1977), do not stand up as a valid criterion for distinguishing in-court from out-of-court responses. Testimony from a government witness is a form of deliberate elicitation, and if the defendant chooses to respond by making a statement, the statement counts. The fact that the defendant's counsel advised against making any statements in court does not nullify the statement, and the fact that a counsel advised his client not to talk to anyone about the case should not nullify a defendant's out-of-court statements to friends or informants.

Such changes by the Supreme Court and Congress would instigate debate within the states over their internal criminal procedure policies. California has already decided by state constitutional amendment not to suppress evidence unless required by the federal courts. Other states should follow suit by judicial or legislative action. The idea voiced by Justice Henry Billings Brown in 1897 that the states have the ability to discover better solutions within the framework of the Constitution is still sound:

> While the cardinal principles of justice are immutable, the methods by which justice is administered are subject to constant fluctuation, and that the Constitution of the United States, which is necessarily and to a large extent inflexible and exceedingly difficult of amendment, should not be so construed as to deprive the States of the power to so amend their laws as to make them conform to the wishes of the citizens as they may deem best for the public welfare without bringing them into conflict with the supreme law of the land. *Hardy v. Holden*, 169 U.S. 366 (1897).

A Supreme Court repudiation of the rule would encourage states to place more emphasis on other remedies for police misconduct, and the states could experiment with new programs to improve police performance and to restore confidence in the justice system. States that want to provide greater protections for their citizens than those required by the United States Constitution can waive their sovereign immunity and can allow citizens to bring lawsuits against them on the basis of their state constitutions.[13]

In the most recent decades, innovative solutions by private attorneys, judges, and law enforcement administrators have provided satisfactory remedies for wronged individuals. These solutions have provided meaningful deterrents to unlawful police conduct and have proved far more effective than the exclusionary rule. It is time to stop unnecessarily immunizing criminals. The hard evidence has shown that the exclusionary rule has been ineffective as a deterrent to police violations and has also set free thousands of criminals, thereby exponentially increasing crime, solely because "the constable has blundered."

---

13. *Brown v. State*, 89 N.Y.2d 172 (1996).

Appendix A

Selected Amendments of the Constitution of the United States

Fourth Amendment

The right of the people to be secure in their persons, houses, papers, and effects, against unreasonable searches and seizures, shall not be violated, and no Warrants shall issue, but upon probable cause, supported by Oath or affirmation, and particularly describing the place to be searched, and the persons or things to be seized.

Fifth Amendment

No person shall be held to answer for a capital, or otherwise infamous crime, unless on presentment or indictment of a Grand Jury, except in cases arising in the land or naval forces, or in the Militia, when in actual service in time of War or public danger; nor shall any person be subject for the same offence to be twice put in jeopardy of life or limb; nor shall be compelled in any criminal case to be a witness against himself, nor be deprived of life, liberty, or property, without due process of law; nor shall private property be taken for public use, without just compensation.

Sixth Amendment

In all criminal prosecutions, the accused shall enjoy the right to a speedy and public trial, by an impartial jury of the State and district wherein the crime shall have been committed, which district shall have been previously ascertained by law, and to be informed of the nature and cause of the accusation; to be confronted with the witnesses against him; to have compulsory process for obtaining Witnesses in his favor, and to have the Assistance of Counsel for his defense.

Fourteenth Amendment

Section 1. All persons born or naturalized in the United States and subject to the jurisdiction thereof, are citizens of the United States and of the State wherein they reside. No State shall make or enforce any law which shall abridge the privileges and immunities of citizens of the United States; nor shall any State deprive any person of life, liberty, or property, without due process of law; nor deny to any person within its jurisdiction the equal protection of the law.

Section 5. The Congress shall have the power to enforce, by appropriate legislation, the provisions of this article.

Appendix B

Problems for Classroom or General Discussion

The following problems are offered as a means to clarify existing exclusionary rule practices and to examine the merits of the rule.

Problem One

Officers respond to a domestic violence incident at a residence. A woman is waiting in front of the residence and tells the officers that her boyfriend, who sometimes shares the residence, threatened to shoot her. She states that he keeps a gun somewhere in the house and that they should go in and find it. The officers knock on the front door, and the boyfriend comes to the door but does not open it. Speaking through the door, the boyfriend denies that he threatened the woman and refuses to allow the officers to enter the residence to search for a gun. He further states that his girlfriend is mentally ill, off her medication, and has made false accusations in the past. Moreover, he says that as soon as he gets dressed, he will come out and go to the station house with the officers.

Questions

1. Should the officers forcibly enter the house to search for the gun?
2. Should they arrest the boyfriend?
3. If they decide to arrest him, should they forcibly enter the house to do so?
4. If they decide to wait for the boyfriend to come out, how long should they wait?
5. If the boyfriend does not come out in a reasonable time, should they forcibly enter the house?

6. If the boyfriend opens the door, should they enter on the basis of the woman's consent for them to search the house?
7. If the boyfriend comes out and agrees to go to the station house with the officers, should they handcuff him?
8. If they handcuff him, does that mean he is under arrest?
9. Should they search him?
10. If they arrest him outside the house, can they enter it to search for the gun?
11. Should they get a search warrant before entering the house?

References

Payton v. New York, 445 U.S. 573, 100 S.Ct. 1371 (1980).
Brigham City, Utah v. Stuart, 547 U.S. 398,126 S.Ct. 1943 (2006).
United States v. Matlock, 415 U.S. 164 (1974).
Illinois v. Rodriguez, 497 U.S. 177, 110 S.Ct. 2793 (1990).
Georgia v. Randolph, 547 U.S. 103, 126 S.Ct. 1515 (2006).

Problem Two

On a rainy December night, after midnight, Police officers Quick and Sharp responded to a 911 call regarding a fight in a bar. The caller to 911 had stated that he had been threatened by three males, each about nineteen years old. They threatened to hit him with pool cues, and one threatened to shoot him. The caller hung up without giving his name or any other information.

When the officers arrived at the bar, they saw three young men playing pool in the rear of the premises. The only other persons present were two elderly patrons at the bar, and the bartender.

The young men were each dressed in short-sleeved muscle shirts, and they looked like bodybuilders. The officers approached them and asked whether anyone had called the police. They said they had not, but after a brief conversation, one of them said that "a wise guy had been there earlier causing trouble but he left."

Officer Sharp asked, "Did you guys threaten him with anything?"

"No," each young man said.

They identified themselves as John Stabile, Joe Vitale, and Bumper Morone.

Officer Sharp noticed three jackets hanging on coat hangers near the pool table, two black leather jackets and one blue denim jacket. The denim jacket appeared to have a heavy pocket that was pulling the jacket to one side. Sharp did not let on that he noticed the heavy pocket. He positioned himself between the denim jacket and the men and said, "We'd like you guys to come to the station house so that we can make out a report."

"Why do we have to go to the station house?" Stabile said.

"It will only take a few minutes. We need to make a report and check your identification. We'll drive you right back."

"Okay, if we have to," Stabile said as he took one of the leather jackets and put it on.

Vitale took the other leather jacket, put it on, and walked to the front of the bar.

Morone also walked to the front of the bar, but he did not take the remaining jacket.

"Don't you have a jacket?" Sharp asked.

"No," Morone answered.

"That's not your jacket on the hanger?"

"No."

"Whose is it?"

"I have no idea."

Officer Sharp asked Stabile and Vitale whether the jacket belonged to either of them. They said no. Then Sharp reached into the pocket of the jacket and took out a semi-automatic handgun. As he did, Morone tried to run out, but Officer Quick tripped him to the floor.

"You're under arrest," Quick said as he handcuffed Morone.

The officers took all three men to the station house. They charged Morone with possession of the gun, but they released Stabile and Vitale.

Questions

1. Did the officers have the authority to question the young men?
2. Was it lawful for the officers to ask the young men to come to the station house with them?
3. Was it lawful for Sharp to search the denim jacket?
4. Did the officers have probable cause to arrest Morone?
5. Did the fact that the officers never saw Morone in possession of the gun preclude them from lawfully arresting him?
6. What facts and circumstances in this incident could be relied upon to establish the necessary probable cause to justify Morone's arrest?
7. At his trial, could a jury convict Morone of the unlawful possession of the gun on the basis only of the above described evidence?

8.   If the jury acquitted Morone, would that mean that his arrest was unlawful?

References

Terry v. Ohio, 392 U.S. 1 (1968)
Alabama v. White, 496 U.S. 325 (1990)
Beck v. Ohio, 379 U.S. 89 (1964)
Peters v. New York, 392 U.S. 40 (1968)
California v. Hodari, 499 U.S. 621 (1991)
United States v. Carrasquillo, 877 F.2d 73 (D.C. Cir. 1989)
Draper v. United States, 358 U.S. 207 (1959)
Illinois v. Gates, 262 U.S. 213 (1983)

Problem Three

Federal Drug Enforcement Administration agents received an anonymous letter regarding an expected shipment of ten packages of cocaine. The letter stated that the cocaine would be hidden inside television sets that were going to arrive at a warehouse the next Sunday when the warehouse was closed to regular business. On that Sunday, six agents in three cars parked at a distance from the warehouse and watched the entrances and exits. The warehouse was closed, but they observed a panel truck parked in the delivery bay of the warehouse. The panel truck was marked "Acme Televisions."

Agent Able walked to the warehouse, climbed onto the loading dock, and found an open door. He looked inside and saw four men opening boxes that contained televisions. One of the men was dressed in a business suit; the other three were dressed in casual attire. Agent Able left the warehouse and relayed the information to the other agents.

When the man wearing the business suit left the warehouse carrying a briefcase, two agents arrested him, searched the briefcase, and found a kilo package of cocaine.

The agents conferred, then entered the warehouse, and arrested the other three men. They did not conduct a search, but sent one agent to obtain a search warrant for the warehouse.

The judge issued the search warrant, and when the agents executed the warrant, they found nine more kilos of cocaine in the television boxes. All four men were arrested and charged with felony possession of cocaine with the intent to distribute.

Before the trial, their attorneys moved to suppress the cocaine on the basis that the defendants' Fourth Amendment rights against unreasonable search and seizure were violated. A hearing was held in which all of the above facts were disclosed. How should the judge rule on the motion to suppress the evidence?

Questions

1. Did the anonymous letter meet the requirements necessary to obtain a search warrant?
2. Did the anonymous letter give the agents a justifiable reason to place the warehouse under surveillance?
3. Did the anonymous letter give Agent Able the lawful authority to enter the warehouse?
4. Did the anonymous letter combined with the observation of the panel truck parked in the delivery bay give Agent Able the lawful authority to enter the warehouse?
5. When Agent Able saw the four men opening the television boxes, did he have sufficient confirmation of the details in the anonymous letter to give him probable cause to arrest the men?
6. Assuming he had probable cause to believe a crime was being committed, could he lawfully enter the warehouse without a warrant?
7. Did the observations of the agents that confirmed the details in the anonymous letter give them probable cause to arrest the man in the business suit?
8. Assuming they had probable cause to arrest him, did they have the lawful authority to search his briefcase without a warrant?
9. Was it necessary for the agents to have seen the actual packages of cocaine for them to have probable cause to arrest the man in the business suit?
10. After the agents found the cocaine in the briefcase, did they have probable cause to arrest the other three men?
11. Assuming so, was it necessary for them to obtain a warrant before entering the warehouse to make the arrests?
12. When the agents arrested the three men inside the warehouse, could they have immediately searched the television boxes without a warrant?
13. When the agents arrested the three men inside the warehouse, could they have immediately searched the entire warehouse without a warrant?
14. Was the issuance of the search warrant by the judge lawful?
15. Assuming Agent Able's first entry onto the loading dock of the warehouse was unlawful, should that fact render all the subsequent actions of the agents unlawful, thereby, requiring suppression of the evidence?

16. Assuming Agent Able's first entry onto the loading dock was unlawful, should the evidence nevertheless be admissible because the agents acted on the basis of other separate and independent facts?

References

Carroll v. United States, 267 U.S. 132 (1925)
Draper v. United States, 358 U.S. 307 (1959)
Illinois v. Gates, 462 U.S. 213 (1983)
Segura v. United States, 468 U.S. 796 (1984)
Murray v. United States, 487 U.S. 533 (1988)

Problem Four

Detectives Snarley and Plodder were assigned to investigate a warehouse burglary at the Acme Trucking Company in which several million dollars worth of laptop computer notebooks had been stolen. A few days after the burglary, they received an anonymous tip identifying Johnny Mack as one of the burglars. The detectives investigated Mack and found that he had an extensive criminal record for burglaries and larcenies, and also a long association with other known criminals. From a confidential informant, the detectives learned that Mack was a heavy marijuana user and hung out at a local bar, *The Hot Spot*, where the informant believed illegal drug transactions continually took place.

Detective Snarley enlisted an undercover narcotics officer, Willie Lowe, to begin frequenting *The Hot Spot* in an attempt to gather information. In the meantime, Mike Boozer, a person known as an associate of Mack, was arrested for driving while intoxicated; in the trunk of his car, the arresting officers found ten of the computers that had been stolen from the warehouse. The officers notified Detective Plodder about the computers, and he attempted to interview Boozer. However, Boozer had an attorney and refused to answer any questions. Detective Plodder asked the officers to arrest Boozer for intoxicated driving only, not to arrest him for criminal possession of the stolen property, and not to let on that they knew the computers were stolen. The officers agreed, and they told Boozer that if he brought in a sales receipt, the computers would be returned to him.

A week later, the undercover narcotics officer called Detective Snarley to inform him that Mack had just purchased marijuana.

"Where is he now?" Snarley asked.

"He's still at the bar," the narcotics officer said.

"Where's the grass?"

"I think he stuffed it in his underwear."

"I'll be right there," Snarley said. "If he leaves, follow him."

Snarley arrived at *The Hot Spot* in time to see Mack leaving the bar with Officer Lowe following him. When Lowe signaled that the person he was following was the suspect, Snarley drove ahead of Mack, got out of the car, and displayed his badge. "I'm a detective. I want to talk to you."

"Who, me?" Mack said.

"Yeah, you."

"I don't have much time. What do you want to talk about?"

"Come over here to the car." Snarley held Mack by the arm. "Someone called in and said you had a gun on you."

"Me. No way. Look for yourself." Mack opened his jacket to show that he was not carrying anything.

"I'll check for myself," Snarley said. He made Mack place his hands on the top of the squad car and frisked him.

"You see, I don't have any gun," Mack said.

Snarley opened Mack's belt buckle, reached into his underwear, and pulled out a clear plastic baggie containing marijuana.

"What have we got here?" Snarley said.

"That's nothing. It's just for personal use," Mack said.

Snarley handcuffed Mack. "This looks like a lot more than personal use."

"It's for me and my friends. I don't sell."

"We'll talk about it at the station house."

In the station house interrogation room, Snarley advised Mack of his Miranda rights, and Mack signed a form indicating that he agreed to answer questions and to waive his right to have a lawyer present.

For twenty minutes, Snarley questioned Mack about who sold him the marijuana and how the transaction occurred. Mack gave ambiguous answers, saying that he only knew the person he bought from by a nickname, "Chuckie." He did not know his real name and gave a vague description.

During the questioning, Detective Plodder arrived. He had the ten computers that had been seized from Boozer, and one by one he brought them into the interrogation room and placed them on the table in front of Mack.

Plodder turned to Mack. "Tell us about the warehouse burglary."

"What warehouse burglary?"

"The Acme Trucking Company. We know you were in on it. We recovered the computers from your accomplices, and we've got your fingerprints on the computer boxes and in the warehouse."

"You can't have my fingerprints," Mack said.

"You apparently took your gloves off for a few minutes," Plodder said.

"I never took them off." Mack then put his head in his hands. "Maybe I should get a lawyer."

"If you want a lawyer, we'll let you call a lawyer. We'll be outside. If you want a lawyer, call us," Plodder said.

The detectives left Mack alone in the room with the computers next to him. After fifteen minutes, they went in and asked him whether he would tell them about the burglary. He said he would cooperate.

Detective Plodder read him the Miranda rights and had him sign another waiver form.

Mack confessed to his participation in the burglary, although he downplayed his role. He identified his accomplices and told the detectives about a garage where most of the stolen computers were stored. The detectives asked him to write out and sign his confession, but he refused.

On the basis of Mack's information, the detectives obtained a search warrant for the garage and recovered the stolen computers.

Mack was indicted, and his attorney moved to exclude from evidence the use of Mack's verbal statements, the marijuana, and the recovered computers.

Questions

1. Was Snarley's arrest of Mack for possession of marijuana lawful?
2. Did Snarley have probable cause to arrest Mack?
3. Did the fact that Snarley did not inform Mack about the charge that he was arresting him for and that he lied to him about the reason for the frisk invalidate the arrest and the search incidental to the arrest?

For the remaining questions assume the arrest for possession of marijuana was lawful.

4. Was the search of Mack's underwear lawful?
5. Should Mack's admissions that the marijuana was "just for his personal use" and "It's for me and my friends" be admissible against him?
6. Should any incriminating statements regarding the marijuana that Mack made at the station house after Snarley gave him the Miranda rights be admissible?
7. Is it lawful for detectives who obtain a suspect's waiver of the right to remain silent without advising him of all the crimes about which they intend to question him?

8. Are the police allowed to lie to a suspect during an interrogation?
9. Should Mack's statement regarding wearing gloves during the warehouse burglary, "I never took them off," be admissible against him?
10. Were Plodder's initial questions to Mack regarding the burglary legally covered under the umbrella of the first set of Miranda rights given to Mack by Snarley?
11. After Mack said, "Maybe I should get a lawyer," was it lawful for the detectives to question him again without a lawyer present?
12. Did the fact that Detective Plodder waited fifteen minutes before reading Mack another set of Miranda rights make his questioning about the burglary lawful?
13. Did Mack's refusal to write out and sign his confession invalidate the confession and render his verbal statements involuntary?
14. Assuming the interrogation regarding the burglary was unlawful, should the computers be excluded from evidence as the fruits of the poisonous tree?

References

Whiteley v. Warden, 401 U.S. 560 (1971)
Edwards v. Arizona, 451 U.S. 477 (1981)
Oregon v. Elstad, 470 U.S. 298 (1985)
Colorado v. Spring, 479 U.S. 564 (1987)
Connecticut v. Barrett, 479 U.S. 523 (1987)
Davis v. United States, 512 U.S. 452 (1994)
United States v. Patane, 542 U.S. 630 (2004)

Problem Five

A police department received a 911 call from an anonymous caller that two men were standing on a street corner outside a bar and they both had guns. The caller described them as two male whites in their early twenties, one was very tall and one was shorter. The caller hung up before giving any further description or information.

Police officers Able and Dunkin were patrolling in the area in their marked patrol car, and they were dispatched to the street corner to investigate the call. The officers saw two young men, approximately 20 or 25 years old, one about six-foot-three-inches tall, the other about five-foot-ten. The young men were engaged in conversation.

The officers double parked in front of the bar, and Officer Dunkin waved to them to come over to the police car. However, the taller young man, later identified as Gary Kooper, began walking away. The shorter young man, later identified as Billy Nelson did not walk away, but he did not acknowledge the officer. With that, the officers got out of their car. As Officer Able walked after Kooper, Officer Dunkin approached Nelson and asked him what he was doing there. Nelson answered, "I'm not doing anything."

Officer Dunkin asked, "Why is your friend walking away?"

"He's not my friend," Nelson said.

"Weren't you just talking to him?" the officer asked.

"No. I don't know him," Nelson said.

With that, Officer Dunkin frisked Nelson and found a loaded automatic pistol in his jacket pocket.

Meanwhile, Officer Able caught up to Kooper, but when he tried to talk to him, Kooper began to run. The officer tackled Kooper, handcuffed him, and found a loaded revolver in his pocket.

The officers arrested both men and sent the guns to the police ballistics laboratory, where they were test fired.

The test-fired bullets from the two guns were compared to bullets in a ballistic evidence computerized data base, and they were both matched to bullets removed from a murder victim, who had been killed during a robbery several days earlier.

Forensic evidence was developed placing both Kooper and Nelson at the scene of the murder/robbery.

On the basis of the ballistics and forensic evidence, Kooper and Nelson were indicted for murder, robbery, and unlawful possession of the guns. They were tried separately, and each of their attorneys moved to have the guns and the ballistics reports excluded from evidence because the guns were obtained in violation of the defendants' Fourth Amendment rights and the ballistics reports were the fruits of the poisonous tree.

Questions

1. Was it lawful for Officer Dunkin to approach and question Nelson?
2. On his initial approach, did Officer Dunkin have reasonable suspicion sufficient to stop and frisk Nelson?
3. After Nelson lied about conversing with Kooper, did Officer Dunkin have reasonable suspicion sufficient to stop and frisk him?

4. Because Kooper walked away from the police, did Officer Dunkin have reasonable suspicion sufficient to stop and frisk Nelson?

5. If the court determines that Dunkin did not have reasonable suspicion sufficient to frisk Nelson, must it suppress the gun and ballistics report?

6. In Nelson's trial, if the court suppresses the gun found on Nelson, can it nevertheless be used as evidence in Kooper's trial?

7. Did Officer Able have reasonable suspicion sufficient to stop and frisk Kooper on the basis of the anonymous call?

8. Did the additional factor of Kooper walking away from the officers, instead of going to the police car, give the officers reasonable suspicion to stop and frisk him?

9. Should the gun that was taken from Kooper be excluded from evidence at his trial?

10. If the court determines that Officer Able did not have reasonable suspicion sufficient to stop and frisk Kooper, must it suppress the gun and ballistics report?

11. In Kooper's trial, if the court suppresses the gun found on Kooper, can it nevertheless be used as evidence in Nelson's trial?

References for Problem Five:

Draper v. United States, 358 U.S. 307 (1959)
Terry v. Ohio, 392 U.S. 1 (1968)
Florida v. J.L., 529 U.S. 266 (2000)
California v. Hodari D., 499 U.S. 621 (1991)
Illinois v. Wardlow, 528 U.S. 119 (2000)

Problem Six

Three 20-year-old young men, Vinny Johnson, Johnny "Bag a Donuts" Fatsom, and Henry Malevolento were driving around in Vinny's car. Malevolento suggested that they rob a florist shop to get some money to buy cocaine. Vinny did not want to do it, but agreed to drive Malevolento and Fatsom to the florist shop. Vinny did not have a gun; Malevolento had a stolen Glock 9mm semi-automatic pistol; and Fatsom had an unlicensed .38 caliber revolver he had bought on the street. Malevolento and Fatsom went inside, each took out their guns, announced a stick up, and told everyone not to move or they would be shot.

Mr. Florentino, the owner of the shop, and his daughter, Maria, were behind the counter. Two male customers were also in the store. Florentino handed Fatsom $200 from the cash register. Then Fatsom said to Malevolento, "Let's go." However, when Malevolento tried to search under Maria's clothes to see whether she had any money hidden on her, Mr. Florentino came to his daughter's defense. Malevolento shot Mr. Florentino in the heart, killing him. Maria screamed and pleaded for someone to help her father, but neither of the customers moved.

Just as the shots were fired, two more customers came into the store. One of the customers, Mrs. Church, knew Fatsom. She had been his den mother when he was a boy scout. She shouted, "Johnny, what are you doing?"

Fatsom told Malevolento, "She knows me. She knows my mother. What are we going to do?"

Malevolento told Fatsom to get all the customers into the back room and to tie them up, which he did. Malevolento tried to drag Maria into the back room, but she would not let go of her father, so he shot her in the head, killing her. Then he told Fatsom to shoot all the customers.

"I can't do that," Fatsom said.

"You have to," Malevolento said. "That woman knows you. It's either them or us."

"I don't care," Fatsom said. "I just can't do it."

Malevolento went in the back room and shot all four customers in the head, killing them all.

As the two robbers ran out of the store, got into Vinny's car, and drove away, a dog walker noticed them running from the store and made a note of the license plate number.

"What happened?" Vinny asked.

"Nothing, just drive," Malevolento said as he slipped his Glock automatic under the passenger seat.

Fatsom began crying. "He shot six people," he said. "He's crazy."

"Shut up," Malevolento said. "Drop me at my house."

Vinny drove Malevolento to his house then dropped off Fatsom at his house.

"I'm getting out of town as fast as I can," Fatsom said. "You should do the same."

Within an hour of the robbery, based on the plate number taken by the dog walker, the police had identified Vinny as a suspect, and five detectives staked out his house. As Vinny pulled up in front of his house, the detectives stopped and questioned him. Vinny immediately began to cry and blurted out that he did not know anyone was going to be shot, but he did not say anything else. The detectives arrested him, read him his Miranda rights, and took him to the station house. They also searched the car, and found the gun that Malevolento had used to shoot the six people.

Laboratory tests found no fingerprints on the Glock, but a ballistics comparison showed that it was the gun used in the killings.

No fingerprints or other physical evidence was found in the store to identify the perpetrators of the crime.

At the station house, Vinny gave a truthful videotaped confession, identified Malevolento and Fatsom, and admitted that he drove them to the florist to commit the robbery. He insisted, however, that he did not know they were going to shoot anyone. He also said that Fatsom was planning to get out of town as soon as possible.

The detectives immediately went to Fatsom's house. When no one answered the door, they broke into the house without a warrant to search for him. They found him hiding in a closet, and found a gun hidden in his sock drawer and $200 in a jewelry box. The detectives questioned him, and he admitted that he had been at the florist shop, but then lied, saying he stayed outside in the car while Vinny and Malevolento went in. He said he did not know they were going to commit a robbery. When they came out of the store, Vinny gave him the revolver and the $200. Fatsom was arrested and taken to the police station where he was given Miranda warnings. He repeated his story, and gave a videotaped statement.

Fatsom's fingerprints were on the revolver that was found in the sock drawer, but a ballistics comparison test showed it was not the gun used in the killings. Later, the $200 was analyzed at the police laboratory and fingerprints belonging to Mr. Florentino were found on several of the bills.

Other detectives went to Malevolento's house. They knocked on the door. Malevolento answered through the door, but refused to open it. The detectives decided to surround the house and to get a search warrant. While the detectives were waiting outside, Malevolento washed his hands thoroughly with Borax soap to get rid of any gunpowder residue.

When the search warrant arrived, the detectives broke down the door, entered the house, and arrested Malevolento. He did not resist. The detectives searched the house, but did not find any incriminating evidence. At the station house, the police conducted a gunpowder residue test on Malevolento's hands, and found no residue. Then, after Miranda warnings, they interrogated him. He would not admit anything, saying, "You've got nothing on me, no witnesses, no evidence, no nothing."

The detectives put Malevolento in a lineup for the dog walker to identify him. However, the dog walker could not.

The dog walker was also unable to identify either Vinny or Fatsom.

Vinny, Fatsom, and Malevolento were indicted for the robbery and the six murders. They were each tried separately because of Supreme Court rulings prohibiting the use of incriminating hearsay statements of one accomplice as evidence against another accomplice. At their trials, all of the defendants chose to remain silent and none testified against the others.

Before the trials, all the lawyers brought motions to exclude their clients' confessions or admissions and to exclude any physical evidence that had been seized, claiming that the police had violated their clients' constitutional rights.

During these motions and at the trials, the following questions were raised. How would they be answered by the judge?

Questions

1. Did the detectives have probable cause to arrest Vinny?
2. Did they have probable cause to search Vinny's car?
3. Did they need a search warrant to search Vinny's car?
4. Can the Glock found in Vinny's car be used as admissible evidence against him?
5. Did the detectives need a search warrant to break into Fatsom's house to search for him?
6. If they needed a search warrant to enter Fatsom's house, can the revolver and the $200 be used as evidence against Fatsom?
7. Assuming they did not need a search warrant to search for Fatsom, can the revolver and the $200 be admissible as evidence against Fatsom?
8. Did the detectives need a separate search warrant to compel Malevolento to submit to the gunpowder residue test?

Assume for questions 9–16 that at their separate trials, none of the out-of-court statements of the defendants can be used against the other defendants. Their statements might only be admissible against the person who made them. Assume further that the defendants may only be convicted on proof beyond a reasonable doubt.

9. At Fatsom's trial, if the judge ruled that neither the revolver nor the $200 were admissible evidence, could Fatsom properly be convicted without other unequivocal incriminating evidence against him?
10. At Malevolento's trial, since neither Vinny nor Fatsom testified against him and no evidence or foundation connected the Glock to him, could the Glock be admitted into evidence against him?
11. At Malevolento's trial, assuming that neither the guns nor the $200 were admissible against him, no one identified him at or near the crime scene,

and neither the confession of Vinny nor the self-serving statements of Fatsom were admissible, could he properly be convicted?

12. May Vinny's statement that he drove the car to the robbery be admissible against him?

13. At Vinny's trial, assuming the judge admitted the eyewitness testimony identifying Vinny's license plate and his car fleeing the crime scene, Vinny's incriminating statement and videotaped confession that he knew there was going to be a robbery, and the murder weapon found under the front seat of his car, could he properly be convicted of the robbery and all six murders.

14. Are the costs of the exclusionary rule, here the possible acquittals of Malevolento and Fatsom, worth the potential value the rule may have in deterring improper police searches?

15. If these events occurred in a state that had capital punishment for such crimes, would it be fair to say that the exclusionary rule might cause Vinny to receive the death penalty while Malevolento and Fatsom might be acquitted?

References

Chambers v. Maroney, 399 U.S. 227 (1940)
Warden v. Hayden, 387 U.S. 294 (1967)
Arizona v. Hicks, 480 U.S. 321 (1987)
Schmerber v. California, 384 U.S. 757 (1966)
Miranda v. Arizona, 384 U.S. 436, at 478 (1966)
United States v. Wright, 991 F.2d 1180 (4th Cir.1993)

Problem Seven

Police were called to a residential home by a desperate mother who told them that her nine-year-old daughter, Polly, was missing. She said that when she went into Polly's room to wake her for school, she was not there. The police immediately began a full-scale search to find the missing girl. Polly's mother told the police that Polly's favorite teddy bear was also missing. The police checked their database for known sex offenders living in the area. The database revealed that a registered sex offender, Allen Schumer, who had a previous conviction for a sex crime against a child, was living in a trailer home across the street from Polly's house.

Detectives went to the trailer to interview Schumer. He would not let them into the trailer, so they asked him to accompany them to the police station. Schumer agreed.

At the police station, the detectives conducted a recorded interview of Schumer. They told him he was not under arrest and they did not give him Miranda warnings before questioning him about the missing girl. At first, Schumer said he knew nothing about Polly's disappearance, but said he was aware that she was missing and had been taken from her bed. His statement that she had been taken from her bed raised the detective's suspicion because that information had not been publicized. They continue to question him, and he told them that he had seen Polly many times. He said she was a very nice girl, and she was very attached to her large white teddy bear. The detectives each had a strong feeling that Schumer was involved in Polly's disappearance, and they decided to advise him of his Miranda rights. He waived his right to remain silent and agreed to continue speaking with them.

When they questioned him about his prior sex crime conviction, he became extremely nervous. He began shifting in his chair and clenching his fists.

He said, "I think I should talk to a lawyer."

The detectives ignored his statement and continued the interrogation. They believed a chance existed that Polly was still alive and that Schumer knew where she was located. They felt he was on the verge of opening up and if they stopped the questioning at that moment, they would lose the chance to learn of Polly's whereabouts.

The detectives continued to press him, and Schumer eventually admitted that he kidnapped and raped Polly, kept her locked in a closet for three days, then buried her alive. He said, "I dug a hole and put her in it, buried her. I pushed. I put her in plastic baggies. She was alive. I buried her alive." He explained that about 3:00 a.m. on the morning of the kidnapping, he simply entered Polly's house and took her. He said, "I got high on drugs. I went over there and took her out of her house. I walked back into her room. I just told her to come with me and be quiet. I sexually assaulted her. I went out there one night and dug a hold and put her in it and buried her … She was still alive. I buried her alive, she suffered. I don't know why I did it."

Based on the information, the police dug up the shallow grave in the yard behind Schumer's trailer and found Polly's body. They found her body kneeling and clutching the white teddy bear, her hands tied with speaker wire, and her fingers poking through the garbage bags in which she had been buried alive. She had been raped, and had died of suffocation.

All of the facts of the case indicate that Schumer's confession was reliable and truthful. The details he provided before the body was found matched the physical evidence found in the grave. The body was found buried in his backyard, and a mattress in his trailer home had blood stains that matched Polly's DNA.

Schumer was charged with first-degree murder, sexual battery on a child, kidnapping, and burglary. His attorney moved to suppress the confession because of the violation of Schumer's right to counsel. He also moved to suppress Polly's body and the other physical evidence because that evidence was the fruit of the poisonous tree of the unlawfully obtained confession.

Questions

1. When the detectives had Schumer accompany them to the police station, did that constitute an arrest?
2. When the detectives first began questioning Schumer, were they required to give him Miranda warnings?
3. Was Schumer's statement, "I think I should talk to a lawyer," an unequivocal request for a lawyer that required the detectives to cease questioning him?
4. When Schumer said that he thought he should talk to a lawyer, was it a violation of his Sixth Amendment rights for the detectives to continue questioning him?
5. When Schumer said that he thought he should talk to a lawyer, was it a violation of the *Miranda* rule for the detectives to continue questioning him?
6. Is there a difference between a violation specifically written in the Sixth Amendment right and a violation of the *Miranda* rules?
7. Should the public safety exception to *Miranda* apply to the statements obtained after Schumer requested an attorney?
8. Assuming that the continuation of questioning violated Schumer's rights, should his confession be suppressed?
9. Assuming that the continuation of questioning violated Schumer's rights, should the body and other physical evidence that was recovered be suppressed as fruits of the poisonous tree?
10. Should the inevitable discovery exception be applied to the body and the physical evidence?

References

Oregon v. Mathiason, 429 U.S. 492 (1977)
California v. Beheler, 463 U.S. 1121 (1983)

Davis v. United States, 512 U.S. 452 (1994)
Chavez v. Martinez, 538 U.S. 760 (2003)
Edwards v. Arizona, 451 U.S. 477 (1981)
Arizona v. Roberson, 486 U.S. 675 (1988)
New York v. Quarles, 467 U.S. 649 (1984)
Nix v. Williams, 467 U.S. 431 (1984)
Berghuis v. Thompkins, 130 S.Ct. 2250 (2010)

Case Index

Index